MEN At WORK

An Action Guide to Masculine Healing

Chris Frey has done his own work and now brings deep and original learning to other men.

Bill Kauth, co-founder of The New Warrior Training and co-author of *A Circle of Men*

CHRIS FREY, MSW, LCSW

- ► *Master repressed feelings*
- ► *Overcome anger*
- ► *Let go of losses*
- ► *Move beyond fear*
- ► *Bury guilt and shame*
- ► *Heal yourself*

Acknowledgments

My thanks to:

Tony, Don, and Hal for contributing your writings from the heart;
Sandy and Mary Jo at Islewest for believing I can write;
Sharon at Islewest for her efforts on my behalf;
all the men and women whose stories make up this book and my life;
Mom and Dad, my greatest cheerleaders;
the New Warriors (especially my I-Group) for restoring my passion.

I did not use footnotes in the book, but my work is one big footnote to the work of many; thanks especially to the books of Sam Keen, John Lee, Robert Bly, Augustus Napier, and Jed Diamond, you mentor me with your words.

Last and most, thanks to my family: DiAnne for being the first to read the book and for your never-ending support of my never-ending projects, and Carly, Aimee, and Nathan for being miracles in my life.

Book Team
Publisher: Sandra J. Hirstein
Managing Editor: Mary Jo Graham
Assistant Editor: Sharon K. Cruse
Editorial Assistant: Christy Henke
Cover Design: Mike Meyer
Composition: Kymberly Schmitt

Author's Note: all of the cases described in this book are composites. They have been scrambled or altered to protect my client's rights of confidentiality and privacy. No client found in this book corresponds to any actual person, living or dead.

Contents

Dedication

This writing is dedicated to Jackie Holler and Jim Howard, my mentors, my friends.

Preface

Movement

A work in progress
Unfinished business
A wise man once said
You will write the final chapters
Of your life story
Only when you release the ghost writers
Your journey is familiar to those
Who passed before you
But the journey is your own

You have believed at times
That they formed you
A sponge
Absorbing the love
The pain
A blank slate
For all to etch upon
Their wisdom
Their expectations
Your self

Other times
You have believed yourself
Completely separate
Free of all others
Free in thought, feeling, deed
Acting as a hopeful child
Insisting they see you as a man

Take a moment
Look, hear, know
Could it be

You experienced those essential others
Not formed by the love
Or the calamity, rather
Working with and against their energy
Then and even now
Growing because of, and in spite of
Their efforts and your own

Moving forward to find a safe
And powerful maleness
You carry the love given
Past and present
You carry the uncertainty
Past, present, and future
You carry
Accountability   Chris Frey
                                                          1993

This is a book about men, movement, and healing. For some of you, the healing may mean moving through and beyond the past traumas of abuse, abandonment, or neglect. Some of you will use this material to move deeper into your hearts, to discover the rhythms of your body, to slow yourself down enough to encounter the wonders of near stillness. Whatever the focus, within the pages that follow I hope you will find opportunities to revive your spirit, reclaim your passion for life, and more fully experience the excitement and uncertainty of each moment.

Men at Work is the story of my professional and personal journey: my truth, my myth. Working with men is a direct outcome of my personal road. These pages are full of my bias with information gleaned and interpreted from my culture, my family, my years as a clinician. In my early training, I was encouraged to be objective, to be simply a mirror for clients to see themselves in. I've found this essential at times. But I've also found this style insufficient and a denial of how my strengths, weaknesses, and beliefs drive my mission to help men change. Having owned this, I make several suggestions in how to proceed. The processes you will find are structured to enhance your healing journey. They are put together as a puzzle made from the teachings of mentors and clients, successes and failures. I hope you will put your personal stamp on each activity. When I "give" an assignment to a man, I "give it away," assuming that the man will make it his own. I hope what you find of Chris Frey in these pages may serve you in your efforts. As many Twelve Step friends say, "Take what you need and leave the rest."

This book is also a toolbox, a container of methods for men to safely learn healing skills. Each man is born with a set of beginner's tools: intellectual, physical, temperamental. You are then entrusted with additional tools given by parents, other significant persons, and your culture. You were structured by words and actions, perhaps with love or abuse, with extensive information, perhaps with expectations of blind acceptance. Be aware that many men carry heavy, outdated, inadequate tools for the job at hand—manhood—and for the roles of lover, husband, father. Each activity is an opportunity to cast aside the obsolete, to repair, update, and forge new life tools. This is not information to be experienced passively. More than a chance to redefine the problems in your life, this book is a call to action. Healing is a full experience of mind, body and soul. I will ask you to draw on all of your senses, left and right brain and, in some cases, challenge you physically.

Although *Men at Work* is written about men, I trust that many of you who are reading this book are women: lovers, wives, therapists, friends. There is a tremendous crisis of masculinity in our world. The number of boys growing up without consistent male role models, mentors, and elders in their lives is potentially catastrophic in our society. Sexism is alive and unwell in the adolescent and adult male subcultures. The past several generations of parents have raised a lot of angry young men. On the other hand, a man seeking a better way with the assistance of others is no longer a rarity as evidenced by the proliferation of men's groups and men's retreats. And many of these men will initiate the healing process at the suggestion and with the support of strong women. This book is for you, too. If you are a lover, wife, family member, or friend, these pages may offer a deeper understanding of new avenues of change for the men in your lives. You may even find that with adaptation, some of the exercises in the book will assist you.

The activities in *Men at Work* resulted from eighteen years of professional and personal healing work. I have experienced, been given, have adapted, and combined various therapeutic gifts through my relationships with mentors, friends, colleagues, and clients. Often, the exercises were created within the movement of a therapy session. The synergy of the men who came before us creates the power of the healing. What does this mean as you read and begin to put this material into action? It means that you will give your own special flavoring to each process. Take them, try them on for size, bring others you trust into the process, and move on.

Introduction

Using *Men at Work*

There are a variety of methods for using the tools that I will describe. Many of the processes call for time alone to prepare, write, and process. (Always keep a journal close by.) Some activities can be utilized on your own, some in individual or group therapy. The imageries have a potential for emotional intensity that is best experienced with a trained professional. Certain tools will be designated as best utilized in that environment. In general, the healing process will be enhanced by doing this work in the company of other men (more on this later).

There is a flow to the work that men do. We set out on a quest, judging life as a journey through time, not overly focused on specific events. The order of the chapters reflects that flow. Beginning with information I call Key Aspects of Masculine Healing, the progression will move from uncovering the male wounds through anger work, grief work, sexual and body healing, and moving beyond the pain. Special attention will be paid to the father-son relationship. **Remember:** There are often no discrete separations in the flow of a man's healing road. The progression of these chapters may not be the exact road you need to follow. You may move in and out of sections, plucking from each the activities that fit you. Some of you will read the table of contents and be led to the heart of your work. Many of you have been on this journey for some time and will not need certain pieces of the text. Often you will repeat activities in multiple settings (alone, individual therapy, group therapy), reaching deeper levels of experience. **Beware of Male Myth 101: Get It Right the First Time!**

Some of you will not feel safe entering into all of the territory described within. Go with your heart, the heart of the man you are *today.* Review all the material, concentrating on the experiences that take you to that zone between comfort and danger. *Take Risks* and Stay Safe!

Definitions

Three terms you will find throughout this text are "men's work," "healing work," and "Shadow." **Men's work** is a shorthand phrase used in many circles to describe a wide range of gatherings that have the common focus of men working with other men on gaining a deeper sense of mature, healthy masculinity. These gatherings include leaderless support groups, men's therapy groups, male religious retreats, male initiation retreats, and other physically, emotionally, and spiritually oriented men's experiences. For the purpose of this book, most of the processes for Men's Work that I describe may be used individually or in support groups, therapy sessions, and many types of retreats. Men and women who read the material will find that many processes are adaptable to women's work, but the energy and focus may need to change.

The energy of this book is directed toward masculine healing. **Healing work** is another short form used to describe a broad range of reflective and expressive tasks I use that are directed toward assisting men in my current life mission: To teach living in the present through healing and honoring the past. For some of you, healing work is cognitive, for some emotional, for others spiritual. For me, it is all of the above. It may also be important to say what I do not mean by this term. I am not describing the perceived magic of a healer, but outlining recovery that comes from a man's efforts—his sweat, tears, wounds, and pain offered up in a strong, safe container of men he trusts. Healing work, your work, will often be facilitated by a skilled, experienced, specially trained man. He is a man, not a god. Even a true shaman, a Merlin, a man of God, is a facilitator, at best. In my best work I combine my gifts with the energy of the men in the circle and we set off on what to me often seems like a magical healing journey, remembering that the magic only occurs if the safety and integrity of the leader is intact. Beware of "healers" who do the work *for* you rather than *with* you. Beware of Shadow Magicians with perfect solutions, who coax you to follow them without question. Be alert for men who are on this journey themselves, and who through their love, dedication, experience, and sense of mission offer you tools, stand by you, and challenge you. These are true healers, mere humans. So, men's work is the healing work that men do.

A few words on **Shadow.** My use of the Shadow comes from my straightforward understanding of the Jungian term. As I moved through childhood I found there were aspects of my behavior, even my personality, that were deemed as unacceptable by certain significant others, aspects that I interpreted as not OK, aspects that brought me enough pain that I suppressed them, tucked them behind me, a shadow of myself. Through the course of life this Shadow has leaked out, usually when I least wanted or expected it. For example, in a time before conscious memory I decided to never be angry. I spent a lot of time being scared, a fair amount of time feeling ashamed and guilty, more than a bit of my time happy, and truly convinced myself that I could eliminate anger. I was nice, polite, and mostly obedient, and only on rare occasions did I punch out my younger brother when no one was watching. In those moments I was truly shocked. In the millisecond after the outburst I promised myself that I would never do this again. As in the story of Peter Pan, there is a connection between my denial of my Shadow and my difficulties with growing up. It was years later, after feedback from several women close to me, after several occasions of scaring my children, and with loving confrontation from men, that I began to own this part of me—Shadow—and change. As you will read throughout this book, a great healing comes from knowing and confronting your Shadow, placing him in front of you, owning him as a previously secret part of yourself, and learning how to move beyond your shame of this childhood you.

The Creative Man

Healing is still an art. One of the most beautiful aspects of this art is that it is interactive. I enjoy looking for the interactive artist in every man that takes me on as his assistant in his work. Often the first place I see this creativity is in the man's daily vocation, the artistry of a man describing his carpentry, his computer, his clients. I hear it as men talk about their hobbies: fishing, golfing, painting, music. In the process of healing lives, it is essential to tap into this creativity. Early in my work of leading men's groups, I met Gary Richardson and Dan Richards. Gary is a wonderful, lyrical guitarist who supplies the backdrop for the words of Dan's guided imageries in men's workshops. For years I had played my guitar in the solitude of my living room, writing lyrics and prose that only I heard. Gary's encouragement brought my music out of my living room. As I played my basic chords, he laid beautiful notes on top, saying, "you sound good!" Since that time, my guitar and dulcimer have supplied the backdrop to my partner, Jim's, imageries. Through our creative interactions in workshops, we have time after time created a powerful atmosphere for healing that is not based on virtuosity, but on working from the heart.

You may be wondering how this story speaks to creativity in your work. There are several levels. First, the permission from a man to openly use your gifts is a powerful experience. Second, locating and practicing right brain skills can lead you into levels of emotion and expression that cannot be accessed by the spoken word. And, it's fun! Often the work of men, be it doing your job or repairing your life, is solemn, repetitive work. Well, it helps to lighten up! With my guitar I can experience tears at the touch of a single minor chord, fear of the mistake that will ring loud enough to distract from Jim's words, and anger at my limited talents. But, perhaps most important, I feel the joy of my fingers on the frets, the sound of the notes, and the beauty of the sound of the stillness—the space *between* the notes. I am a man of many words, many gestures, effusive in my expression. The silence teaches me much.

The activities in this book will encourage you to move toward new forms of expression. You will be invited to write, to visualize, to draw, to drum, to move your body. At this point, some of you are tapping into your inner skeptic, thinking, "I can't do this stuff (i.e., would be embarrassed or ashamed). I'm not an artistic man." Others of you will resist because you are artistic, but struggle with perfectionism and a need to perform, not simply create. I challenge you to test these beliefs. Remember, this is not a competition among men. It is a means of reaching another part of who you are.

Throughout the following chapters, you will find opportunities to create. You will also read examples of others who have brought forth their artistic spirit. In most cases, these will be men who do not create prose, poetry, sound, or art as a profession. We all know the power of a practiced, developed, professional artist who speaks from the heart. The power in your artistic life may or may not be steeped in skill. Its worth is measured by your heart.

Drumming

Many men will tell me, "I have no musical ability, I can't dance, I have no sense of rhythm." Drumming is a way into the emotion, chaos, and symmetry of creativity and the connectedness of men. I play a simple drum from New Mexico. There are beautiful drums I have heard men play from all parts of the world. I drum alone, quietly to meditate, loudly to energize. I drum with men, to feel and to connect. I cannot fully describe the experience of a fire, a group of drummers and an experienced drummer to lead! The drumming begins as a search for common rhythm, disorganized, perhaps frustrating. The sound builds to a clear, coherent, powerful beat. Over time, this rhythm runs its course. Chaos, again, until gradually a new common beat is found. This can go on for hours. Men who can't drum, do. For me, this is a lesson, without words, in trust—opening myself to feelings, power, and being a vital cog in a very large wheel of masculinity, celebration, and spirituality.

Visualizations

Throughout the book, the terms **visualization** and **guided imagery** are used interchangeably. There are several options that may be used to move through an imagery. The options are as follows:

- someone may read it to you,
- you may learn it to the extent that you can walk your own way through,
- you may record my words on a cassette to be played back.

To prepare, find a quiet, dark, safe space. Lie down or sit in a position where your body is fully supported. I recommend closing your eyes, which will increase your focus, and for most men, take you to a deeper level of experience. If you do not feel safe, keeping your eyes open and turning on a light will decrease the intensity. Pick an object that is safe or powerful to you as a focal point. Breathing is of particular importance. Many of us learned in childhood to hold our breath to shut down feelings, or we turned to shallow breathing when afraid. When you begin to feel during imagery, hear the word *breath* slow and deep; you will feel, and you will proceed.

Journaling

Your therapy journal is a place to write your thoughts, your feelings, and what you learn. Writing will help you understand yourself and how to heal. In addition, you will be able to look back and see a written history of how you have grown and changed in your therapy.

When journaling, it is helpful to always include the date, and time of day when you are writing. Also, you may want to include the date and time of the event, thought, or feeling you are writing about, the specifics of the event, thought, or feeling, and what you learned, changed, or will work on as a result of the happening.

Role-Play

There are many ways that role playing can assist a man in Men's Work. The role-player exists to serve the man who is doing the work. The role-player must encourage the man doing the work to give specific guidelines for the role—words, phrases, attitudes, body positions of the person being played—that will assist the man in his work. The role-player can be a catalyst—be creative.

Always de-role after a piece of work. It is important that no man go home in the role he played. He may carry too much pain that is not his. By example, clearly verbalizing at the end of a piece of work, "I am not your father, I am your friend...," and having the worker repeat it back to the role-player allows the worker to see the role-player again as he really is. This also reminds the man doing the work that the group has been operating in actual time and space, the person being role-played is not physically in the room and neither the worker nor the role-player has suffered any harm in present time.

1: Key Aspects of Men's Work

Men and Feelings

He was. . . a good boy, a gentle son
Kind, polite
Careful, helpful
His anger tidy, kept tucked neatly away
Only on rare occasions exploding outward
Like a ghost
Jumping unexpectedly from the dark
Then pushing away
Back into the shadows
With the ghost's bedfellows
Fear, sadness, shame

Excerpt, "Gentle Sons, Frightened Fathers"
Chris Frey, 1992

Begin this section by joining me in a brief visualization. Close your eyes. Breathe slowly, deeply. Clear your head of thoughts of the present.

Begin to look back to your childhood messages about feelings, as if you are watching a movie of your past. Be aware of what you were taught about males and feelings. You were given this information by the words and actions of significant persons, who made decisions for you about what the information meant. Picture yourself as you are today. Begin to look back, reviewing the past as an adult gazing from a safe distance. Pause between each phrase to reflect. What did you learn about:

males and sadness

males and fear

males and anger

males and shame (Remember, the difference between guilt and shame. Guilt is feeling bad about what you've done; shame is feeling bad about who you are. Guilt is simply a feeling, shame a state of being.)

males and happiness

Breathe, remain safe as you realize you are in the present, looking at the past. Be aware of who gave you this information. What did you learn from women? What did you learn from men? What conflicting information did you receive? Who did you believe? Having gathered this knowledge, return to the present. Bring what you have learned with you. Continue to breathe evenly and relax. When you are ready, open your eyes as the count reaches: 1, 2, 3, 4, 5, open eyes.

When you feel ready, take your journal and write what you learned about yourself and others. This introductory imagery will help you begin understanding the messages you received about emotions and the decisions you made about those messages. **Note:** Identifying the effects others had on your growth as a male is not about blame. This work is to become aware of and to grow beyond childhood. Each human, including you, is accountable for his or her choices.

If you are ready and want to extend the process, return to the visualization and ask yourself: How do I use this information in my life today? How do I use the messages in ways that work? How do I use the messages in ways that don't work? How have I changed, or tried to change, the way I approach my feelings?

Men and women, alike, have often suggested a "man's problem" is not being in touch with his feelings and how to express them. I see many men who are feeling all the time, especially their pain. Many of us are not in clear contact with the specific feelings we are having or expressing. We deny, repress, and sublimate certain emotions, ashamed that we are a man who feels. Others seem to magically change every feeling into anger. And, as many of you who are reading are acutely aware, we have alcohol, drugs, sex, work, gambling, food—a wide array of methods—to numb and redirect emotion. Rather than simply

2

suggesting that men need to learn to feel, I believe there are many men, hence, many needs.

> *Joe came to therapy stating, "My wife says I'm out of touch with my feelings." He then describes a myriad of ways that he passively expresses anger, guilt, and fear—being late, procrastinating, drinking. His secret is that he knows this about himself, but tells no one.*

> *Mel feels all the time. If he is angry, sad, scared, guilty, he expresses anger. Like the men he grew up with, and now socializes and works with, Mel thinks emotions other than anger are "weak." He will cautiously admit to feeling guilty when he explodes at his family and is angry about that.*

> *Tim is so sad and scared that he has difficulty remembering when he felt happy. He cries when alone. He has a long list of secret fears.*

Men's Emotions

Let's look at some of these needs by examining several key emotions in mens' lives.

Anger

In the current culture of violence, more than ever before as men we must look at what we have learned, and at what we are teaching our sons, about anger. In the chapter on anger work, I will offer activities directed toward healing old anger and safely expressing present-day anger, but for now, I will briefly discuss the process of healing rage.

I remember when I first owned that I am an angry man, without shame, without pride! Many of you will understand that men are commonly raised to see anger as bad and/or as a badge of courage that "real men" must wear. Our culture teaches a mixture of disdain and admiration for men of violence, implying that violence is abhorrent (although there are exceptions to this rule). As boys, we are to understand that it is not OK to beat up little sister, but war is necessary. The examples are many; my point is that few of the men who come for healing work received consistent messages about anger.

Be not proud, nor ashamed. Anger is a reality for men. Face it, embrace it. The problem men have is not anger; that is a legitimate feeling. The epidemic is in teaching our boys to turn anger into control, violence, and heart attacks. It is necessary to let go of old rage and learn skills to safely express present-day anger. The work will take place on two levels. Some of you will become more aware of when you're angry, how you express it indirectly, and how to learn clear, direct anger skills. Others will first need to build a safe container for your rage, a corral for the raging child in a man's body that damages you and others.

Fear

Do you feel fear? When? What do you tell yourself about feeling afraid? If you are following common cultural scripts, you deny fear or secretly feel afraid much of the time. Men who deny fear are dying and killing in great numbers (gangs, war, parachuting off bridges). Men who secretly sleep with their fear are frozen from making basic life decisions about family, career, life, death. Only a man who is numb or already dead inside feels no fear. The man who openly owns his fears can face them and move beyond. To begin this work, take out your journal and write down the name of one man you have feared. Facing this man in your heart is one brick in the foundation of your fear work. For some, writing the name will itself be intensely frightening. Others have tried to conquer this fear by physically, vocationally, or financially beating the man, only to feel the fear again. As you write his name begin to know you will only beat him with your heart.

Sadness

"I only saw my dad cry once." This story has been related an untold number of times in my office and among my friends. Many of us have a very limited framework for sadness, the male grief process. Sadness is presented as a feminine emotion, to be expressed only in the most desperate of circumstances. Shame and guilt frequently follow crying. The amount of grief many men carry is so massive, they don't have words to fully describe it. In my lifetime, I have heard story after story of war, child abuse, alcoholism, death, and abandonment, along with less dramatic tales of the absent dad who traveled for work, to boys who never knew Dad's story, the sons who did not feel wanted. The grief is real. Big boys do cry, and big men need to.

Guilt and Shame

As described earlier, guilt is based on behavior; shame is a state of being. Guilt is internally correctable:

Stop the guilt-inducing behavior
Own your mistakes

4

Make the changes necessary to stop repetition of the harm to self and others.

Because shame is "I am . . ." not "I did . . ." a man may feel it is ingrained in his soul.

It's A Shame

It's so easy
a word
a phrase
a glance
a gesture
Shut up, quit being stupid
You drive me crazy
You're a wimp
You'll never amount to anything
Hey, you want this kid
It's so easy
A word, phrase, look, gesture
I see you
I hear you
I accept you
I love you

Chris Frey, 1995

Take a moment and write down words, phrases, and non-verbal signals that cause you to say: "What's wrong with me?" or "I'm bad." Next to each, label how you got this message. Common shame inducers are Dad, Mom, other adult family members with power, the church, school. How do you live this shame in your present life (work, lovers, spouses, friends)? How do you shame yourself? What secrets do you carry? How have you used your shame to shame others?

As you proceed, you will have opportunities to dislodge both levels of shame that you just expressed in your journal. The first is shame from significant others, an intergenerational passing of the shame baton. Anger and grief shake loose this shame, finding a new reality for the child you were. By this, I do not mean the golden "inner child" that much of the literature describes. I mean the real boy, lovable and at times, a little pain in the posterior. No one is born bad, but no one is born perfect. The second type of shame, "self-generated shame," is the cycle of using the shame you were handed earlier in life and continuing to use it against yourself and others. Recall any time you did or said something that reminded you of your parents in a way you promised yourself you'd never repeat. Another example is to review the secrets you keep, how you are hurt by these, how you believe these secrets have or could hurt others. This shame is healed through remorse (grief work), owning your behavior, stopping it, expressing your feelings, making amends from the heart where appropriate. More on this later.

Happiness and Joy

One purpose of Men's Work is to feel better. Obvious, you say. Perhaps not. Many of us believe life is a constant struggle: "Don't feel good until the work is done and the work is never done." How many of you have started a task that you didn't really understand, getting angrier and feeling increasingly inadequate as you struggled. Healing is also about humor, play, recognizing strengths, being grateful for the good stuff, expressing love, reveling in the positive changes. When a man "graduates" from group, we celebrate with food, cards, gifts, poems, and glowing reports of how the man has grown. Men's work is as much about the celebration of our connections, our survival and our evolution, as it is about healing the pain.

Open your journal. Write the last time you laughed a good, real, loud guffaw. Do you remember? Was it recent enough? Decide how long you will wait to feel this good again. (If you're stuck, I recommend Marx Brothers movies, especially the song "I Must Be Going" in "Animal Crackers".)

Men's Gatherings

"Coming from a broken home as a young boy and never having that lost feeling replaced, this gathering was the most moving male experience of my life."

Workshop Participant, 1993

Most of us were taught not to share our deepest fear, shame, sadness, joy. Many of us were taught not to share our deepest anger. The masculine script that many boys learned is:

Don't communicate feelings openly—If you do, make sure this is with a female, not a male—If you share with a female, make sure you can dominate her so you don't "lose" control.

I believe fear and shame are the foundation of men avoiding the love and support of other men. This suggests that the loving acceptance of a man who knows my secrets can be life changing. Male gatherings such as groups and workshops are the cornerstone of the healing work of men. Following is a partial list of what such experiences can provide; it is a compilation of feedback received from men over the years.

> Men can love me.
> Men listened to me.
> I realized my love for my father.
> I can be with men and not compete.
> There are older men who can teach me things I still need to know.
> I danced.
> I drummed.
> Men can touch me in ways that don't hurt.
> I'm less angry at women.
> I'm accountable for my choices, feelings, actions.
> Other men were beaten and molested.
> Other men miss their fathers.
> Straight men can accept gay men (and vice versa).
> Other men don't like "macho" stuff.
> Some men who do like "macho" stuff are also loving men.
> The power of the men is greater than my power alone.
> Other men are confused, scared, and insecure about sex.
> It's OK to cry.
> Belching and farting are not sins.
> I don't have to know everything.
> I can connect with men who are different from my. . . race, religion, sexual orientation, background.

What Men's Gatherings Are Not

Men's Work Is Not a New, Private Men's Club

I emphasize to men I work with that many of us who are attracted to these gatherings are the boys who felt "I don't belong." The goal of the work is not to provide a safe place for some men, where we can belittle men who don't join us or value what we do. Any man who wants to do the work can find a safe place to participate. Groups, workshops and men's centers are spreading throughout the United States, Canada, and Europe. This work has been most available to men with funds to attend events that are often substantial in cost, but efforts are moving forward to reach men of limited finances, along with men of various spiritual orientations and races. Finally, I will quote a man I love who struggled through childhood physical abuse, rape, and addictions: "It's great for me to come to group and get through all this pain. But, if I don't take it home, it's not worth much."

The message is: men's gatherings exist to **change** your life, not **escape** from your life. The greatest change I have felt internally from my own work among men is a deeper, more passionate commitment to demonstrate my love as a husband and father. Moving beyond being a "responsible" family man, I've learned to enjoy these roles. The final highlight of each gathering I attend is going home.

Men's Work Is Not about Blaming or Bashing Women

One of the immediate shifts when only men are in the room occurs when men realize there are no women to nurture, to dominate, to depend upon. Men provide the verbal and physical support, and the feedback. Men role-play mom and other females for feeling work. Men bring the hand-made gifts, the poems, the food when someone leaves group for the next stage of his journey. We honor women for their strength, love, and separateness. We honor that the women's movement blazed the trail for some of the work we do. Contrary to some of what has been written by people who are fearful of and angry at men, I do not believe most men see this work as an opportunity to return to the past when a man's power meant primitive dominance over others. (In fact, this dominance by men is not in the past; it is alive and unwell in our corporate, political, and poverty subcultures.) The foundation of masculine healing, instead, is accessing personal power to join with other men and women to create a safer, stronger world.

Men's Work Is Not a Religion or a Cult

I am a facilitator and a leader, not a guru. I do not have one road map or a magic prescription for masculine salvation or spiritual reclamation. The material in this book is adaptable; men from a wide range of backgrounds, cultures, races, and creeds can use these processes. This work does not replace your belief system; it asks you to evaluate where your beliefs come from, how well you practice them, and how well they operate in your life and the lives of the people you're accountable to. In your travels among men, you may hear about King energy, a Jungian archetype that for me symbolizes, in its simplest form, leadership. The true King leads by modeling strength and stewardship, not for control over others, or accolades, or approval. One Shadow of the King is the evangelist, presenting a male model of perfection to gain power, money, disciples. In men's work, the leader is a real man, perhaps a man with special knowledge and skills, but also with tarnishes in his armor and bearing his own woundedness.

Ritual and Beyond

"Do you do drumming."
"Sure."
"That probably scares some men away."
"Probably."
"Sounds like fun."
"It's great fun."
"Keep up the good work."

Conversation about men's retreats
with a woman at a health fair

Every culture, society, generation has essential rituals that provide transitions for males into new life stages, as broad based as religious ceremonies, as simple as the family meal. As times change, so do some rituals. Traditional, time honored rituals can be life giving. Western culture has drifted toward many weak, control-based Shadow Rituals, which are reflections of our dark side. These Shadow processes range from child-like and dangerous (fraternity hazing) to those that potentially threaten every male (alcohol and drug abuse, sex without intimacy, gangs). These adolescent and adult male rituals often foster isolation through competition, or offer connections only through acceptance of rigid authority.

In men's gatherings, we often combine tradition and invention to create rituals that enhance the growth process. These rituals have several key components. They are always voluntary and contain an element of emotional risk. Some rituals enter the realm of the sacred; ceremonies such as honoring elders have been repeated by men of heart since the beginning of time. Others are simple processes to engage each man in the healing circle. For example, each week the men's group I facilitate starts with check-in, "What I'm feeling and what I came to work on tonight," and ends with check-out, "What I got tonight and any contracts of what I will work on this week." As you can see from the examples, the purpose of ritual can range from the sacred, spiritual, and time-honored to the simple practice of male connectedness. Many of the rituals used in men's work cannot be explained without losing some of their power. Others can be described, but their strength is truly known only by experiencing them. Many of the rituals I use involve what I call "physicalizing the process": walking, standing, drumming, dancing, writing, moving. As boys, many of us were most in touch with our feelings when we were in movement: climbing, running, falling, lifting, throwing, catching. The rituals of talk therapy are insufficient for many men to reach down to their passion and pain. And so, we remove the competition but keep the physical challenge and increase the emotional challenge.

Some men fear ritual and ceremony, and verbalize that by skepticism. Common messages I hear as a male working with masculine healing in a relatively conservative mid-western city are:

> "Don't say in the workshop brochure that you drum. Men will be scared off."
> "Is this the weird stuff, where guys run through the woods in loincloths?"
> "Is this like a cult?"
> "Is this like church?"

Not all men will be attracted to all rituals. As you move through this book, find the activities that you're drawn to. In some cases you will sense a need to repeat certain processes over and over: they will become rituals in your journey. As you begin to find healing, powerful, fun rituals for your life today, some will fit the needs of friends and family. You may expand your holiday rituals, build a positive ritual to start each day, design traditions with your lover, children, and friends. Do take risks. Suspend for periods of time your skepticism, embarrassment, ridicule (your "look good" masks) and enter the journey of healing rituals.

Honoring the Original Child

"All I know is that I survived long enough to get here. What a gift."

Man, 1992

Words and behaviors of significant adults during our childhood significantly influence each of us today. Through the interaction of child, parents, and culture, decisions about love, self-esteem, relationships, sexuality, spirituality, feelings, career, and more, are formulated. When men come to do the work of healing, they often carry along a traumatized Inner Child. Much has been written in recent years on Healing the Inner Child. (One current book I found particularly interesting is Stephen Wolinsky's, *The Dark Side of the Inner Child.*)

My clearest conceptualization of this view is that within me are the messages, beliefs, memories, feelings, and prejudices I established as a child, formulated through an interactive process between myself and my environment. I am not simply a victim of others' shortcomings; I am a participant in my entire life cycle. I do not get a second childhood. Healing my Inner Child is not synonymous with letting him run amok. My job is to move beyond that childhood stuckness. And to let go of the past, I must first honor it.

> *"When I was a kid, after Mom and Dad fought and somebody got hit, I would hide in my room. I decided they were not really my parents. Dad had said once when he was mad that they must have brought the wrong kid home. I imagined my real parents were these great people who would realize they had the wrong kid and they'd come to get me."*

I've heard varying versions of this story over and over: men who describe feeling trapped in an emotionally, physically, or sexually dangerous family, who developed extraordinary survival tools to stay alive and sane. Some of these methods of coping were dangerous in themselves; raging, constant fantasizing, drinking and drugging, running away. Some were quiet and secret: hiding in closets, hiding in science fiction, dissociating. Many of the men reading these pages found solace in sports, early sexual acting out, fighting, gangs, and any other form of achievement or competition available. Many of these tools we carried into adulthood, at times without a conscious understanding of that choice. As the boy grows to manhood, perhaps as part of that journey he arrives in my office.

> *"My life doesn't work. I've pushed for years to prove that I'm not . . . (stupid, hopeless, crazy, worthless, weak) and to feel. . . (wanted, loved, good enough). I've accomplished (or not accomplished) what I wanted, but something's still missing.*

In listening to the story again, I always hear part of what's missing—the Honoring of the Original Child. Simply, the man must go back and give himself several messages that he was either not given as a child, or he was given but lost through abandonment or contradictory experiences. These messages are:

> *"You've always been good enough. I love you."*
> *"I want to thank you for doing all that you did to survive childhood."*
> *"Some of what you did to survive doesn't work in adulthood; it's time to learn new ways."*

11

Go to a mirror. Look deeply into your own eyes. Say these three messages out loud, at least twice. Journal your responses. What you journal will tell you if you've heard these messages before, if you believed them, if you believe them now.

Honoring your past self may mean thanking the child that ran away, took drugs to numb pain, threw tantrums to get noticed, hid in a fantasy world, masturbated to go to sleep every night. This means thanking the child who tried to always be perfect, who never got a "B," who injured his body in sports to express his rage, who never let anyone get close, who never cried, who never laughed. This does not mean absolving yourself of the harm you've done to others! Rather, you regain contact with a boy who knows remorse, not shame, and uses his mistakes to grow.

As we move onto the next Key Aspect, remember, Honoring the Original Child is a two-step process: one, accepting and loving the boy you were, and two, knowing that many of your boyhood survival skills are no longer effective, or even necessary. This may be a painful process, accomplished not in one glorious moment of healing, but in numerous hard-fought battles of anger work, shame release, grief. Take the time; do the work.

Beyond The Inner Child

To reach the Light Beyond Your Shadow
To go to where my inner darkness lies
My eternal boyhood longing
That you supply the magic answers;
Only in letting go of the fantasy
Am I able to become a Man
Who is a part of and apart from Father

Excerpt from "The Man in the River"
Chris Frey, 1994

It is important to Honor the Original Child—regaining a belief that you were a lovable kid regardless of the messages you received. As you re-read the previous section, I hope you will see the word "Honor," not "Revere." One of the errors I perceive in Inner Child work is that some folks believe the process translates into seeing a perfect, precious child who was traumatized and should get another childhood. I have begun to hear the excuse, "I did that because I was stuck in my Child," and the justification to remain a perpetual victim, "I can't deal with (him/her) when I'm in Child." Any therapeutic conceptualization is presented with healing in mind. My work with men is not to simply explain the trauma, or to feel the trauma, or to excuse present and future behavior because of trauma. The goal is to move beyond the constraints of childhood. To simply set loose the Inner Child and give him permission to be free is to set loose emotions without safe boundaries; it is to ignore the updated information available in the current environment. The Inner Child is a therapeutic construct, not another self. My real external self still looks a lot like a forty-year-old man with a few wrinkles who puffs up that last hill no matter how expensive the running shoes are. In the work that men do, I must see the options that the man has, options the boy may not have seen, or to which he may not have had access. Only then can the man save the best part of childhood, and grow beyond. Some examples of being stuck are:

> "Mom used to say 'Always prepare for the worst,' and I do." Joe then gave several examples of how his wife says he "creates" the worst by believing it will happen. His kids have begun to say they might as well mess up; he constantly suspects that they are anyway.

> Fred says, "My boss is angry because I started procrastinating. I'm tired of following the rules. My Child needs to finally be free to play when he needs to. I'm learning I have to put myself first for a change." Fred gets fired for verbally abusing co-workers who complain about his procrastination to his boss.

> "People have victimized me all my life. Why would Sue be any different? Maybe I deserve it. Maybe all women are like that. Why bother?"

Examples of being unstuck are:

> It was suggested that Mike "interview" his dad; get a better grasp of Dad's history and his perceptions of the father-son relationship. Mike returned amazed. "I thought my dad never supported me in my music. He told me that he used to come and listen to my band, but stayed in the back so he wouldn't intimidate me." Dad had been an excellent musician and didn't want Mike to feel pressured. Mike moves from resenting his dad for "never" supporting his efforts, to grief work about never knowing of his dad's support. He realizes that he, too, makes his father's mistake at times: by assuming his kid knows Mike supports him. Mike begins a

more open communication with his father and his own child.

Bill spent his life beating men or being beaten by them; literally and figuratively. "My dad hit me, and from there it was football, then bar fights." Bill's decision to change came when he began hitting his kids. His first challenge was to look at each man in the group he attended and honestly say, "I'm a violent and dangerous man." He was shocked when first confronted by the men about his anger: "I always saw it as hit or be hit; strong, like my Dad. I didn't want to remember how scary he was. Now I know I'm that scary, too."

Sitting in the circle, several men remembered the shame that accompanied masturbation; the messages at church, Mom calling it "dirty," dad not talking about sex, except, in a joking way. "If I couldn't talk about masturbation, how could I talk about . . . (being molested, my attraction to females, my attraction to males, my wet dreams, etc.)." Each man, in turn, asked a question he had always needed to ask about sex. The group worked together to find the best answer available. "It's time to quit waiting for mom and dad to deal with my sexuality. It's time to move on."

Mentors, Elders, and Initiation

"As the oldest man in the group, I was able to appreciate all the things mentors have given me, and I was able to be a mentor to others."

Workshop participant

I will never forget the first Elders Ceremony I attended at a men's workshop. Honoring the men ages fifty-five and above touched me deeper than any other process. I was flooded with memories of men who took time to teach me, including my father. In my time doing men's work, I have come to truly value mentors and elders. Even as I write, I visualize men who have taken me on as a pupil of life, not on my direct request, but for reasons of their own (mentors). I am struck by what I learned, positive and negative, from the older men of my tribe (family),

14

and how pivotal this instruction was in the man I have become. Let me offer several brief definitions:

A **Male Mentor** is a man who selects a younger boy or man, teaching him his most valued knowledge. Often the mentor's selection process is a mystery to the one who is selected. One clear purpose of mentoring is the hope that men who have been mentored will grow within the knowledge, in turn, passing it on to another generation. In this way, important stories and lives are given a certain earth-bound immortality. (I wish to note the importance of female mentors. While not a focus of this volume, many of the concepts in this section will apply to key women in your life who teach a sense of feminine power.)

Elders are men of the tribe, family and community who take responsibility for initiating a young male from boyhood into manhood. Elders may be blood relatives or simply men of honor and experience.

Initiation is the process by which boys symbolically pass through the gate to manhood. Many cultures have time-honored, organized rituals of initiation that boys experience at predetermined ages. In some cultures, such as the Native American, elders have stimulated a renewed interest in ceremonies that were in danger of extinction due to assimilation into other cultures. An interesting addition to this process is the common use of ceremonies based on Native American and African rituals in men's healing gatherings, which are often heavily attended by Caucasian men. This indication that Western culture lacks essential initiation experiences will be discussed later in this section.

A brief exercise may help you get a clear fix on your place in these issues.

Take out your journal. Begin a review of your life, starting today and going backwards in five-year increments. Review the men you have had significant interactions with. As you drift back, list the names of men who "took you under wing" in a positive way. Make a notation next to each name that indicates what you learned about manhood and life.

Some of you may believe you got nothing positive from men. I am reminded of a client who was abused verbally, physically, and sexually by men as a child. But, he remembered a summer when a group of carpenters gave him attention, a few skills, a place of safety away from home, and an awareness of kindness from men. This gesture from a few men, for a short time, was critical in creating a window of opportunity in my building trust with this client.

Now take a moment to finish this sentence: "What I was taught growing up about elders was. . . . Looking through your messages about elders, was their behavior consistent with their expectations of you? How did this affect decisions you made about older men and how you viewed relationships between men in your world? How do you honor elders in your world today?

Having looked at your history with mentors and elders, I believe it is important to look at the Shadow side of this Key Aspect and how to utilize mentors, elders and, initiation in your present life.

As you review your journaling, you may recall the presence of Shadow Mentors—men who chose to instruct boys toward emotional, physical, and sexual danger. Extreme examples include child sexual offenders and adults who introduce children to substance abuse. On another level are men whose agenda is to control youth: abusive coaches, repressive clergy, teachers, and therapists, and bosses who steal the spotlight from the student or client in his moment of glory. When making my own judgments about this Shadow, I use the following tenet:

I stand in the Light if my goals in mentoring or being mentored are to teach and be taught, not to become or find a guru.

In applying the Shadow view to elders, several guidelines are useful:

- Respect is earned and given.
- Trust is earned and given.
- A true Elder earns respect and trust through his words and deeds each day.

Over the past century a number of factors have contributed to the lack of the formal, healthy initiation of males. In the United States, many families left their traditional cultures behind in the "Old Country." A number of men have told me tales of a father who forbid the children from learning the native language and customs of their ancestors. The parents were looking to leave a past of repression or poverty behind, mistakenly eliminating the key positive aspects of initiation. The Industrial Revolution drew fathers and other elders away from the family. Men began working away from home in increasing numbers, in hard times such as the Depression, working long days every day. Fathers, grandfathers, and uncles drifted farther from the family system. Increasingly, boys have turned to mothers and peers for socialization and initiation. This movement had expanded as families became more geographically mobile, as mother wanted or needed to work outside of the home, and as many parents exited the family by divorce. None of these issues is presented as an indictment of men or women. Simply, many of you who are reading these pages have been dramatically affected by these events.

As emotional trauma is accompanied by survival behavior, the adolescent culture empowers through rejection of the processes of eldering and initiation. Boys have turned to peers for rites of passage, as our view of elders has evolved toward statements like, "His time has passed," "Old people are like children again." "Retire and play golf." Increasingly, adolescent males have migrated to Shadow rituals of alcohol, drugs, sexual acting out, or violence. In the most extreme situations, gangs have replaced family and community, with older inappropriately initiated youth mentoring younger boys in need of fathers and elders.

All the while, efforts have continued to properly initiate young men into a strong, powerful, loving masculinity. In listing Initiation as a Key Aspect in a book for adult males, I am suggesting these efforts are often valiant, but many fail because uninitiated men are attempting to initiate boys. I challenge you who have sons, nephews, neighbor boys, and also you who are fathers, grandfathers, uncles, coaches, clergy, Big Brothers, gang interventionists, and scout leaders. Face your own Shadow and your secrets. An old therapy adage is "you can't take anyone farther than you've gone." Do your own work as you seek to make your mark on the world and teach boys to be men. As you seek to be listened to and respected by boys and younger men, find the mentors and elders in your life. Honor them. Thank them. Say to them all that you have wanted to, but hesitated. If some of these are men from your past with whom you no longer have contact, write letters to be read aloud with new, trusted men in your life. There are men who passed before me, who taught me, who gave me gifts of knowledge of the head and heart, that I speak to regularly in my thoughts.

It is essential to mention again that adapting historical rites of male passage, as described here, is **not** a return to attitudes of male dominance over women and children. I don't suggest that all ways of the past were right, simply that capturing the best parts of our past is a necessary process in healing, as necessary as letting go of the worst parts of our past. In our work we also honor our healthy female mentors and elders. We let go of the dependence on, and blame of, women that has resulted from the movement of men away from families. We honor the women who daily, often without adequate assistance from responsible men, do their best to teach their sons to become good men. I, for one, have learned much about good fathering from my wife, DiAne, but the female energy is not enough.

Continue to find mentors and key elders in your life, whatever your age. Be available to men of knowledge, experience, and gentle, powerful masculinity in your workplace, your community, your church. Find a men's group; attend a men's workshop that honors elders; create a men's support group. Whatever your age, someone calls you "young man."

Fathering

My pledge to you. . .
Generations of men have wounded
Borrowing the power of their sons
Hoping to rekindle their own flame
Keep, guard your strength, son
Each to His Fire
This being so
I see
Snarls, growls, howls, loving battle
And laughter
The embrace of separateness and
The embrace of connectedness
Welcome!

Excerpt, "Keeping the Flame"
Chris Frey, 1991

The crisis of absent fathers has reached epidemic proportions in cultures throughout our planet. As described earlier, a major factor was more fathers moving into the industrial workforce. In current times many fathers and mothers must work long hours, even multiple jobs to keep the family afloat financially. Economic necessity is not the only driving force in the detachment of fathers. Many committed fathers find time with their children limited through divorce. Even in the best custody arrangements both parents lose opportunities. Fathers are often physically present in the family but overcommitted to career, are alcoholic and drug dependent, or simply emotionally disconnected. Finally, more boys and men are fathering children, then abandoning them to the mothers, the extended family, and the community. This crisis has increased dramatically over the past several decades. At the same time, the role of a father has been minimized to little more than hunter (provider) and ruler (disciplinarian). This is a common experience with men who come to my office:

> *Chris: "You've spoken a lot about your mom (be it her love or her dysfunction). What about Dad?"*
> *Man: "I don't think Dad had much to do with this stuff. He was... (never around, left when I was young, died, worked all the time, never paid attention to me, always drunk, a great guy but didn't talk much)."*

Strangely enough, the most powerful wound in the father-son relationship may be the issues used to discount the father's importance—his absence. As the man's work continues, the conversation with a man often begins to sound like this:

> *"Until I focused on my father, I didn't see how much I missed him, wanted to be with him, wanted him just to hold me or accept me. There's a lot I don't know about being a man, stuff Mom couldn't teach me").*

So, I propose that *the first mission of fathering is to be present, physically and emotionally.*

A while ago, my friend Jim and I presented a professional workshop on Men in Therapy. We covered a number of the issues I've discussed in these pages. When we reached father-son relationships, the intensity of discussion reached a new level. The entire day could easily have been devoted to this issue, as entire books have been. One heated debate was on the best methods of fathering. But, much of this discussion gave way to the larger, more fundamental concern on which I will focus: the importance of the father as a consistent, safe, powerful presence in his child's life, what I will call the Three Principles of Fathering.

My Story

Principle 1: As a father, I need to show up and find the joy of fathering.

In 1993, after some years of working on myself and with other men, I completed the New Warrior Training Adventure, a powerful male initiation experience. The one primary purpose of my decision was a desire to uncover my passion for fathering. I have been a good dad (good provider, a hugger of children, a sayer of "I love you," an organizer of fun). However, I had always focused more on the responsibilities of being a parent, and less on the joy. I had daughters, Carly and Aimee, with a good mother and ex-wife, Renee, and a new son, Nathan, with DiAnne. Due to my choices about marriage and work, I had often been one of those absent fathers. Time for change.

I did find that passion for fathering that I was looking for. What does it mean in my life? Beyond the concrete behaviors such as spending more time with my kids, I feel different. My emotional approach to being a father has changed. I feel a joy beyond words. I enjoy the good times more. I am more present and effective in the rough times. I feel at once more protective of my children, yet more able to let them go. I listen better, get in fewer control struggles with them, play more, and own my mistakes. (Yes, I still make plenty.) I am present more often.

My wife sometimes looks at me as if she cannot grasp that this passion is not a natural process. It seems to be for her, and I used to feel shame about that. Somewhere between the ecstasy of the moment I first saw each child and my views of being a "responsible" father, I misplaced a lot of the joy. I share this because I believe many of you have experienced a similar loss, as did many of our fathers. Most important, you can rekindle that joy, perhaps locate it for the first time.

Principle 2: As a father I must seek to provide a safe haven for my children.

Although men have been dominant in our culture physically, vocationally, and financially, we have often lacked essential male power in our families. You might be saying, "Oh yeah. My dad had all the power. What he said was law. He hit us. Even Mom was afraid of him." This is dominance and control, not positive power. True male power is used to protect and guide, not control and abuse. This power starts with being a strong role model, not an errant dictator. One of the most heated discussions in one workshop involved children, parents, and fear. More than one man argued that if children did not fear their fathers they would not accept limits; they would engage in inappropriate and dangerous behaviors. I believe that as fathers we must teach an awareness of appropriate fear in certain life choices: playing with matches, the first day in a new school, naked bungee jumping from suspension bridges. We listen to, support, and reassure our children when they are scared. We assist them in making judgments about potential life danger. We **do not** seek to become one of life's dangers or the focus of control in the child's life. If a child is conditioned to make choices based primarily on fear of retribution, what happens when the father is not around, or if he dies? What happens when the child is thirty-five years old?

Looking from the other end of the tunnel, how many of us as sons felt compelled to make more, not fewer, dangerous choices to escape the control and intimidation of a parent? Finally, how many of us engaged in dangerous behavior because the danger present in our childhood home created an immunity to feeling the fear of "life on the edge"?

Principle 3: I use my power as a father to protect, to create opportunity, and to model accountability.

Power in men's work is an internal process: the intent to feel and project a sense of strength, awareness, passion, and integrity. The father is not a thief in the night who seeks to feel powerful by stealing the powers of others who are weaker or smaller, those who depend on him, who will not or cannot stop him. I see many men who have a strong sense of powerlessness, strength stolen from them by an abusive past or present. Our corporate economy often uses people as parts of a machine, not as humans. Our systems of "helping" the indigent contain an unwritten requirement, "to receive you must feel ashamed." Men who no longer "produce," our elders, are pushed aside. One outcome of these abuses I see is the man who feels his powerlessness each day outside of the home, and returns to those who love him with resentment, shame, and a desire to get control. Too often this translates into controlling others. Another scenario is the man who successfully dominates others and believes that real power is calculated by how many people obey him, or at least fear him.

In this less than perfect world, we each have an opportunity to father from a position of strength, not control. I hope you will learn from several healing stories in my life.

> When I was twelve years old, my sister, Lisa, and I were accused of shoplifting. The store owner would not search us, as we suggested. He simply accused and abused us. Upon arriving home we told Dad the story without expecting anything. Dad piled us into the car, took us to the store and had us watch as he confronted the manager. The gist of the confrontation: the cowardice of a man who seeks to scare and shame children without any intention of resolving the conflict. That day, as I stood behind my dad, I felt safe and trusted by a very powerful father.
>
> Twenty-seven years later, I sat down with Dad to do some face-to-face, father-son work. He had agreed to meet with me, heard me out as I recounted my questions and anger from childhood. He spoke of mistakes he had made and guilt he had wrestled with. It was a loving, healing time for me. But, perhaps, the most important moments were toward the end. He stated that having expressed his remorse, he did not plan to grow old feeling guilty for his past, that any residual anger in me I was accountable for resolving. I felt an initial sense of shock, then anger, followed by an understanding that my dad was echoing hundreds of conversations I have had with

men. A man's power lies in his accountability. Confronting my past was not about blaming Dad; it was about stating my truth, learning his, and moving on.

A big component in my personal work has been strengthening my belief that I can protect my children. Much of my early life was about shrinking from conflict. Later, I became unsure of naturally taking the kind of action my father did when I was twelve. I've focused a lot of energy on this in finding my power. Several weeks after a powerful men's weekend, I took my family to the zoo. I was carrying my son, Nathan, and not really paying full attention to the moment. I stepped off the edge of the sidewalk, tripped, and fell. Without time to think, I felt the need to put my arm out, hitting my elbow on the ground instead of Nathan's head. I later cried knowing I had protected my child out of my heart, not my head. I carry a scar—the scar I'm proudest of. As I write, I'm thinking about the parents who this day will literally put their lives on the line for their children: starving so a child eats, shielding a child from a bullet. And I consider the many less dramatic ways that millions of parents every day work to give their children a safer world. That's power!

Mothers

I have focused a great deal of personal effort on my understanding and letting go of my boyhood relationship with my mom, which allows me to give this section in the book a place of honor and significance. I am most personally familiar with the over-dependent mother-son relationship. I was the sickly son of a traditional stay-at-home mom—a mom whose male role models had been severely lacking. I see many men with this problem in my practice today. I also see many men, whose personal relationships have suffered from a lack of men in their lives, due to abandonment or neglect. A third story I often hear seems to combine the worst of these two styles: the son who was expected to be with Mom when Dad was absent or "bad" (drunk, angry, etc.) and then expected to back off when Dad reappeared. In styles one and three, the son is often left with too much mother energy. Common life decisions that come from this overload of the feminine include:

"Mom needs me to take care of her."
"I am the man of the house."
"Men are bad."

"Mom (all women) will take care of me."
"I will be the kind of man that women (Mom) want me to be."
"I must make women accept me and must make Mom and my
lover/wife accept each other."

(If you are a man who felt too close to Mom, write down in your journal other ways this affected you.)

In families with a significantly traumatized mother (chemical dependent, abuse victim, mentally ill) this enmeshment can take the form of abuse and/or feminizing of the son, in an effort to make him different from the mother's fearful, angry view of men. This boy may then long for, and feel short on, masculine energy; or he may turn to the other extreme, expressions of false masculinity, "machoism." I see this scenario in many fatherless households.

From the enmeshed relationship comes many "Nice Men (boys)," men who are dependent on pleasing and merging with past, present and future females. If you are one of these men you may be aware of secret rage at women that comes out quickly and explosively, only to be quickly tucked away with more niceness. I was determined to be the nice male that I did not see in my mother's extended family, the nice male that got complimented by everyone, the nice male that my father was. Those gentle, soft parts of me are valuable components of who I am and have often served me well in my work and life. Over-emphasis on these facets of my personality also served to cover much of my masculine power and created an under-development of traits such as courage, healthy expression of anger, and boundaries with angry men and most females. Repression of my Shadow led me to harm myself and others in many ways, particularly as an adolescent and young man. Even now, people are sometimes surprised to find I am not always "nice" (my daughters' mother and my wife are not in this company).

I have no better way to summarize this view of the merged mother-son relationship than through a writing I offered, in part, earlier in this chapter:

Gentle Sons, Frightened Fathers

He was . . . a good boy, a gentle son, kind, polite
Careful, helpful
His anger tidy, kept tucked neatly away
Only on rare occasions exploding outward
Like a ghost jumping unexpectedly from the dark
then pushed   away
With the ghost's bedfellows
Fear, sadness, shame

23

He was . . . a good boy, a gentle son, sensitive, loving
Motivated, NICE
A mother's pride and joy
A teacher's pet
A talker, a thinker
A reader, a listener
Your father doesn't understand
Your mother doesn't understand
Able to give the illusion that he did . . . understand

A master of illusion, he becomes a good man, a gentle man
His anger tidy, kept tucked neatly away
Except, of course, in sarcasm or criticism, advice or isolation
Silence or talking . . . talking . . . talking
His fear deep in the belly
Except, of course, in his drive for the 4 Ss
Success, Sincerity, Substances, and Sex
Building walls as others try to touch him
Wondering, if he becomes good enough then . . .

Unable to finish the sentence he takes the next illogical step
Fatherhood
Praying for a son, determined to improve on the model
Praying for a daughter, afraid he cannot father a real man
Instead he receives a gift, a Child who needs no improvement
The man asks himself
What does this child need? What do I have of worth to give?
What will I do knowing I cannot give perfectly?

In answering the final question he enters his shame
Fear, sadness, anger, His Grief
In this haystack he finds a needle; Hope
The intimacy of his real self
Letting go of the myth of perfection
Not just his own
But those who gave him the best they had

I knew I was truly becoming a man when I stopped trying to convince my mother I was a man! One of the greatest gifts my mother gave me was persistence. I do not have to stay where I am, nor do you. Some of you may be thinking, "I don't know how to be if I let go of Mom? What if I lose her completely? What if I fall apart completely? What if she falls apart?" To you who share these fears, I offer another gift my mother gave me that I was unwilling to see until I was well into adulthood: Moms are often the strongest, bravest, most resilient humans in our lives. If you're willing to grow up, Mom's going to be OK. My Mom and I have had several discussions about who I *really* was as a boy. Although it is not my mom's style to say this, I believe she's ready for me to be a man who can stand in his own power. It took a lot of time and energy to mother me, and she has other stuff she likes to do with her time.

Perhaps you don't fit the description of the enmeshed relationship; your mother may have left, physically and/or emotionally. Maybe she was a good, even great, mom but she died or worked long hours. Perhaps she was chemically dependent, depressed, chronically ill. Some of you never met your biological mother; you are adopted or lost her at birth. As with the man who has too much mother, you who had too little are at risk to move through manhood seeking Mom in wives, lovers, and friends. Another risk is to become so self-sufficient that no women can get in. How many of you have found a lover who is very maternal, only to both invite and reject efforts to take care of you:

> *Doug had lost his mother at an early age. Without much direction from his father, he hit the streets early—drugs, deals, fights. He came to therapy with a great amount of confusion about his relationships with women. His lovers always seemed to be women who wanted him to change and who constantly gave him advice. After a while he decided that he both wanted to be taken care of, loved and accepted by a women **and** he wanted to do the opposite of almost anything they suggested to him.*

In short, the man with too little mother energy may also function at the extreme edge of male stereotypes: the son who becomes the pseudo-mother in the family and denies his own need for nurturing; the son who denies all aspects of the feminine in himself and becomes a cartoon cutout of John Wayne; the son who submits to every women in his life, willing to trade his sense of maleness to fill that mother hunger.

If you are this man, be aware of several essential aspects of men's work. In the company of men can be found Male Mothers, men who possess a great strength combined with the gentleness, nurturing, and safety of a mother's arms (with a male flavoring). Further, in your journey you will have the opportunity to meet many good, strong women who can provide support and nurturing, but are not available for us to hook up our emotional umbilical cords. Take time to form non-romantic relationships with females. Connect with women who have children. Find out what you missed, how to grieve the loss, and how to put loving feminine intensity in your life.

What makes this information so vital? I believe looking at Mom serves you on several levels. One, resolution of your anger, grief and shame about Mom allows you to create a place in your heart for loving your mother without feeling you two must be "as one" or that you could only deeply love her if you knew her well and saw her often. Second, this work offers the opportunity to love and honor women as wives, lovers, or friends without having to be "as one" with them. Third, as a father you may create the chance to break the cycle, assisting the mothers of our children in learning to be present, available, but separate from their sons.

As you prepare to finish this section, open your journal and answer the following questions :

Do you compare lovers, favorably or unfavorably, to Mom?
Do you avoid women, particularly women like Mom?
Are you particularly attracted to women or lovers like Mom but these relationships don't seem to work?
How does your mom feel about your choice of lovers or wife?
When Mom has struggles in her life today, how do you react? Do you help her, feel responsible, avoid her?
What are you still angry at your mom about? What about Mom saddens you, scares you, shames you?
If you could be different in your relationship with Mom, how would you be?
If you could be different in your relationships with your lover, female friends, or wife, how would you be?

In the journaling, you will find clues that will assist you in the later chapters.

I close this section with several statements of healing from men:

"I knew I was becoming a man when I quit trying to convince Mom that I was a man."
"I knew I was a man when I accepted Mom as she is, rather than working to make her accept me."
"Mom did the best she could, but it's OK that I'm sad and angry that she wasn't there much when I needed her."
"Mom seems smaller, not so scary and powerful."
"I know I had a biological mother. Even though I didn't get to know her; she gave me life."
"I can keep the good parts of my time with Mom and give her back her anger, fear, and guilt."
"I had a good mom, not perfect, but really good."
"I didn't get much of anything from Mom, but she is my mom."

Thanks to my mom for getting me into this world and teaching me about persistence, giving to others, strength, volumes about love, and how to do my own laundry.

Race/Ethnicity/Sexual Orientation

"Welcome, brother"

a greeting common to men's gatherings

I placed this Key Aspect toward the end of the chapter for two reasons: First, issues of race, ethnicity, and sexual orientation are absolutely critical to men who choose to move "Beyond the Inner Child," and secondly, this may be the Key Aspect in which I feel the least focused.

Although sexual orientation may seem somewhat removed from race and ethnicity, I found myself centered on a similar dynamic in each: prejudice. As men, we're taught to compete and win. We are also taught that for each winner, there must be a loser. And we are taught that a quick and easy method to identify who the loser should be is to select a man who is *different*. Often the difference men select is racial, ethnic, or sexual. To justify conquest, the historical warrior mentality identifies a foe who *deserves* to lose, more often based on prejudice than fact. In masculine healing, the enemy must be the bigotry, not the man who is different. The battle of the modern warrior is *internal*.

The "men's movement" has largely been a movement of Caucasian men, but the work is becoming multicultural. As a white, college-educated professional I have been provided opportunities that relate not only to my hard work, but also to my membership in what has been a privileged group of men. In recent years I have been fortunate enough in this men's work to stand with men of African, Hispanic, and Asian descent; to find my commonality with men of Jewish, Catholic, Protestant, Morman, and other religious backgrounds; to be held by, and to hold, gay men, heterosexual men, men who are struggling to decide. In each circumstance, the other men and myself were forced to confront our Shadow sides: our prejudice, our assumptions, our stereotypes. Sadly, I do not always like the attitudes of the man I have become, but it is only through looking at how I diminish and shame men who are different that I change. In that change I face my fear and shame that I do not belong, that I am different. In that change I face perhaps my greatest myth, that to be a "real man," I must make another man less than me.

Take a moment to journal. Finish these sentences:

Fill the blank with a race other than your own: . . .*men are.* . . .

Fill the blank with your race: . . .*men are.* . . .

Fill the blank with another ethnic origin:

   (*Irish, German, Italian) men are.* . . .

Fill the blank with a sexual orientation.

   (*Gay, Heterosexual) men are.* . . .

Finally, select two religious orientations other than your own (if you consider yourself a religious man, you may want to select "atheist").

Men of the . . .religion are . . .

Men of my religion are. . . .

As an interesting related activity, consider what "permissions" you may have been given in your life to place responsibility on your ethnicity or religion. For example, my background is primarily German and Scandinavian. In the community where I live, being German is frequently used to excuse rigid, stoic, uncommunicative behavior in men. Some men blame their German ethnicity when no family member has set foot in Germany or stayed connected to their German heritage in positive ways for several generations.

One of the great joys of life is experiencing diversity. One of the great joys, and challenges, of men's work is experiencing men of different colors, origins, and orientations. This will certainly push you. You'll probably not like all of what you learn about yourself, but you will learn.

Several suggestions as you seek to change:

Pay attention to your words. How do you demean others or yourself due to race, ethnicity or orientation?

Pay attention to the words of others. How do you react when others demean someone due to race, ethnicity, or orientation?

Pay attention to assumptions you make before you know men who seem different from you.

Open yourself to what each man can teach you about yourself.

Finally, as you prepare for this work, consider the mix of the men you will seek to accompany you. Are there suficient numbers of men who know this cornerstone of your pain from their own experience? Is there suficient diversity, the opportunity to create love and respect with men who have walked other roads? Over and over, I have seen men who would never consider speaking in the grocery line become lifelines for one another in group.

Moving On

"If I don't take this home, it's not worth much."

Anonymous, 1992

A favorite saying of mine is, "therapy is only as good as what you do between sessions." Healing is recovering the best parts of the past, getting unstuck from the negative aspects of the past, and moving on as stated in my mission: "To teach living in the present by healing and honoring the past."

Movement includes not only the work of internal healing, but taking this new male self into the world, improving relationships with family, friends, and strangers. It means practicing this new me. It means understanding that healing work is not a guarantee of happiness and security. However, it is a guarantee of mature masculinity. For many of you, moving on will carry with it a stronger spiritual life. Perhaps, you will slow down to see, smell, hear, and taste life, rather than trying to beat time. You may search for a purpose to your life greater than healing your pain, greater than getting what you want out of life.

No guide to healing would be complete without a discussion of forgiveness. Among the many models of healing—religious, Twelve Step, therapeutic, other spiritual approaches—forgiveness is an issue of great debate. My offering is not a judgement about forgiveness as a necessary or unnecessary process in trauma healing. Rather, I would like to offer a perspective to those of you who have someone you desire to forgive for past conflicts.

Forgiveness is best found in relationships with one person in the spirit of forgiveness and another in the spirit of remorse. In the healing of past trauma, anger work is often a prerequisite to feeling this spirit of forgiveness. Too often I have seen men who are attempting what I call *instant forgiveness*. This man makes forgiving an intellectual process, stuffing often long-standing anger with statements like "I know they did the best they could," "I understand nobody's perfect," "I just need to let go of my resentment." While these statements are all strong truths, and may even be sufficient at times, many of the wounds boys suffer cannot be simply thought away. In these times, forgiveness must come from the heart, which means feeling the anger and grief first. As for the individual who is experiencing the forgiveness of another, an attitude of honesty, understanding, and remorse is essential.

Of course, you may create forgiveness in relationships that don't offer optimum circumstances: the other person may no longer be in your daily life; it might be unwise, even dangerous, to have direct contact with him or her; or there may be no remorse. In these situations, the work will be symbolic. I will talk at length in later chapters about this part of the journey.

Finally, I believe each of us will face the challenge of self-forgiveness in this work. The path of healing may include forgiving those who shamed you. Significantly, we each have also experienced "self-generated shame," the process of shaming yourself through choices that are destructive to yourself and others. Again, the cycle of honesty, understanding, and remorse are essential.

> *Bill grew up in a violent, alcoholic home. As a young man he became violent and alcoholic. "Sometimes I believe the most important part of my work was admitting first to other men, then to my family, that I had become what I hated in my father. For years I said, 'I'm sorry,' but I didn't change. Even when I got into recovery, it didn't work to ask my kids to forgive me because I hadn't forgiven myself. When I felt all the sadness of how I hurt them, hurt myself; when I realized how much I had missed, I wasn't so guilty and ashamed. I was very sad. That's when my deepest change began."*

As you finish this chapter, and prepare for the action steps of what remains, open your journal and reflect on several questions about moving on:

What is my greatest challenge in getting on with my life?
Who and what do I believe keep me stuck?
How do *I* keep myself stuck?
As a man, what is my life purpose; what will my contribution be to this world?

As you prepare to enter further into the action steps of this book, I want to thank you for your openness, and your skepticism, this far. For today, moving on only means turning to the next page.

2: Uncovering and Expressing the Wounds

A childhood lesson powerful as the fire
Which wailing, damned souls could never tame,
Returns to haunt the middle aged with ire,
And singe the present's eyelash with its flame.
The boy who has forbidden thoughts is less
Than all the heroes strong and brave and true;
He must deny all sadness, anger, stress
And of the sin of weakness give no clue.
He leans to the flame, yet feels no pain;
And when reality burns cold and wet,
Confusion, dread, and apprehension reign,
While hot, dry thoughts, and cold, now make him sweat.
The flame has fully burned his senses numb;
He cannot feel the fire, or hear the drum

Hal Maples, 1993

Tim came to therapy to look at how he expressed anger. More specifically he came because his wife told him she would not live with him unless he changed. When questioned about his anger Tim called it "expressing my frustration." When asked to define his ways of giving voice to that frustration he acknowledged name-calling, throwing objects, and hitting walls. In apparent confusion he reported, "My wife says I yell all the time, I don't think I do. She says I'm abusive, but I've never hit her." In discussing family of origin history Tim said, "My dad was pretty strict. It wasn't like he abused us or anything; he only hit me when I deserved it. It did seem like I could never do anything good enough. He called me stupid a lot. He

31

*was a really big guy with a loud voice." When asked to de-
scribe the physical punishment, Tim reflected, "I haven't
thought about this for a long time. The belt he used really hurt,
and if I cried he kept hitting." After a time Tim agreed to join
men's group. He began to reconnect with memories of Dad using the buckle end of the belt, of the time Dad threw him
against the wall, and one night in group, with great sadness,
the promise he had made to himself to never scare his wife and
children the way his dad scared him. In his grief and shame,
Tim began to own that the similarities between him and his dad
were far more numerous than he let himself know.*

To "feel the fire, or hear the drum," a man must touch his wounds.
The writer of the poem that opens this chapter, Hal, was one of the first
men to submit writings to me when I put out my request to include in
these chapters the words of men I love. I was immediately drawn to this
poem and knew that it belonged with this chapter. I have not asked Hal
to interpret his poem. Instead, I found myself writing: To express the
wounds of childhood, manhood, of generations past is to feel the fire,
to **be** fire, to beat the drum, to join a community of drummers.
Uncovering woundedness often involves processes that allow men to
observe any or all stages of the life cycle, pre-natal to the present. Men
are working on the grief of not being wanted before birth, a birth
process that prevented bonding with mother and father, and numerous
other birth traumas. Other men are healing the pain of childhood neglect, abuse, and abandonment. From these efforts, men are learning
new skills to express the adult wounds of divorce, addictions, death of
loved ones, war, and other seemingly catastrophic losses. Some of you
who read this material will wonder if you belong in this work. You had
a childhood with loving, healthy parents free of the traumas often discussed in men's work. Perhaps your trauma came later (war, loss of a
loved one or a job). Or, you may simply be a man looking for a deeper
soul connection with yourself, other men, your community, your world,
maybe your Higher Power.

Many of you are already acutely aware of the pain that you carry,
and you have made considerable progress in recovery. For you, this
chapter may offer new strategies for continuing your work. For the men
who are relatively new to this journey, review the exercises and determine (with a trusted group or person) your best method of proceeding,
both keeping yourself safe and stretching yourself. Keep in mind that
you are uncovering your perceptions of your pain. Others, even those
who were present for some of the events you are working on, may re-

member and interpret those occurrences differently. Memories are affected by age, your style of gathering information, and by the passing of time. Some of your most significant struggles may originate from unintentional acts of people who believed they had your best interests in mind. The intentions and remembrances of others aside, this work is about how you remember your life and how you actually experienced these moments. The wounds are yours; the perceptions belong to you; the feelings are your truth.

A controversy over the concept of repressed memories is raging among therapists and has become a legal question. Sadly, few issues that relate to the emotional, psychological, sexual, and physical well-being of children have ever found much worth in our legal system. This is not an attack on the good intentions of many; I simply speak to the realities of an institution by adults, for adults. Memories originating from childhood, uncovered in adolescence or adulthood, are difficult to prove. The good news about this text is that it isn't a court of law. I believe in repressed memories, and perhaps most important, we are seeking in this work to heal the pain, not create a narrative of historical fact.

I was trained in a model that focused on recovering and working through specific memories of trauma, but my perspective has broadened. I know that babies are abused in our world. I know that some of these babies grow to adulthood with the effects of this abuse, but no specific memories. I have worked with men and women who go down to feelings so deep they have no words, only sounds and guttural noises. If you have key memories to work on, go for it! If you have a sense of things that will forever pre-date conscious memory, this book encourages you to go to the feelings to heal them. Still others have impressions, guesses and questions; again, go for the feelings! In many of the exercises that follow, you will locate the fear, shame, anger, sadness, and joy. You may, in turn, uncover memories of events, people, and places. But, the memories are not the key, the feelings are. You are reading this book, or involved in men's work, not to satisfy a therapist's curiosity, or to be told what happened in your childhood, or to assign blame to those who raised you. This work is about healing pain and changing life choices and behaviors.

Preparing for the Work

I believe deeply in the potential of the processes I will be describing in the following pages. I also believe that like many other activities men participate in, a man must condition himself for the tasks ahead. As such, I offer several guidelines and several commitments that many of you need to consider before forging ahead.

Note: It may be helpful at this point to read the section on couples (pages 219-225) before beginning the next section.

Addictions

There are at least three substantial risks in proceeding with work of the heart if you are in the throes of an active addiction: the feelings you uncover will either be muted or exaggerated by your addiction, the memories you uncover may be of questionable validity to yourself and others during and after your active addictive process, and you will recycle your pain.

> *Sid came to group with a disclosure, "I started drinking again three months ago." In the course of the discussion, Sid shared that his decision to tell the group was in large part due to his feeling stuck in his grief work. "I'll do pieces of work, feel better for a few days and then go right back to where I started. I don't really understand my feelings; I don't trust that I've made any real progress, and I'm tired of rehashing the same old pain."*

If you have not made a commitment to abstain from your addictive behaviors and to create a program of recovery that gives you a basic foundation to live differently, you will find limited success from the pages that follow. I recommend that all men doing this work of the heart abstain from alcohol during the time they are in a men's group. It is not my purpose in this text to assist you in assessing whether you are an addict or in describing a basic program for recovery. However, if you are reading and find yourself resisting the idea, take a look at yourself before going any further. As you are reading this, if you are saying, "I don't have a problem with . . . (alcohol, drugs, sex, food)", take another look before you proceed. I also recommend you do this work in the company of a skilled professional if you take prescription medications for emotional or psychiatric disorders. The interplay between medications and feelings work can be of considerable benefit to some men, and should always be approached with you and the professional operating as a team.

Sobriety Contracts

I encourage all men who are recovering to set contracts for sobriety in the company of other men who are doing this work of the heart. Typically, the contract includes:

The specific addictive "bottom line" behaviors that the man is giving up.

The specific activities (Twelve-Step, men's group, etc.) that the man will engage in for recovery.

The actions the man will take (extra Twelve-Step meetings, use of phone list, extra therapy sessions) in the event the stirring of his emotions stimulates a desire to relapse.

Some professionals believe that working on issues of past trauma and pain has no place in early recovery. I have often found that my clients just won't follow a progression of recovery as prescribed by the manual of rigid performance. Delving deeply in past abuse and the core emotions resulting from early trauma can be futile at best. It may even encourage relapse in many chemically and sexually addicted men. If you are one of these men, I suggest you combine a strong early recovery program with individual therapy or a men's support group. One resource that addresses the issues surrounding early recovery and sexual abuse is my book, *Double Jeopardy*. Although written for treating adolescents, the section on "The Emergency Stage" for survivors is an excellent text for addicts of all ages whose emotions and early trauma are beginning to surface.

No-Harm Contracts

Some of the men reading this book have experienced suicidal and/or homicidal ideation, perhaps even behaviors. A commitment to live and to let others live is essential to the healing journey you are on. For men, this includes not only suicidal behavior, but also the self-destructive and risky behaviors common to many of us who grew up in danger.

Greg worked with children in a residential setting for seriously violent juveniles. He reported, early in group, that he often went against agency protocol, attempting to control and de-escalate dangerous kids without the assistance of other staff. Greg also shared that he often drove his car at dangerous speeds around curves, had been drinking and driving, and had engaged in numerous dangerous sports activities.

So, a necessary step in beginning the journey of emotion if you have any history of these kinds of thoughts or behaviors is a No-Harm Contract. This contract is best made in the company of other men and takes into consideration any specific risks to your safety that you are aware of. I recommend a contract that reads as follows:

I,_____, do agree not to harm or kill myself or others. This specifically includes all of the following

_____

(any physically, sexually, emotionally dangerous behaviors to self and others). I will renew this contract with_____ (who) on a_____(how often) basis.

_____

Name

_____

Witness

_____

Date

Getting Started

I have read many excellent manuals that guide the reader through the recovery process in an orderly, sequential manner. This is not one of those volumes. My own experience, personally and professionally, is that much of a man's work is random, chaotic, and ordered only to the point that it fits who the man is. The closest I could come to order in this book is to make several observations and to then sequence my chapters accordingly.

Many of you have forgotten that at one time you knew exactly what, when and how to feel your feelings. As a child, no one needed to teach you to feel, you just did. Of course, we adults then start messing around trying to control what, when, and how. Starting this work for many of you will include using processes that help you relocate the realm and range of feelings.

Sadness and joy are most often the emotions I see men experience only after going through fear, anger, and shame. It will be common for many men reading this book to become familiar with a transitioning process in feelings work, particularly moving through rage and flowing right into powerful sadness.

All men must feel and move through fear, time after time, to do this work. I have met men, read about men, seen men interviewed that professed to have no fear. If this is true, these men are incredibly dangerous to themselves and to those who love them. I have also seen many men who have faced without fear physical challenges that would terrify me beyond description; they seem to fear nothing in the external world. Untold numbers of the men I described above are truly afraid of one thing—the internal world of emotion. I call this "Scared Backwards"; the propensity of men to risk death without fear physically, yet run from emotion, commitments, accountability, relationships, as if these were some form of living, breathing death.

Relationships, sexuality, and spirituality are issues that are foundational in masculine woundedness and the healing of men, women, and our planet. Without the work of the heart, these cornerstones of the foundation are built on quicksand.

The flow of exercises and chapters tends to move from my somewhat arbitrary perceptions of least risky toward more risky activities. Much of the early work will be journaling, a potentially powerful tool that provides some emotional distance, yet the opportunity to express some feelings while gathering information. As you move through the volume, many of the processes will be best experienced in the company of support people, for intensity of healing and for emotional safety. Each man is different, and many of you will move in and out of various sections of the work in your own ways. Men I work with often repeat certain processes multiple times, reaching new levels of healing. If this is good for you, do it.

My Myth

I am my history. Men come to me with the goal of erasing their painful histories, others with the goal of recapturing their stories. In my mission of healing and honoring the past, my offering of a place to start is writing your life story as a fable. To the extent that my beliefs, perceptions, and feelings are uniquely created from my experience, my story is My Myth, as is yours.

Take out your journal. At the top of a clean page write, *"Once upon a time there was a boy . . ."* In the first section of this writing, tell the story of a boy who grew up to be just like you are today. Describe his birth, his family, his struggles, the other significant people in his development, his victories, his defeats, his key life events, his thoughts and feelings as he grew. Let your pen flow, be impulsive. The goal is to tell the story of a boy like you, not to provide an exhaustive chronology. Who is he? How did he become who he is? As you write, feelings may surface. Stop. Let yourself feel. If the feelings become more intense than you are prepared to face, go away from the journal for an hour, or a day, and return to it. If the feelings are still too intense, reach out to a support person to process your experience before moving forward.

Having completed the story, return to read your myth with the attitude that this is the myth *and* the truth of the boy with my name. In this story, I will find the beliefs, wounds, victories, feelings, and relationships upon which I have based my life. As I read, I will make notes in my journal, answering the question: What does the story of the boy tell me of the healing work that this boy needs? From the answers you give yourself, you will find clear and focused direction of your road to healing. Some of you will also find a clarity about where to start (what issue, event, relationship, wound). If you do not, worry not. "If you stick around long enough and do the work, we'll get to everything."

After writing "My Myth," try these exercises.

Write your story in the third person This activity begins, "If you knew a man who had become just like you, what is the story of how he became who he is?" The story begins, "Once upon a time there was a boy who . . ."

Draw your Feelings Container Get a large sheet of paper and markers or crayons. Draw the container that is in your body, the one that holds your emotions. Draw the feelings that are in your container (use anger, sadness, fear, joy, guilt, shame). Be aware of the following questions and write or draw the answers on the paper:

- What color is the container?
- What material is the container made of?
- What feelings are in your container? How are they organized, or disorganized? What colors are your feelings?
- Is there an opening or a lid? How does someone get to your feelings? Who can get in?
- If you could change anything about your container, or the feelings in it, what would you change? What is the next step of your change?
- At this point, there are many directions you can take this creative venture. You might journal answers to any other questions that occur to you. You might journal what you learned from the exercise. You may close your eyes and visualize where you carry this container in your body and how that feels. Draw a lock on the container with a secret combination, allowing you to decide

who gets in and who doesn't. Share what you experienced with another man. Show him the drawing. Deal with your embarrassment as you say, "I can't draw," or as you hide who you are behind a true artistic talent. (To take the painting/drawing aspect of healing to a new level, a great resource is *Through the Inner Eye,* by Jan Groenemann, Islewest Publications, 1994.)

My Trust Line

Early in life we make decisions about trust. These are decisions made not only about certain individuals that we chose to trust or distrust, but they also are judgments about what I call my Trust Rules—foundational beliefs about trusting what kinds of people, in what types of situations. These conclusions can be made as a result of how we are treated by someone, by a group or culture, and they are frequently molded by the biases of significant others. These conclusions may or may not be accurate perceptions of our childhood world, but they are survival tools. When carried into adulthood, they become the material that weaves sexism, racism, fear of intimacy, isolation, and numerous other emotionally catastrophic choices.

Many of you have seen trust as either-or—I either trust someone or I don't. This exercise suggests that healthy rules about trust are based on evaluating an individual's behavior, that trust is a process not an event, and that we have a wide territory in which to operate when making judgments about trust. As a beginning tool, the Trust Line is directed at assisting you in identifying how you developed your beliefs about trust, how you act these rules out in helpful and destructive ways now, and a basic method for initiating a more mature system for building trust with others:

Take out your journal or a large piece of paper. On the paper draw a horizontal line, labeling it as a scale, 0 at the far left and 100 at the far right.

Distrust   *Trust*

---

0   *100*

Choose at least three people from your childhood that you know well, at least three different people from your adulthood that you know well, and three people from your life now that you don't know well. Using your own system to label who these people are, place each one along the scale on your paper based on the following criteria: *"On a scale from 0 percent to 100 percent, how much do I trust . . ."* Using the same criteria, place yourself on the scale, and answer the following questions on the same page:

- For each person above 50 percent, list specific behaviors of that person that led you to believe he/she could be trusted.
- For each person below 50 percent, list specific behaviors of that person that led you to believe he/she should be distrusted.
- Is there anyone on the list that you trusted or distrusted simply because you were told to, or because someone you cared about felt that way? How did making these choices based on the needs of others work for you?
- Did you put someone high on the scale who has not really earned your trust, perhaps has even earned your distrust? Why?
- Did you put someone low on the scale who has done little, if anything, to harm you? Why?
- Is there anyone on the list whose trust you have trusted much more or much less at some point in your life?
- Have any of these people lost your trust? What would he/she have to do to regain trust?
- Has anyone gained trust? What would he/she have to do to lose your trust?
- What would you have to do to be a more trustworthy person?
- What else have you learned about trust and distrust from this exercise?

Finally, based on the information you just gathered, make a list of the rules you have used to decide who can be trusted. A helpful way to start this is; *"I trust people if. . ."* How do these rules work for you today with friends, co-workers, family?

As you review this activity, be aware of how rigid the rules of trust often are for men who have been severely wounded. Many of you re-experience being used and abused because you trust naively; many of you are isolated because you distrust so naively and easily. Safe and healthy connections are formed one person at a time, over time, with each person being judged on his or her own merits, not something you saw modeled by key mentors and elders. Also, be aware of how much of your own trust Shadow you project on to others. For many years I rigidly and maliciously judged people who lied to make themselves look good, only later realizing my propensity for exaggerating the positive to make myself look more powerful, helpful, altruistic than I had truly been. An excellent adaptation of this exercise is to develop a Trust Line for groups of people based on what I learned as a child and sought to confirm as an adult.

Finally, make a list of groups of people who cause issues to surface in you: men, women, children, African-Americans, heterosexuals, homosexuals, Asian-Americans, etc. Place these names on the Trust Line much like you did before, asking yourself essentially the same questions and anything else you think is pertinent. Be especially aware of how many of your prejudices come from the messages of significant others, rather than your own experiences. Be aware of how these beliefs keep you separate from people you love, from people who could enrich your life, from people whose lives you could enrich.

Finding My Feelings

I have emphasized that much of this work is about going to your heart, locating the emotional stuck places in your life and healing the pain. Some of you are saying, "How do I heal what I don't have?" First, everyone feels, everyone. You may have a myriad of ways to numb those feelings, but when you least expect it, something out of proportion or misdirected or disguised, pops up. When a man tells me, "I don't get . . . (mad, sad, scared, happy)," I hear, "I don't express . . . (mad, sad, scared, happy) directly."

The exercises below are directed toward helping you to identify the feeling and bring it to the surface in safe ways.

Movies

I often recommend movies that touch issues and feelings pertinent to men's lives. With the distance provided by a movie screen, many men have allowed themselves to feel safely at arm's length. Excellent films are available on topics such as father-son relationships, chemical dependency, child abuse, homosexuality, death, and almost every critical issue in family life. Many of the messages are straightforward; other films will touch you in ways that demand deeper consideration.

As a child, I was moved to intense sadness by a scene in the Gary Cooper western, *Saratoga Trunk,* a moment when a little person (then called a midget) is struck by a shovel during a fight sequence and is later rescued by Cooper. This man is small of physical stature but strong of character. I have connected with powerful sadness through movies on many occasions since, but never more deeply than through a movie that for many people would not be associated with grief work. It was only as I was putting this section into print that I fully connected with the meaning of that piece in my life at the time. I was the smallest boy in my age group, entering adolescence without having reached puberty and feeling an intense sense of inadequacy and fear. Not only did I identify with the man of small physical stature, but I also was emotionally assaulted by the image of his being beaten in the movie—my fear of being hurt by the bigger, stronger, more aggressive males of my clan. I also hoped to have the courage of the man in that movie, and the assault highlighted my deepest fears, that by stepping forward as a "real man" of any size, I risk a great deal emotionally and, at times, physically.

As some of you search for your heart, go to the video store. Rent that film you have avoided, the one that speaks about a part of your life. Go to the privacy of your own space, watch, and let yourself feel. Keep your journal by your side. Seek to identify how the movie affects you. Attempt to name the feelings you experience.

Music

There have been times when listening to and playing music was my only mode of direct expression of sadness and anger. Many of you, even those who claim to be out of touch with emotions, are brought to tears and loud, joyful vocalizations by songs that have meaning to you. (Admit it, you've sat in your car at a stop sign, singing at the top of your lungs, only to realize that the person in the car next to you is getting a real charge out of watching you.) Men who don't cry at family funerals, cry to sounds as divergent as Bach and Hank Williams, from Miles Davis to Eric Clapton, Linda Ronstadt to Bob Marley, The Ramones to The Temptations, music awakens the heart, touches the soul, reminds us of better and worse times, reminds us of God. As you seek to reach deeper into your heart, get in touch with a wide range of music and devote time to solitary listening. Listen to jazz, blues, classical, Native American flute, country, punk-rock. Close your eyes and listen to how your heart and body receive the sound. If a feeling comes up, go with it. Express it with your body: cry, laugh, yell, dance. Keep your journal close by: name the feelings, where in your body you feel them, how you would express them more deeply if you were ready.

Drumming

Drumming is a forceful tool in finding and expressing emotion in a truly visceral, masculine mode. I know what you're saying: "I don't have a drum," or "I can't even keep a beat." All you need to start are your ears and heart. Buy or borrow drum music; I recommend *Taiko Drumming from Japan* for power drumming, and a wide range of African and Native American drumming tapes that often cover a breadth of moods. Then, buy a drum. Gather men you know together and experience the wordless connection that group drumming provides. If you really get hooked, take a drumming class. Most often, drumming takes me to feelings of joy, my bond with other humans, and power, yet, I have also found calm and gentle breezes in my drum.

Pillows Exercise

Not all of the processes have catchy names. This exercise is a simple method to look at how you present your emotions, what feelings are most acceptable to you, and how experiencing the full range of feelings may lead you to your joy.

Gather 6-10 throw pillows and stack them in a tower of feelings. As you look at the tower, be aware of the feeling that was most acceptable in the family you grew up in (even families that avoid feelings experience them). Was it OK to be scared of Dad (even if showing it was discouraged)? Perhaps your family subtly or overtly encouraged guilt or shame. Imagine the stack of pillows as the progression of how you experience and/or express your emotions. Is the top pillow (the feeling you are most likely to be in touch with) the feeling that was most acceptable in the family system? Get in touch with that feeling in your body for a moment; put a word, a phrase, or a sound with the feeling. As you make contact with the lead feeling in your life, throw the pillow aside and immediately decide what emotion you find next. If you find numb or nothing, feel that numbness; give it a word, phrase or sound; now, throw it aside and move to the next pillow. Continue the process of making brief contact with each feeling and quickly moving to the next, going with your impulse response. Use any feeling names you have in your repertoire, anger, sad, scared, guilt, shame, glad, or more subtle forms, such as, frustration, hurt, anxious. Some of you will find powerful feelings such as rage, terror, pain, ecstasy. As you move toward the bottom of the pile, be aware of where you find happy, joy, excitement, passion.

Lead Feeling   Many of you will realize from this process that you return to your Lead Feeling over and over in your life, even at times when others find this inappropriate, even when it doesn't make sense to *you*. This habitual response is protective, but inhibits you from the full range of emotion.

Happy   I believe that most of you will not find emotions labeled happy, joy, excitement, or passion until you near the bottom of the pile. I have two guesses about this: one, the natural ability we all possessed to experience and express emotional satisfaction in infancy often becomes overshadowed, even smothered, by the pain; second, *to find the joy many of us must, as told by Robert Bly, "go through the ashes."*[1] My vision of feelings work is the journey of moving through a series of clouds, often dense, sometimes hazy, seldom distinctly separated, and not knowing exactly what comes next until I get there. As I move through the clouds in succession, I am surprised to arrive at my joy at the most unexpected moments!

Another Pillow Exercise

Creating a conversation between what may feel like warring factions within your head will be a useful tool in uncovering, expressing, and understanding your pain. There are three moments when the following exercise can be especially beneficial:

> You don't seem to be able to move forward in your work because your thoughts are racing or you are in an intense state of confusion (what some call, "stuck in Child").

> You may feel a strong split in who you are (the addict versus the recovering man, the "good Child versus bad Child," the self-destructive Shadow self versus the Adult you).

> You need to get a fix on both your rational thoughts *and* your feelings in your healing.

Put three pillows in a triangle formation on the floor. Name one pillow Adult, one pillow Good Kid, and one pillow Bad Kid. Sit on the pillow that can best express the issue you are struggling with, describing the issue from the perspective of that "part." As soon as you get stuck or find yourself taking on the words of another "part," move to that pillow. You will find that the Kids will be expressive of your emotions and the conflict between your Dark Shadow and your Light Shadow. At some point in the work, move to the Adult "part." The adult speaks only from the question of "what makes sense." In this part you are able to see the information necessary to heal the confusion. If your Adult resists functioning, move back to another pillow and have a Kid ask for help. The purpose of the dialogue is to use the strengths of both Kids in assisting the Adult male in making decisions about where to move in the work. Another useful outcome of the exercise for some men is a greater understanding of how bringing your Shadow self

---

1. Iron John. Robert Bly. 1990.

into the light is simply the process of owning parts of who you were as a child. These parts—qualities that were only "bad" because others deemed them so—you suppressed, but they continued to grow in murky, dank, treacherous corners of your being. Stay with the exercise until you find the information you need to work through the issue in front of you. You will find strengths and gifts in what you have named your "Bad" self in the past; you will find pain and shadow in what you have believed is the "Good." If you get stuck, I recommend doing the process in the presence of another man, who may be able to see your stuck points, the places where you give control and responsibility for your work over to the Child. *Note:* If you only find one child, Good or Bad, imagine the other part as if he existed.

Finding the Boy I Was

Dolls

If you have been around the work that has been labeled, "Inner Child Work," you may be familiar with the concept of using dolls as a healing tool. In my work with men the dolls have many utilizations, but all of these are based on two simple concepts: a man's doll is a tangible, physical symbol of the boy that man once was, and the doll is a representation of the man's feeling self, his heart. It is difficult to explain the impression made on a man in pain who goes to the toy store to find the doll that represents his childhood. I will not spoil the moment by describing this process to you. I will only encourage you to put your skepticism in front of you and go find a doll that is you. Having found your little boy, there are numerous ways to begin this healing work.

Getting to Know the Child (Using Your Doll)

Get your journal out, and put your doll in front of you. Picture yourself at whatever age you connect with. See the doll as you at this age. What kind of a child is he? Describe his life. How do you feel about him: do you like him, dislike him, truly know him? What are his secrets? What does he need from a dad? A mom? Imagine that you are his parent. How do you feel about taking on this boy as your responsibility? Other than your parents, to whom have you given him in the hope that he or she would take care of this boy?

Take this boy everywhere you go for a week. How do you let him make your decisions, take over in painful or confrontational situations, decide what, when, and how you feel? In other words, how does your childhood experience still determine your adult choices?

Getting to Know Him Better

Using your journal to dialogue with the dominant and non-dominant hands has a variety of utilizations in getting in touch with your little boy:

Uncovering feelings and issues stuck in your past.

Separating your *feeling self (child)* from your *thinking self (adult)* to gain clarity on resolution of a key issue.

To get a better sense of how your thoughts and feelings might be working at cross purposes and how you can better coordinate your heart and your head.

To practice boundary setting.

This process is best taught by example. Don't limit yourself to the context described below; create your own possibilities.

Zeke's common response to questions about ways to take better care of himself was, "I don't know." He continued to act out sexually, verbalizing a motivation to recover, working what seemed to be an honest program, yet continuing to struggle. The group gave Zeke the following assignment. Open your journal. Take the pen in your non-dominant writing hand and write the question, "What keeps you from taking care of me?" Now switch to your dominant hand and answer the question from your adult, rational self. Be aware of sharing feelings from your non-dominant hand and information from your dominant hand. Imagine this as a dialogue between a knowledgeable adult and a small boy. You don't have to have all the answers for the boy; you do have to write from your full intelligence as a man.

A variation of this activity (another pillow exercise) that I often use in group, and teach men to use at home, utilizes physical movement to help the man *shift gears.*

Put three pillows on the floor in a triangle. One pillow represents your Child (feelings), one your Adult (rational thinking), one your Parent (love, nurturing, and boundaries). Bring forth an issue that is causing you great confusion. Sit in Child and begin by sharing your feelings, concerns, questions about the problem. When you have shared, move to either Adult or Parent and respond. Each time you switch states of being (feelings, thinking, nurturing), switch pillows. Here is an example:

C: *I'm afraid to admit I still miss my mom.*

A: *A lot of men miss their moms for a long time after they've died.*

C: *Yeh, but I'm not really a boy any more and I feel like a wimp.*

A: *Remember, you were never allowed to cry about her death. Everyone said you needed to be strong for the other kids.*

C: *I'm really pissed off at Dad and Grandma for telling me that.*

P: *Its understandable and OK to be sad and mad, even after all these years.*

C: *Great, so it's OK, what good does that do.*

P: *It's also important to know you don't have to stay sad and mad forever. I'll help you get through it.*

The above dialogue is not an invention of my imagination. It can continue to the place in a man's work when he gains significant clarity about struggles previously lost in obsessive, circular thoughts and emotions. The act of physically moving from pillow to pillow forces one to begin developing the plan (Adult), the feelings (Child), and the commitment (Parent) to engage and resolve the pain. From this simple exercise I have seen men grasp healing concepts that had been bouncing like an emotional pinball machine inside of their minds and hearts.

Recommendation: Learn this exercise in the company of at least one other man. An objective person will often see and hear you make subtle shifts that necessitate moving to another pillow, shifts that your Shadow will not allow you to readily notice. Remember, this Inner Boy is golden. He is also all boy and may be a manipulative little guy. Remember, this Parent is **learning** to be loving and **learning** boundaries. This will not always come naturally if you grew up in an atmosphere short on these. This Adult is smart, but he may have learned a tendency to play dumb or play know-it-all (these are actually subtle shifts to the Child).

How I Give Myself (My Child) Away

Often, as a step in demonstrating how a man gives his power, safety, and accountability away, I will use the following technique in group.

You have said that when you were growing up you did not get what you needed from . . . (Dad, Mom, significant people or institutions). Pick a group member to role-play that person or persons. Give your doll to...(he then gives the doll to the role-player). How are you still waiting for . . . to take

care of you? Who suffers, and how, because you are still wait-
ing to be taken care of by . . .? What would you have to do to
take this boy back and be responsible for the rest of his
growth? Are you willing to do that work?

This exercise will often be the prelude to an intense piece of anger, grief, and/or shame work. As a man progresses in his healing there will be essential differences in his responses to this exercise.

There's no way I'm giving you my kid unless you explain
how what you plan to do and commit to keep him safe.
I'll just keep him with me; I know the work I came to do tonight.
I'll take care of my kid during my work; he's my responsibil-
ity and I love him.

When a man has reached the place where he sees his Inner Child (his heart) as his responsibility and is pleased with this choice, he has accomplished one of my primary tenets of healing: This child is not only my responsibility, he is my opportunity. I don't *have* to take care of him, I *get* to take care of him. The goal is to heal him, not become him and attempt to have a second childhood.

Finding My Family: My Life Movie

The form of guided imagery that I have termed "My Life Movie" is a powerful method to look into your past, gathering information from a distance that is often inaccessible to the conscious mind. I have created, and been mentored in, many variations on this theme. The one I will walk you through I call, "In My Father's House." You will notice as you move through the visualization that the flow can be adapted to innumerable situations and people in your past: Mom, school, church, places and people where abuse occurred. This imagery is equally valid in discovery about a person you interacted with, or even a person who was not physically present. The setting I ask you to create is in the manner I suggest you always set the tone for your work. The atmosphere I will ask you to create is to maximize the opportunity to learn and to experience your feelings. It is also to keep you safe. Imagery is a potent tool, not a game or a method to play fast and loose with your heart. Follow the introduction closely. I will not repeat it in every imagery throughout the text, but it is my intention that you begin each visualization with the following ritual.

Move your body in a comfortable position; unfold your hands and legs, make sure each part of your body is supported, either by laying down or resting in a high back chair. Close your eyes (if the images become too intense during this process simply open your eyes and there will be a de-intensification). Become aware of your breathing. Begin breathing slowly and deeply, filling your lungs and breathing out. As you breathe, feel yourself establish a rhythm that you will maintain throughout the work. If you experience feelings during the process, focus on this rhythm. This allows you to move through the feelings rather than suppressing them or becoming overwhelmed by them.

Now, see yourself as you are today, the age, size, strength you are in your adult self. You will be looking into the past from the perspective of the adult you are today. You will not be returning to relive the past again as a child. This provides a safe distance and the groundedness of your adult skills, yet allows the intensity of information and emotion to surface. When you have a strong, solid picture of your Adult, see yourself going into a movie theater. As you enter you are the only person in the theater, and you are aware that the movie that will be shown is about your life. Today's movie is about your relationship with your father. You sit in the seat that provides you both safety and enough closeness to understand what you are ready to see and hear. As you prepare, be aware of two things: if you believe you need support in this process you may choose to invite others into the theater to sit with you, choosing only those that you know are safe; you have a video control in your hand to stop, pause, or slow the action, and to raise or lower the volume at any time you chose. Always take the time you need to answer the questions and feel the feelings.

When you are ready, press the play button.

You see a house that you grew up in (this exercise can be done several times if you grew up in multiple locations). As the door opens, you decide to find your father. Where do you find him? What is he doing? If you cannot find him, go to each room in the house looking. How do you feel as you look? If he is nowhere in the house, where is he? How long has he been gone? Does he ever come back? Does he ever come for you? What are you feeling?

If he is in the house, how do you feel as you find him? Describe your father on the outside, his physical self. What age is he; do you see him at different ages? What age(s) are you at these times? Now, describe how your father sounds: his voice, the volume, what he says to you, what he says to others, his tone. Describe your father on the inside. What are his dreams? What does he value? How does he spend his time? As you watch and listen to your father, he may begin to move around the house. Follow him to any place in the house that you need to go in your quest to learn about your relationship with Dad. By his words, his behavior, his presence or his absence, what is dad teaching you about:

work	*love*
women	*money*
parenting	*being a real man*
anger	*religion and spirituality*
sadness	*people of other races*
fear	*listening*
guilt and shame	*asking for help*
happiness	*violence*
sex	*success*
alcohol and drugs	*trust*
children	*marriage*

If your father is not present, who do you go to for this information? How does this work? Is your father loving, critical, abusive, mysterious, safe? What is it like to be the son of this man? Are you important, loved, seen, heard? Did you decide to be like dad? How? Did you decide to not be like Dad? In what ways, and how did this work for you?

Just for a moment you are able to talk to your dad. What would you like to ask him? Ask. Listen to his answer. Tell him, "I just wanted you to . . .". Listen to his response. Watch his reactions.

Finally, look at your dad and decide what you still want from him. What are you waiting for? Will you ever get this? How does that feel? Realistically, what can your dad give you? How does waiting serve you in your life today? What work of the heart would you have to be willing to do to be ready to move on?

Taking note of all that you have learned, it is time to return to the present. Pushing the fade button, you see yourself out of the house that you grew up in, no one else left the house. You move the movie forward into the present until the images completely fade from the screen and you are aware of being in the theater, the age that you are today. The movie is over now; however, you have learned a new skill and can return for more information any time you choose. Now, refocus on your breathing, and be aware of the present. Let yourself open your eyes and stretch, taking time before you speak to any one. When you feel ready, take out your journal and write whatever you need to about what you just learned. (If you go deep into the imageries, try finishing up by counting from 1 to 5, opening your eyes on 5. If you know from experience or believe that you may have difficulty coming out of visualizations, it is important to complete these exercises in the company of a group or trained professional).

I will reiterate that if the person you are imaging was physically absent from your life, this tool can still be used in a powerful way. You may reach essential information and emotion as you attempt to answer questions about someone you had little or no direct contact with, or have learned about through the eyes of others. Second, many men who did not know their fathers due to death, adoption, or abandonment, create a fantasy Dad. This exercise may allow you the opportunity to see how you magically created Dad, and what thoughts have feelings lurking underneath this survival strategy. Finally, this is an opportunity to look at the other influences in your experience, to move beyond our culture's tendency to lay it all at the doorstep of Dad and Mom. As you move through the information-gathering process, be aware of grandparents, other family, teachers, clergy, neighbors, and perhaps most important in our time, the effect of media and culture.

My Toolbox

One of my favorite processes is a combination of imagery and journaling that I titled "My Toolbox." The purpose of this piece is to provide another method to uncover the skills that you were born with and the skills you learned in your environment (what Keen termed your software). This activity is focused on the skills that you received and learned from your father figures. In this process, you open doors to maximize your God-given talents and to begin anew the journey of accepting, rejecting, replacing and adapting the life tools you were given as a child. Jim Howard and I experimented with several names when I wrote this exercise and the masculine image of a toolbox gives me great pleasure.

For this work you need the largest sheet of unlined paper you have, markers, a pen, and a packet of self-adhesive notes. As always, the activity is structured in such a way as to be useful to men who have no active memory of a father. In addition, this work can be repeated if you lived with multiple father figures; some men give each man a place in the exercise in the first completion.

As you breathe and relax, follow the protocol for all imageries. Be open to learning, to feeling.

> See yourself as you are today, an adult. Find yourself in a lighted room with a toolbox in the center of the room. You recognize this as your **father's toolbox;** It contains the tools he will give you toward becoming a man. Every man has a toolbox, even if he never met his father. The tools were created by what he said, or didn't say, his presence or his absence, the behavior he modeled, and what others taught you about your father. Today, you are here to become aware of the tools you were given. See your father at the toolbox; see him as you best remember or imagine him to be. Behind him are the people who helped teach you about your father and your manhood. Dad beckons you to come and receive his tools, then steps away. You move to the box. What is it made of? How big is it? What do you feel as you draw near and begin to open it?

> Now, look inside the toolbox and see how it is arranged. In it are tools of all kinds. First, physical. What are you physically inheriting from your dad: size, appearance, handicaps or illnesses, intelligence, addictions? What aptitudes or lack of aptitude were you taught that you inherited from Dad? What mythical genetic qualities were you taught you inherited from Dad (i.e., Irish temper). Now, look into the section of the box that holds the emotional and spiritual tools that you received from Dad. Each of these tools describes what you were taught about becoming a man, rules to live by. What do you find in the toolbox that tells you:

A real man is . . .	Trust is . . .
Family is . . .	Work is . . .
Women are . . .	Anger is . . .
Children are . . .	Sadness is . . .
Real boys are . . .	Happiness is . . .
Success is . . .	Fear is . . .
Sex is . . .	Shame is . . .
Alcohol and drugs are . . .	Life is . . .

Now look in the toolbox and see what objects Dad is giving you to use as tools to implement what you are learning: money, liquor, weapons, gifts, tools of his chosen trade, anything you see? What's missing from the toolbox? What are the best tools? As a child, which tools did you accept, which did you reject? What secrets are there about Dad's tools? Now, begin the protocol for bringing yourself back from the visualization, returning to this room and slowly getting centered in the present.

Taking your paper and markers out, draw your image of the toolbox. Tapping into the imagery, write each tool that you accepted and began living by, both positive and negative, on a self-adhesive note, sticking each one inside your drawing. Now, write the tools you rejected by saying briefly on a note what you believed or lived instead. Put each one inside the toolbox. Then, write the tools you learned and accepted from others about what a boy and man should be, both positive and negative, when Dad was absent or you judged him inadequate. Having done this, take time to look; this toolbox contains the definition of a man that you left childhood with. Finally, if you noticed that you have replaced some of the tools from childhood, remove them from your toolbox and add a new note for the healthier tool you have learned to use in your journey. Be specific and place them in your toolbox. This is the toolbox you work from in today's world. How do you feel as you see the big picture?

And now, close your eyes again and safely re-enter the visualization.

*Return to the room where you first found Dad's toolbox. As you re-enter, you realize that Dad and all of the others are gone. The toolbox is still there; it may be slightly different based on what you have learned through your work today. This toolbox contains your manhood as bequeathed you by your father. This is your load to carry, be it light or heavy, useful or outdated. You must lift it, carry it. As you bend to hoist it, how old do you feel? How heavy is the weight of your manhood, of continuing in your father's Shadow. Do you give up under the weight? Do you try to prove yourself a better man than Dad, carrying more than he did or pretending you can reject all that he gave you? What will happen if you cannot carry the load? From what and whom do you stay separate while you concentrate on this task? Which of these tools do you resist giving up, even though you know they are worn out, outdated, broken, even dangerous? Who do you turn to, female and male, to manipulate into carrying part of the load for you, and what happens when they fail? **How do you feel when you realize that** *the people who gave you tools that don't work cannot or will not help you carry the weight?*

In a moment of powerful awareness, you realize it is time to change this toolbox, to get better, stronger, lighter tools. As you stand in the room, unsure of what to do next, a man enters— a teacher or mentor who is safe, smart, creative—it is as if you both know him and are meeting him for the first time. He says:

"I see your father, and the others, gave you some tools that simply don't work. Perhaps they used to be good tools; perhaps they worked for others. I see that they do not serve you. I know you have tried to use these tools and to find others. I see your successes and honor you; I see your failures and honor you. Together, we are going to look at this old toolbox. You will keep the tools that still work, adapt some for better use, discard some, build new ones with the help of others you trust, and borrow some that have been missing. I will help you carry the load. For the rest of this day, stay with me and learn."

And now, using what you have learned, return to this moment from the imagery. As you open your eyes and are centered in the present, take your journal and write what you learned today. Take another look at your toolbox and ask yourself these questions:

What tools work that I want to keep? (Thanks, Dad.)
What tools need to be removed, replaced, updated?
What tool will I focus on next? Share this information and commitment with another man.

I close this section with the words of a man who completed My Toolbox in a workshop several years ago: "I realized I had too many tools (rules); most of them didn't work. I found I only need a few good adult tools that I will stick with."

Safe Places and Safe People

My Places

Many of you did not feel safe in your own homes. Let me correct that: **many of you were not safe in your own homes!** What some of you did was to find a safe or semi-safe haven, somewhere in or out of the family home. It may have been a closet, a part of a room, or a treehouse.

As you became more mobile, some of you found safer places: staying at school, or hanging out at a friend's house with a family you "adopted." In the extreme, some of you created safe havens on the inside when there was no place outside to go. You built extravagant fantasy rituals, becoming a super-hero, deciding you were given to the wrong parents at the hospital and that some day the "good parents" were going to come for you, or getting lost in music, science fiction novels, computer games, or (*you fill in the blank*). The exercise below is offered to help you uncover the functional and potential risky elements of using your safe places in the healing work. As you proceed, remember one axiom of mature healing: survival tactics that were necessary and functional in the environment of my youth may become antiquated and even harmful to myself and others when used in the adult world.

Begin by getting your doll and following the ritual of safety for guided imageries. When you are comfortable, close your eyes.

> *Be aware of the age and size you are today. Hold your doll and be aware that you are in the present, looking at the past. Your doll is your representation of that past. Where did . . . (your childhood name) go to feel safe? Was there a place that he went to hide? As you see him in that place, what ages is he? Who or what is he hiding from (it's OK to feel)? How safe is this place? Is he ever found? Is he really safe here? Often at this point, a realization occurs that even the safe place was not always safe . . . feel that. There may be a realization that there was no safe place . . . feel that. Both of these issues are powerful ways for rescuing and healing that little boy. Were there any other places, through the years, that this boy went to feel safe? How successful was he in finding places? Validate him for doing what he could do, in a child's body, to find safety.*
>
> *Now, look to the inside of this boy, the places he goes in his imagination to cope, to feel safe. How did he use his imagination to get away from his pain, to detach from what was happening around him? Remember the games, the thoughts, the fantasies, the activities that he used to soothe himself, to escape. At this point many of us will begin to connect with memories of reading, computers, games, masturbation, early chemical use, etc. Be aware of how these activities helped him.*
>
> *Be aware next that the boy you have been learning about is you at an early age, maybe at several ages. As you understand this, decide which of the places and activities of*

the past have become habits that you still engage in today. Are there similar places where you go to hide when you are struggling? Are there similar activities to which you turn to cope in your present life? Name how these places and activities are still helpful. Name how these old coping skills interfere today in your work, your relationships, in your sense of being a powerful adult. Does hiding ever cause you to be less, not more safe?

Finally, picture the safest place for you. This could still be the place of your childhood. If it is, bring your picture of this place into the present; put your safe place in today's world. It could be a place you have been since then, a place in your life right now. If there were or are no such places for you, paint a picture in your imagination: a secret safe place where you cannot be found unless you wish to be, where only those you invite can enter. Secure this space in your consciousness. Throughout your work, you will have the opportunity to use symbols to heal. One such symbol is a safe place you have created in the adult world. In your mind's eye, you may chose to return to this space many times in your healing journey.

Here are the rules:

You can only go to this place when you are in a secure environment—not in the car, not in a business meeting, not in the middle of being sexual.

Your Adult must always know that your Child went to the safe place, and must be able to retrieve him.

This is not a place to hide from accountability, from work, from life. It is a place to do work.

If you have a dissociative disorder, this process must be used with a trained professional.

Begin the steps to move out of the visualization: breathe, slowly open your eyes, count up if you need to. When you are fully present, stretch, take out your journal, and write what you learned from this exercise.

As I wrote this imagery, which I have walked through with men many times, I reacted as a reader and my reader said, "I really don't get this imagery. I don't get what it means or how to use it in my healing." For the benefit of those who feel the same way, I'm going to give an example of a man using this material.

Ted came to men's group talking about his tendency to withdraw into his bedroom when he felt overwhelmed by the demands of others. His wife was becoming increasingly angry with his isolation from the kids and from her. He also reported a fear of confrontation with his boss because he had withdrawn into his office, neglecting conflicts with the staff he supervises. When asked about this, he recalled this pattern went as far back as he could remember. Ted was asked to participate in the imagery about his safe place.

As he held his doll he described a scene when he was seven years old, a scene that may have occurred before he was seven and certainly occurred many times after. Stepdad and Mom are fighting: yelling, swearing, seemingly oblivious to Ted's presence and his fear. Threats of violence build to pushing and hitting. Ted flees to his room. He covers his ears, eventually crying himself to sleep.

As these incidents re-occur, Ted begins to anticipate. He comes home from school, goes to his room, does his school work, reads, begins to write science fiction stories, and only comes out when he has to. As long as Ted "behaves," nobody seems to care if he comes out. Ted struggles with many feelings. He feels less afraid of the fighting when he hides out. He is both relieved and devastated that no one ever comes to see how he is after the fights. He grows increasingly comfortable in his room and increasingly uncomfortable with people. He begins a lifelong pattern of "behaving" and withdrawing in conflict situations, even situations where he anticipates conflict might occur.

What was a highly functional and logical choice for Ted as a child had become a style of conflict management that threatened his marriage and his job. Before proceeding any further, Ted was instructed to honor his Child for doing what he could do to stay out of the line of fire. Then, his Child was informed that Ted's childhood safe place had served its function, but now it was backfiring. With the support of the group, Ted reassured his Child that it was time to find new safe places and new ways to be safe, and that there were people to help with that process.

The initial strategy that we adopted involved the rules of safe places. Ted made several decisions that directly addressed these rules. First, he selected a time limit for withdrawal at work and at home, allowing himself to go to an old, *familiar safe place but not to get stuck there. Second, he agreed to use his withdrawal time to journal about his feelings, to problem solve, and to commit from his Parent to keep his Child safe, rather than drifting into fantasy, obsessive thought, and self-recrimination. Third, he discussed his plan with his wife to gain her support, ease her fear and anger, and demonstrate that he was accepting accountability for changing what had become a destructive pattern. Finally, Ted began to plan his fear and anger work around the violence and neglect in his family of origin.*

In this example, Ted found the best of both worlds. He updated his childhood concept of coping and created something in his adult life that accelerated his healing, replacing isolation with time for contemplation. As his work progressed, Ted found there were safe places throughout his adult world.

My People

Mentors are older (usually) males or females who select, often for reasons not apparent to the person chosen, someone to teach, to pass on valuable information and, at times, to provide valuable nurturing. It is not uncommon in my work with men to hear, "There was no one, Chris, no one that was safe or took time or taught me to be a man." As our time together passes, many of these men come upon a story one night, the story of someone who made an impression on a child, someone in real life, someone in a book, perhaps a role model on TV, a man or women who imparted life-giving knowledge at a time when it was desperately needed. Let me share a few of the brief moments of Safe People from men I have known who survived on mere morsels of mentorship.

My neighbor, Mr. Jones, taught me how to work with wood. He had a little workbench for me, next to his big bench. It was always safe at his house; it wasn't safe at mine. He never yelled. He seemed to know something was wrong in my family, and he encouraged me to come around. I remember what he taught me about doing things. I remember his kindness, and I remember one time when my dad was mad at me, Mr. Jones was the only person in my entire childhood that stood up to Dad for me!

I never had a man take time with me. Dad was usually drunk; I remember the time he beat Mom until I actually thought she was dead, then he left. That's how it was; he was drunk or gone. Then one summer, men came to build a house down the street. I started hanging out there. One guy talked to me; I don't even remember his name. He showed me how to hammer a nail, and we talked about all kinds of stuff. I went back every day until they were done. It was hard to believe there was a man who didn't mind having me around, who didn't yell at me or hit me, who didn't try to molest me. I hung on to something from that summer. It has helped me see that not all men are bad.

I was new in town, didn't have many friends, and Dad was really busy. The man that lived across the street, Mr. Black, knew a lot about the woods. I was a city kid. I never forget that day. It had snowed quite a bit and he dropped by to invite me to walk in the woods, to track. I don't remember how long we were out there, but I remember seeing one deer. He led me as we found the tracks in the snow, followed them until we spotted the deer, got as close as the deer allowed. Then, we sat and watched: that's it, we watched. I felt as if I was being taught some sacred art unknown to urban kids.

My dad was pretty far progressed in his alcoholism by the time I came around, and it seemed that Mom was always busy with so many kids. When I was young, I just tried to stay out of the way. I still have that problem today. But, as I got older I made friends with Jerry. I hung out at his house a lot; his parents never seemed to mind. I kind of adopted them as my substitute family, ate meals there, went places with them. I watched how Jerry's dad acted toward Jerry's mom and the kids. I thought he was like my image of Ward Cleaver, the perfect Dad. I'm sure he had his problems—everybody does— but he was nice to his wife and kids: he was funny, he played with them, he even hugged and kissed his wife in front of us. When I grew up, if I ever did, I felt like all I had for role models were TV and Jerry's dad. That helped some.

These are the stories of men who had few safe places and few safe people, but they were able to connect with memories of someone who made a difference. Many of you have stories like these, or perhaps were fortunate enough to have safe family, friends, teachers, coaches, or others who gave you emotional shelter. I believe it is important to identify these people and anchor the love you got from them in your Child. It is important to identify what you learned, however small, from each and anchor these moments in your Adult, to be used in those times when you claim, "I don't know how to . . . (love, take care of myself, be responsible, etc)." Here is an exercise to assist you.

Take out your journal. Break your life down into five-year time increments, beginning at birth. Take each five-year time slot and review and list the people in your life. Include family, friends, neighbors, teachers, baby-sitters, clergy, any person older than you that you can recall. Don't limit yourself to people you have always seen as significant. Brainstorm and list people you have not thought much about over the years; you may not even remember a name. List people during that time that you learned about and became interested in through reading or TV.

Having gone through each five-year time frame up to the present, go back through the list and check the people you would term "safe." Taking a fresh page, put two headings at the top, "CHARACTERISTICS" and "LEARNED." List each of the safe people along the left side of the page. Next to each, write the characteristics he or she possessed that made him or her a safe person. In the second column, write a brief description of what you learned by being in the company of that person: about yourself, about other people, skills you developed, pain that was permanently or temporarily relieved, gifts you were given. When you have done this, turn to another fresh page. Compile the characteristics of a safe person. Then, compile all that you have learned from safe people. Remember, whether you received these people in childhood or more recently, you have access to their gifts now!

There are two addenda to this journaling task that may be useful.

Gratitude to My Safe Person

In my own healing, I have found it necessary to express my gratitude to several mentors and other safe people. In some cases, I have been able to speak directly to the person; in others I have sent letters; in some situations I no longer had knowledge of thier whereabouts and either shared the letter with a friend or with the wind. I would encourage you to select the most significant safe people and communicate your appreciation. Further, I encourage you to do this without expecting anything other than to give back a message of love. The receiver will often not even be aware of the gift he or she gave you in the past and/or gave it with no expectation of getting anything in return. To emphasize this point, I will share my last contact with my greatest therapy mentor, a safe person who didn't appear in my life until I was twenty-one years old.

After nearly fifteen years in the field, I decided it was time to share with Dr. Bob Brundage what he meant to me. I had not seen Bob for several years, and a friend told me he was terminally ill, which I could not picture in a man I saw both eternally old and eternally young. Bob was the Chief of Psychiatry on the Adolescent Unit at the state hospital where I spent the first three years of my career. Bob took time to teach me, to listen to me, to notice my work, to nurture me before I could fly. We used to do "co-therapy" with families, which consisted of Bob working with the family, me watching and learning, and Bob telling me later what a good therapist I was becoming because I cared, I listened, and I was hungry to learn. He let me call him Bob—the boss thirty-five years my senior. He had a great sense of humor, he was incredibly disorganized. He often drove to work and walked home, at any given time having two or three of his old beat-up cars in the staff lot. Best of all, we shared a common interest in junk food, and when Bob left our country town to consult, he brought bags of Big Macs back to be reheated and eaten on break. Perhaps my greatest testimony to Bob is that he instilled therapeutic genius in many fledgling clinicians. I was only one of many people he mentored.

It was time to write Bob. I learned he could no longer read to himself, and had great difficulty speaking, so I sent the letter to my good friend, Tom, who agreed to be my messenger. Mine was a heartfelt letter, full of the feelings I expressed above, culminating in my truth: that Bob had more to do with the kind of therapist I became than any other teacher. I knew that Bob would be touched deeply by my feelings; he had given so much and so infrequently been thanked. I waited to hear from Tom about his response. When Tom called several weeks later he told me he had read the letter as requested. Bob's response was something like, "It wasn't any big deal." Vintage Bob—and a reminder to leave my expectations at the door when thanking those who selected me to help for their own good reasons.

Imagery from My Safe People

Close your eyes. Create the safe container for imageries that you have learned.

See the little boy that you were, sitting in a room, a room of his choosing, a safe place. How old is he in this place? As he rests, he becomes aware that he is going to receive guests, people he is excited to see, people who have been helpful and loving to him. He becomes aware of the people entering, one by one. Each is a safe person who has been there for him, perhaps for a long time, perhaps for a short time, perhaps a long time ago, possibly someone who is available even today. Let each person give him a gesture of love. Let him receive, again, the nurturing, information, and guidance that each provides. Let him feel the fullness of this safe time. The last person in the room is you, as an adult. Give this little boy your love, your commitment to keep him safe. Tell him, "Others have loved you as you are and so do I. Put all this into your heart and take it with you wherever you go." Go to the boy, pick him up. Be aware that he does not have to see these safe people each day; he carries the gifts they gave him in his heart. Turn to them and thank them by saying . . . (finish this thought). Now, holding the boy, leave the room and begin to walk back into the present, into this safe space. When you are here in the present, open your eyes.

Closing

Someone out there is saying those last two processes were not about uncovering the wound; they were healing pieces. This chapter evolved as a microcosm of how I see the healing road, as it pertains to historical pain. If you moved through the entire chapter, the progression was awareness → early experiential learning → deeper experiential learning → resolution and moving on. Although this section is primarily about exposing the pain, the final two exercises provide a picture of using the information you gather to heal. Finally, all of the information related to safe people and safe places will now be available to you as you proceed on your pilgrimage. Return to these images whenever necessary in your work.

We have ventured into the territory of the heart. It is time to connect this with what I call "Physicalizing the Pain" (a term used before in another context). The focus of the next chapter is on how your body catalogs your pain, and how important work on your body is in the mind, emotion, body, and spirit path to healing.

3: Body Pain

I Work
Until my body aches
Until I wear knee braces
Until I have surgery
Until the pain forces me to pay attention

Paying attention,
I drink, take aspirin, sleep
Try to sleep
Then I Work

Used as a tool for others pleasure
My body
A receptacle
A computer
Hardwired as a human

Programmed to believe . . .
A machine

I Hate These Men
Messing with my software
Stop
Slow Down
Ease Up
Nurture
We see flesh, blood, love, pain
And if you persist. . .

I Love These Men
And in this awakening
My Body, My Mind
My Heart, My Spirit
Weep, Moan, Wail
In unison

CHRIS FREY, 1995
Inspired by the healing work of Ed F. and
the words of Sam Keen

There was a pattern to Ben's work in group, to his fear and grief work. Often, when he moved into those feelings, especially if he was dealing with his father's rage, he began to choke. It is difficult to describe the experience of discovering with Ben the origins of this physiological response. I remember in vivid detail his place in the room, the expression on his face, the position of my body as he told his story, his childhood memory of the night that his father choked him to point that he believed he would surely die. In time, that fear was choked up, literally, and was followed by the rage, the sadness, and, eventually, even forgiveness. It was a long journey.

Ben recorded the physical pain from his youth in a dark, distant place, a place in his body that was reached only with trust, courage, exploration of memories and emotions, and with the support of other men. I have a friend who often flinches when he attempts to verbalize intense emotional pain. I have seen an ex-football player watch a bone-crunching hit on a televised game and unconsciously grab the knee he had injured years before. I know that I am visualizing my shame because I habitually toss my head quickly to the side, as if I can shake the memory and the pain out of my head. Our bodies record information: pain, pleasure, memories. Gaining access to "the what, how, and where" of your body's recording process is a potent tool in the restoration of your masculine identity. The explosion of combining therapy with many forms of body work indicates that those of us doing healing work in the West are finally realizing that the whole being is traumatized and must be healed. This chapter offers methods to integrate this understanding into the masculine journey. Men who are acutely aware of body trauma—physical and sexual abuse, war, disability due to accident, illness, or birth trauma—may readily make these connections. Those of you who have been in denial of the link between mind, body, emotion, and spirit— or who have simply not considered the possibility—may be in for an "Aha!" experience. Men who are on this journey without specific events of severe trauma will still uncover subtle, powerful messages being transmitted from your physical to your emotional self.

Before I move on, a second story, recently given to me, illustrates the healing of mind, heart, and body as it takes place simultaneously. I share it with you as an indication of healing that takes places in the moment, not years later in a men's group, in hope that you will carry from this book the knowledge that we are not only here to heal the past, but to learn improved skills to heal the pain yet to come.

[Dad] responded with mock anger that he ought to make me finish the digging. As he picked up the shovel and began his powerful downstroke I said "OK!" and jumped into the hole. I screamed in pain as the shovel hit my leg. I looked up and in the faint light I saw my dad's shocked face turn pale against the black sky. He couldn't see in the darkness of the hole, but both of us could feel his fingers slipping over the blood on my leg. He scooped me into his arms and ran to the house calling my mother's name. . . . I closed my eyes against the stark, bright light of the kitchen and the image of the room. My mother moving toward us remained frozen in my brain while sounds told me everything was still in motion. . . . I sobbed and dribbled tears as Mom applied first aid. Dad watched over her shoulder, went for scissors, helped hold gauze in place, and asked me how I was doing. . . . With the worst of the crisis over, I thought he might get mad at me for jumping into the hole, but he never did. He said [he'd] take a quick shower and maybe we'd play a game of checkers or something.

A few minutes later he stood at the door to the living room with his hair still wet. As he walked toward me he said, "How does it feel?" He sat down next to me on the couch and put his arm around me. His body was warm and damp from the shower, and he smelled like Old Spice. I leaned into him and we just sat there and it felt so good. He was so tired that he fell asleep in just a few minutes, but I didn't care. My dad, my hero, was in camp. And he loved me.

Don Wesemann, 1995

The physical pain experienced by Don is not carried as ongoing trauma. The responses of his mother, and particularly his father, have made this a moment of great love in his life story.

This section is about *re-associating,* reconnecting with your body, your thoughts, your feelings. If you have a need to re-associate, this means to some degree you have *dissociative* in the past, disconnected from your body, your thoughts, your feelings. In the most severe of early trauma, some of you may have learned to dissociative in ways that left you markedly removed from memories, parts of your body, even conscious actions that you take in certain emotional states. I believe that if this is true for you, you must consider these things:

re-association work should be seen as an extended process. It frightens me when I hear about "healers" who do powerful workshops to assist men in reconnecting with their pain, with no follow-up recommended or offered. Every man who does the work in this chapter needs to seek the support of a skilled professional, a men's therapy group or a men's support group with men who are familiar with intense work of the heart. If you have been diagnosed by a professional as living with a dissociative disorder, the work described here should progress within a safe, ongoing therapeutic relationship.

Body Pain, Body Shame

Uncovering and healing the secrets held within your body can be an essential element of the masculine journey. This is a powerful exercise in beginning this process. I have used this exercise primarily in the context of an imagery; however, I was taught a variation using a body drawing. I will lead you through both versions. Use the one that best fits your learning style. In fact, try both! In this process, pay particular attention to the affects of physical limitations and disabilities. If you experience anger, shame, a sense of betrayal in terms of your bodies limits, go with the emotions; this is your work.

Imagery

Begin as you have learned to create the safe, ritual space of the visualization. As you are breathing and relaxing, see your body as a whole, from head to toes, the age you are today. Be aware that in understanding your body and how it has worked, you will now gain valuable information about your pain, your shame, your strengths. Decide to know as much as you are ready. It is OK to see and to feel and to understand. Plan to view what you are learning from today's perspective, not to relive the past.

And now, let yourself see your Brain. How big is your brain? How intelligent are you? Did anyone tell you that you were dumb? What did you believe about yourself? Can you think clearly? Do you have a good memory? What, if anything, prevents you from remembering? What parts of your life or your experiences do you have difficulty remembering? Do you rely more on your right brain (abstract/creative) or your left brain (analytical/logical)? Do you get lost in your thoughts, get easily confused, have difficulty getting out of your head?

*How much of your brain do you use for your own well-being;
how much is dedicated to thinking for others? How much of
your brain is dedicated to thoughts that you don't want to
have? How much of your brain feels empty of memories that
you believe are not there? What healing would you have to accomplish to have more complete use of your brain?*

*Now, review your face. First, your eyes. What have you
seen, as a child and adult, that you carry as pain? Who did
you see that you remember with pain? Who or what have you
looked for, hoping to find, to see, to understand? Look to
your third eye, the inner sight. How willing are you to look at
yourself? How much of your vision do you use for yourself?
Do you pay attention? How difficult is it for you to see
others as they truly are? What do you miss because you are
unwilling or too ashamed to look up and see, or be seen? Are
there any physical difficulties you experience with your eyes
that have affected your life?*

*Your nose: Be aware of smells that have meaning in
your life. Name your favorite scents. Name the smells you
avoid or dislike. Name smells that trigger childhood memories. Can you "smell trouble"? Are there any physical difficulties with your nose that have affected your life?*

*Be aware of your mouth. How does your mouth carry
and express your pain—your shame—with words, with the
ways you use your mouth? What are you unwilling to speak
about yourself: your memories or your feelings? To what
people are you unwilling to speak your truth? What have you
expressed that you wish you could take back? Are there physical problems with your mouth that have affected your life?*

*Review your entire face and see the years, the pain, and
the strength expressed there. See the age you truly are.*

*Be aware of your neck, your shoulders, your upper back.
How are you weighted down by your pain? What past pain do
you lift and carry every day that you can now feel in your neck
or shoulders or back? Whose weight do you feel resting on you?
What responsibilities, what shame, what anger, what sadness,
what fear do you carry? As you feel, stay safe; it is OK to know
your truth. Are there physical problems in these areas that affect your life, and how are these connected to your life story?*

*Be aware of your arms and hands. What pain do you
lift and carry? What does touching and being touched mean
in your life? Can you touch others; can they touch you; can*

you touch yourself? Who holds you, who do you hold? Do your hands express love, fear, rage? Do they create or destroy? Are you "good with your hands"? Are there physical problems in these areas?

Sense your chest, and on the inside, your heart. What pain do you carry in your chest? Be aware of any tightness, heaviness, emptiness. Is this fear, shame, anger, sadness? What portion of your heart is locked away, guarded, secret, shut down? What portion of your heart will not love others, will not love you? Where do you hide your joy? Who do you let into your heart? Who do you keep out? Who would you like to let more into your heart? It is OK to feel this: Remember, a secret heart carries shame.

Move to your stomach. What "fire" do you carry in your belly? What is in your stomach when you connect with anger, fear, or not being good enough? Do you experience any physical problems in your stomach?

Now, be aware of your buttocks, your anus, your bowels. Do you carry any pain here? Were you hurt in these places? Do you experience any physical difficulties in these areas today? It's OK to know.

Move to your genitals. How do you see your genitals? Are you proud? Are they an integral part of your body or have you treated them as separate from your brain, heart, and spirit? Do you carry any physical pain in your genitals; do you carry any emotional pain? How do you use this part of your body to act out joy, excitement, anger, fear, shame, sadness?

Now, see your legs and feet. How have you tried to run from yourself, from others, from life? What pain, physical and emotional, do you carry here?

And now, review your entire body. Have you loved your body, let it be loved in healthy ways, used it to connect or to disconnect? Let yourself know how you have used your body to cope, to survive through times of trauma. You may have childhood and adult hurts, ailments, scars, weight, or injuries that reflect how your body was traumitized in the past and how you overworked your body in response to what you came to believe from these events. You may have fed your body with alcohol, drugs, violent sports, food, work, or sex to cope, only to find you caused further damage. You may have treated your outer body with great respect (exercise, diet, fashion) to protect and hide the pain of your inner being. You may also have strength, resilience, and power in your body, having developed your brain, heart, and other limbs toward your quest for healing.

Thank your body now. It got you here. It carried the spirit of the little boy you were. It holds your strength; it holds your Shadow. Part of recovery is to learn new, life-giving ways to nurture this vehicle that transports your soul and spirit around the earth. With this knowledge etched in you, become aware of moving back to the present, following the ritual of returning from the imagery.

Immediately after the imagery, journal what you can about what you learned, or process the experience with someone who was present. Describe any memories you uncovered, any connections between the past and present, and any connections between certain people, events and emotions with certain parts of your body. Pay attention to how the past has affected the way you treat your body, and to physical maladies, which may have originated and been maintained as part of your dysfunctional early experiences. For example, I know that I have anger and fear work to do when I feel what I call "The Brick on My Chest" (a heavy pressure seeming to push from the outside).

Drawing

Another method (I do not know the origin, but I credit my friends and teachers, Jackie and Connie) is to begin this exercise with large paper and have someone trace the outline of your body, or simply draw an outline. It does not have to be artistic. You draw your brain, eyes, nose, mouth, heart, stomach, genitals, and any other necessary body part inside of the outline. With a marker, color in the portion of each body part that you have healed, the portion that you have full access to. Use the same questions asked in the imagery above to make these decisions. In the segment of each body part, list the events that interfere with your having full access to your body—the people, places, and times associated with those events—and the feelings that you carry. Use the following example as a guide:

For years, Larry was told by his stepfather that he was stupid. His mother used to often tell him he had no common sense. His mother also insisted he sleep with her until he was almost sixteen and rub her back and legs while in bed. In spite of a college education and successful business career, he colored only half of his brain in and wrote "STUPID" in the other half. He colored in only a small portion of his hands and wrote "AFRAID TO TOUCH OR BE TOUCHED" and "MASTURBATION" in the uncolored portion.

69

Using this information, make decisions about how you will recapture use of your body, or grieve the losses you experienced.

Important Note: In my work with chronically ill clients (diabetes, cystic fibrosis, asthma, Lupus, multiple sclerosis), I believe that facing the anger, grieving the loss, and accepting the importance of self-care must be accomplished, but it must be within an understanding of the emotions and childhood messages that often exacerbate the person's physical limitations. Being labeled in childhood as a burden, as limited in ways totally unrelated to the disease, even as punishments from God, have had devastating effects on people. This exercise has the potential to give an individual information to move beyond the early, unhealthy emotional limits inflicted upon him by others.

My Body as a Metaphor

A picture may be worth a thousand words in the work that men do. Being a man of many words, I know that a man in his pain can get lost in lengthy discussions of meanings, feelings, and issues. A man afraid or ashamed of his pain can use these prolonged discourses (his own or mine) to avoid and resist. At times, simply having a man move his body in such a way as to highlight the memory, the pain, the response, even the resistance, can transport him quickly and powerfully to new awareness. Physical movement to create insight and healing are time-honored traditions in many therapeutic methods. I would like to offer several simple techniques that may assist you in using what is one of a man's best mechanisms for this work, physical movement.

Standing

As Ken worked on his shame, he would shrink before our eyes—hanging his head, slumping his shoulders, pulling into himself, invariably ending up at confusion and passive resistance to his stated goal. After several group sessions like this, each time Ken went into his shame he was asked to stand. At different times, he was asked to state his physical size, which was substantial. He was asked to maintain eye contact during his work with a man as tall as he. The group encircled him, and he owned his shame by rotating around the circle, naming the shame and receiving each man's feedback.

Assume the Position

Putting your body in the position that illustrates a particular feeling, event, relationship, or life stance can be effective in creating a deeper insight, and even release pain.

The Pedestal

Terry often talked about the expectation in his family that he be better than the other boys: smarter, well behaved, harder working. He described his life today as superficially successful, but empty in terms of relationships. In group he was seen by most of the men as aloof, bordering on arrogant. He began to report a sadness that he was in group, but did not belong with the men. That night we set up a physical manifestation of what he had been living. The group all gathered in one end of the room. Ken was asked to stand on my desk at the other end of the room. As he stood he gave verbal expression to the paradox he had lived, "I'm lonely and I want to join you, but I'm better than you, and so I can't come down to your level and you can't come up to mine." As Ken spoke, the men began to ignore him and carry on an energetic discussion at a volume just below Ken's ability to hear. In this, Ken connected with his truth. He could maintain his superior stance, and most men cared little—they simply excluded him. He reached the awareness that a King without a kingdom is just a boy at play. From this, Ken moved to his intense sadness at being so alone and, eventually, to his anger at the members of his family who hid the alcoholism and sexual abuse behind the facade of Ken, the All-American Boy, or, in the lingo of codependency, The Family Hero.

Carry The Pain

Mark often spoke of a lifetime of managing responsibilities. He still took care of his alcoholic mother, ran his business, had gone back to school, and, admittedly, functioned as a marginal husband and father. While he engaged in what the group terms, "macho whining" about his life, he also seemed to derive great pride and his only sense of esteem from carrying this load. During his work one night, he was asked to stand and put out his arms. As he did this the men began to slowly stack pillows on his arms. Mark was asked to name each pillow as a person or situation he was responsible for in his life. After a time he began to tire but was encouraged

to sustain his effort, as he stated he must in real life, and be-
cause he had yet to receive the pillows which represented his
marriage, his children, and himself! Through the course of
the exercise Mark moved from compliance, to complaining,
to anger at the men, to anger at his mother, to shame about
his neglect of his wife and children, to sadness about his ne-
glect of himself.

In a group setting, where the trust and safety are secure, variations of the above may be created that are specific to the man. For a man who feels the tension in his neck, shoulders and back, someone may stand behind him and press firmly until he resists and starts to fight against the burden he is bearing. For a man who feels "smothered," he may agree to be covered with pillows while lying on his back, with firm pressure applied from above until he fights his way to freedom and fresh air. In learning the true difference between responsibilities and burdens, be creative, but be physically and emotionally safe.

Body Emotion

Several of the exercises earlier in this chapter helped you locate the pain, the joy, and the feelings in your body. Another step in this process is giving voice to these feelings within specific pieces of healing work. The following is not an exercise in and of itself; rather, it is a method to locate and express feelings that can be utilized in many of the expressive processes described in the book. As you prepare to work on a specific issue, you may find it difficult to move to the feelings about the event, person, or pain you are seeking to resolve. This method will tap into your body's way of knowing.

As you prepare, name the work you are here to do. As you discuss the memory, the relationship, or the pain that is associated with your work, close your eyes and look into your body. Describe any body sensation you are experiencing. Although the possibilities are limitless, I often hear about heaviness in the chest, pressure in the neck and shoulders, pain in the stomach, emptiness inside of the chest, moving feet, pain in the head, lightheadedness, tingling extremities, pain or tingling in the genitals. I often observe moving feet, various movements of the hands and head, change in facial expression, and shift in body position. I will often ask the man to describe the physical sensation that goes with what I'm observing and then ask him to name these sensations as sad, mad, glad, scared, guilty, or ashamed.

Through this simple process, men are often able to name the pain that was unclear to them on a purely intellectual level. Another common realization is that the inside and outside manifestations of the pain have been with this man for years, labeled only in vague terms such as "stress" or completely ignored. In the next stage of the work, the man is asked to proceed. Having named the feeling, you choose to give it your voice, to express and release it. If ready, go to all the places in your body where you keep this feeling about this issue. Collect all of the feeling in one place in your body, and compact it into energy you will express. When you have done this, decide where you will need to move all of this emotion to release it.

I was amazed when I first used and then taught this technique. People actually visualize moving the pain in their bodies, and their bodies respond, in kind. By example, a frequent occurrence in anger work at this moment is the twitching of arms and hands, which is consistent with the desire of many men to hit when angry and with the group rule that it is OK to hit the big pillow that is on the man's lap during abreactive work. At this point I return to several basic techniques for assisting the man in releasing the pain.

Anger

Hit the pillow or put your arms straight out, with palms out, pushing another man's palms who is across from you. In settings where there is a large physical space and extensive safety measures, other methods may be used. Most groups and workshops do not provide the space or adequate numbers of trained staff to insure safety if a man is mobile, so I encourage men to work sitting or kneeling on the floor. I will describe this work in greater detail, in the chapter dedicated solely to anger work.

Fear

Breathing and giving voice to the fear are essential to get the pain out of the man's body. A good place to start is to simply yell repeatedly at the event or person ((e.g., "You Scared Me!") until more words and feelings come. Remember, on the other side of fear you will most often find rage, and at times, sadness, before you find peace.

Sadness

I find sadness to be generally the most personalized of emotions. Many men are masters of holding the sadness back, keeping the finger in the dike. When the sadness is gathered in the body, the tender touch of a shoulder, one magic word of validation or understanding, one key disclosure of a boy's desire for love, will trigger sorrow that words cannot adequately describe. Each man has his own window to sadness. As you progress, let yours be known to you and to the other men.

Joy

When a man gets to his joy, he often needs permission to express it. After an intense piece of rage or grief, the joy may simply look and sound like relief. At times, the man needs to hear, "If you're feeling good, put it on your face." And remember, laughter, loud, raucous laughter, is allowed.

I made reference above to a man's voice. Putting sound to the feeling is an essential part of clearing the system of the pain. As a man begins to give physical expression to the work, I will then ask him to add noise. Give that feeling a sound! Use words or just a sound. Put that sound out now . . . louder . . . louder . . . stay with it. As you use your body and voice to express the pain, sense it move out of your body. Release the . . . (anger, sadness, shame, fear) through your voice and out through your . . . (hands, heart , etc.).

In other situations, a man might reverse the process as described above, beginning with his voice and moving to his physical expression; this is common among men who are fearful of their rage or feel embarrassed by the process. If this fits you, I encourage you to gather the feeling in your body, go inside, and find a sound or a phrase that names the pain. When using words, I recommend brief phrases that go to the heart of the pain. Long sentences will intellectualize the trauma, and there is time for intellectual review after the catharsis.

At this stage, you judge how far you push yourself and how much you release. In the minutes, hours, and days that follow, take stock of changes not only in your emotional well-being and in your relationship behaviors, but also in your body, as a result of your work. Your immediate sense of exhaustion after a powerful expression is testimony to your effort; relish it. Revel in your laryngitis after rage work; you earned it. When your voice comes back, some of you will feel like you went through puberty all over again; you will speak in deeper, more masculine tones. Take it in, you earned it!

I mentioned the importance in some men of finding their softness. Much has been said in masculine healing work over the past several years about the preponderance of soft males in our culture, males dominated in youth by feminine energy, unable to fight the good battle for family, self, and our planet. In the responses you are looking for, I am referring to a different softness: the ability to be a powerful man who knows there is strength in speaking to a scared child in a quiet voice, a man who knows when to take a step backwards before giving voice to his anger, a man who learns to hold and nurture children, women, animals, earth, and other men. My task has been not only to rekindle my passion, my power, my Wildman, but also to see the Shadow side of my anger and control, the seething mass that can create and destroy. If you are described by yourself in your secret shame or by others as a scary man, practice the following skills to assist you in creating a container for your rage:

The anger work I describe is for controlled, safe settings in the presence of others who understand this work. Do not practice at home with persons uninitiated in this work.

When you are angry at persons smaller than you (physically or emotionally) take one or two steps back from the person before verbally expressing your feelings.

When you are angry at a child, kneel down to make your body less intimidating before verbalizing your feelings.

As a conflict escalates, be conscious on lowering—not raising—your voice volume one level. You will be more effective, and, many people will concentrate more closely on what you are saying.

Use fewer words.

Make "I" statements, rather than blaming the other person for your feelings.

There will be more of this in the anger work chapter.

Take 5 minutes to close your eyes and review how you express anger to others in your life, paying particular attention to voice and body position. If you appear intimidating in some relationships, begin to practice the skills above. From your five minute visual review, journal other voice or body changes you will begin to carry out.

Un-Bonding

Many of us bonded too closely with someone during our childhood. This bond may have left you with a lasting confusion as to where you (your needs, goals, emotions, body) stop and where the needs, goals, emotions, and bodies of those close to you start.

Tommy's memory of Mom was that she had "nerve problems." Although this vague term was the only information he was ever given, he does remember Mom going away to the hospital to "rest" five or six times before he was a teenager. As he got older, he was often given the responsibility for taking care of Mom because Dad worked long hours. On several occasions, Tommy wrestled Mom to the ground and carried her to her room when she attempted to overdose on medication.

She would often tell him that she struggled because Dad was a bad husband and that she hoped Tommy would always be around to help her. He would then lie with her while she went to sleep. Years later, Tommy came in to men's group to work on his latest failed marriage, again to a woman for whom he had spent thousands of dollars for psychiatric treatment, none on his own therapy. He was sexually addicted, abused alcohol, and had a myriad of health problems due to obesity.

Carl's parents were both alcoholic. Carl was the oldest of three. As far back as he could remember he would get the other kids up in the morning, feed them, and get everyone off to school. He began contributing money from his job to the family by the age of thirteen; he also began drinking that year. Carl came to therapy with five years of sobriety and a lot of rage.

For men like Tommy and Carl, the job of taking care of disturbed others had never ended. In this perpetual focus on the needs of others, each had failed to see that he had become as troubled as those significant others from childhood. For these men, and some of you reading their stories, there is a seemingly indestructible umbilical cord that stretches the entire distance between a caretaker child and the significant people he cared for, be they parent, sibling, perpetrator of abuse, or other. Throughout this text, I will offer ways to "cut the cord." For some of you, the physical feeling of separation proposed in the ritual below will be a first step in freedom from the emotional bondage of a loved one. This exercise must be completed with a partner.

Today you are going to reclaim your body and soul as separate from someone who parented you or abused you or expected more than a child could provide.

Sit on the floor facing your partner. Put your hands out and grasp your partners hands; close your eyes. As a child you depended on adults for physical survival. You had to trust that someone would provide for you. Feel the intensity of an infant's need for that other person. Grasp that other person with a sense of dependency. The plan was for that person to give and for you to take, as it is supposed to be. However, if he or she was too needy, sick, scared, angry, or unfinished to be truly present, you may have begun to reverse the process; the child began to parent the adult. Even if you received excellent care, no caretaker meets every need. As you grew, you may have become needy and greedy, clutching to others; needy but distant, holding others away or even pushing them away; simultaneously grasping on and running away from men, women, children. Let yourself know and feel which you chose in your life: connection, distance, symbiosis. Be aware of when, where, and from what relationships you learned this style.

As we continue to test the bond you have with those who raised you be aware of how these ways of connecting affect you with family, friends, lovers, and children.

Keeping your eyes closed, drop your hands in front of you. As you relax, your partner will become a role-player of the person who inappropriately leaned on you, grasping onto you for survival. As this occurs, the role-player clutches on to the hands of the man, communicating through his hands the intensity of the needy adult. Let yourself connect with the feelings of being needed by someone so much that you feel taken over, unable to refuse, unable to leave. It's OK to verbalize these feelings. (If you are a skilled role-player and know the man well, you may pre-arrange to respond to him as the significant other, which may lead to rage, fear, shame, or sadness work.)

Again, keeping your eyes closed, drop your hands. The role-player now pulls out of the range of touch. Feel the absence of connection. You are alone. How do you feel? Is there relief, fear, anger, all of the above? Reach out and try to connect (the role-player stays out of range). How do you feel as you desire connection, but there is no response? As the role-player moves back into touch range, hold hands briefly, and with anger and fear, pull away. This is the physical sense of approach-avoidance that many of us live today, allowing the past and our emotions to rule our relationship choices.

Now, I want you to experience the more aggressive process of creating distance that some of us use. Put your arms straight out, with the palms of your hands facing out. Your role-player will do the same. When your palms touch the other person's, begin to push, as if you are pushing this person away to give your body, and yourself space. (The partner pushes back; don't give in easily.) When you have finally pushed this person away, what do you feel? Who in your life has crowded you? Who have you needed to push away to get breathing room? Who have you pushed away in error? Now, in your mind's eye, picture someone from whom you still need emotional distance and repeat the pushing exercise. You may feel fear, anger, or guilt in this, but do it anyway. It is OK to put your voice to the feelings as you push, make a sound. (This portion of the exercise can be an excellent warm-up to other feelings work.)

Finally, I am going to ask you to experience a safe connection, a formula for bonding while maintaining your separate self.

Open your eyes and see your partner for who he really is. He will put his arms out with his palms flat and upraised; put your arms out and lay your open palms on top of his. Slowly begin to pull away until only your fingertips touch, then stop. Now, as you look at your hands, slowly move until your fingers are completely separate from his, becoming aware of where he stops and you begin. This is Body Integrity. You can not be engulfed by anyone. You will connect up physically, emotionally, spiritually, or sexually only with people of your choosing.

Now, move back and reconnect with your partner, connecting and separating several times, just to get used to the idea. Mature relationships are like this: you move away and you reconnect, all of your and your partner's free will. As the final stage of the process, remember the many ways you can connect, and try some of them with your partner—eye contact, smiling, handshakes, hugs, kisses—ending each one as soon as you feel the need. Your body, your choice!

My Child's Body

Earlier in your journey I asked you to begin renewing your relationship with the child you were. As a boy, many of you were invaded physically or sexually. Some of you were simply not given good skills in understanding the sacredness of your physical being. We have beaten our bodies with alcohol and drugs, work, food, violent play, and violent sex. Throughout your work, you will have the opportunity to learn new ways of nourishing that boy, applying this love to your adult self, and to the world around you.

At the close of a piece of expressive work, I believe you must make decisions and commitments about how you will live differently because of the work. Emotional release is often insufficient in providing more than short-lived relief from pain. These commitments are the present-day, behavioral assurances of action in your journey through manhood. Below are a number of visual cues that can be employed at the conclusion of many of the processes in this pilgrimage.

As you conclude a piece of work, pick up your doll. If your work has been about times he was neglected, abused, and ill-treated, close your eyes and visualize your adult self doing the following. For sexually abused boys, gently wash from him any remnants of the abuse, help him feel clean, then dress him in clothes he really wants to wear. If the boy has been physically abused or neglected, feed him, give him a good drink, clothe him well. Any boy (not just the ones that were abused or neglected) must be hugged. Promise him that you will keep him safe, that you will listen to him, that you will teach him or find out the information he needs to become a man. Promise him that you will not let his dark side (this is not a perfect boy) take charge, reminding him that in the present day you are a man who is responsible for your behaviors and choices.

Having done this, state aloud and write down the specific, observable changes that you will practice as a result of the work. Translate the physical sustenance you supplied the little boy into how you will treat your adult body differently: chemicals, work, exercise, food, sex, touch, play. It is important to never say never or always **but never** miss this stage of the work. **Always** look at this aspect of your new self-care contract!

Grieving My Disease

I have a special interest in the struggles of the chronically ill, due to a long childhood battle with respiratory problems, exceedingly small stature, and an adulthood of skirmishes with what I now know are minor health concerns. In working with children and adults who battle diseases, I have seen the horrendous self-care generated by rage, fear, shame, and sadness at the unfairness of a chronic condition. I have also seen and heard the full range of responses from caregivers, from the unconditional love of the parents of two developmentally delayed boys, to the rage, shaming, and intimidation of the father of a twelve year old with cystic fibrosis who seemed determined to die before her time. In keeping with the spirit of this chapter, the healing of the whole being, I offer an exercise that is directed toward letting go of self-destructive pain that interferes with a commitment to self-care. Do I believe that this healing can even affect the progress of some disease processes? You bet. In later chapters, variations of this exercise will be used to grieve addictions, another category of disease. In this section, if you are faced with disease or disability, do this work.

Take a large sheet of unlined paper and markers and draw your disease (if you doubt that you have a picture of your illness, close your eyes and repeat the name of it while looking inside yourself). If you are in group, pick a man to role-play your disease, and place the drawing in front of his face. Have him ask you the following questions:

How do I hold you back in your life?

How do I scare you?

How do I anger you?

How do I change how others treat you? Are there significant people who have shamed, scared, or angered you because of me? Who are you angry at because of me (people, God)?

How do you use me to escape responsibility? To avoid relationships? How do you minimize or maximize my affects on you?

Who do I connect you with (family who have the disease, others who have the disease, caregivers)? How are these connections healthy? Unhealthy?

How do I serve you?

How have I betrayed you?

What have you always wanted to ask me? To tell me?

At any point in the dialogue, you may go into feelings. If this happens, heal this feeling, but expect to do more at another time. If you shut down emotionally, the dialogue will often give the role-player clues about your walls against healing. If you trust him enough, let him push the walls with the material you share. If you don't trust him enough, you picked the wrong man to role-play. And if none of this works, *come back and work again next week.*

If you move into feelings, apply the same rules that are offered throughout the book regarding anger, sadness, shame, and fear work. At the conclusion of the work, go back to the process as described in "My Child's Body." For you, the commitments you make must be in direct relation to any ways in which you have neglected caring for your disease or disability: medicine, rest, exercise, education, use of healers, honoring and challenging your limitations. Some of you will repeat this work many times, reaching deeper levels of healing, perhaps dealing with feelings that have been recycled as your disease progresses. Use every tool available: medical, emotional, spiritual.

4: Releasing Anger

the angry man

the angry boy lives inside this man body,
he runs the family, he runs the corporations, he runs the world . . .
    he runs . . . he runs,
little boys are taught to run.
inside he once was golden but he has been tarnished,
and he has forgotten his own beauty.
lost in the family, lost in the world, he runs to get back to the
    safety of the womb . . . woman,
any woman, but she can't heal his wounds . . . they are the wounds
    of a child man.

exerpt, Tony Schanuel, 1994

I am an angry man. If you are reading these words, you are likely either another angry man or someone who cares about an angry man. Perhaps you are someone who spends a lot of time apologizing for your anger, or at least for the ways you express your anger. Perhaps your denial, your anger Shadow, is so strong that you are reading these words believing they don't apply to you. Possibly your anger is buried so deep that you know if you do not heal it, your anger will kill you, or someone else. Your anger may be directed inward, in self-destructive, self-mutilating, suicidal behaviors. Perhaps you are learning for the first time about the pain caused by the rage of others toward you. I can't count the number of times I've heard a man say, "Yeah, my dad . . . (hit me with the buckle end of the belt, broke my nose, left marks on me, threw me against a wall, called me a bastard and an idiot, etc.), but he didn't abuse me."

Everyone gets angry. The question is not, "Am I Angry?" The questions are: "How do I express my anger?" "Am I expressing my anger in ways that are safe for me and others?" "Am I expressing my anger in ways that decrease and resolve it or escalate it?" The myth that all men are aggressively angry is just that, a myth. Men have as many types of anger as any other species. If you believe you don't get angry, ask around about the indirect, possibly passive-aggressive ways you make people who displease you pay a price. If people tell you your anger is scary and you doubt what they say, ask more people who experience your anger.

An abundance of literature has been written about anger. Until very recently, most of this information was on how to control anger. Some writers have suggested that anger is an unnecessary emotion caused by other feelings and issues, and that anger can be eliminated without expressing it. Numerous volumes teach skills of anger management. Other writers have begun to describe the importance of getting in touch with suppressed anger and engaging in cathartic processes to discharge your anger. I see anger work as a cognitive, emotional, behavioral, and spiritual expedition that incorporates aspects of each of the above philosophies. Anger is typically linked to, and often caused by, other emotions. Many men cannot even begin to resolve their anger until they move through the terror of people who abused them and the terror of their own emotions. Many men need to learn new skills to stop violent, angry actions. Most of the men I have worked with have benefited from rage resolution work—processes that allow the expression, release, and understanding of our anger from life trauma. As such, I divided this topic into two chapters, Releasing Anger (this chapter) and Anger Resolution (chapter 5), each with processes to assist in the healing of Shadow anger. This chapter will focus on building a new, safe container for rage. The chapter on anger resolution will offer techniques for reaching into anger when you are blocked by fear, shame, or sadness; there are unique aspects of each in this part of the journey. Certain exercises will be most appropriate for the man who easily touches his anger, often in ways that are destructive to self and others. Other processes will focus on finding, expressing and letting go of toxic anger. Many of you will find that both sets of tasks fit your work at different stages in your life cycle.

The Life and Times of an Abusive Man

I was smiling just before the explosion
Never saw it coming, or so I said
I
Try
To
Hold
It
In
I Love You

82

I'm Sorry
I Didn't Mean It
I'll Never Do It Again
I Promise

Finally . . .
No one cared
Apologies and Promises
Don't stick
To stone
So . . .
I Stopped

I'm an angry . . . dangerous . . . sad . . . beautiful man

Chris Frey, 1996

The Rules of Anger Work

This work is emotionally risky. For those who are facing your violence for the first time or at a deeper level, you may feel intense shame and sadness. Some of you will also touch for the first time the violence that has been committed against you, perhaps as far back as childhood. You may revisit moments in time when your desire to be abusive to yourself was overwhelming. The goals of anger work are not to relive these traumas, not to revive old rage or create new. Your goals are to learn new, safe rules about anger and to provide yourself with methods to permanently discharge your old, festering rage. I offer what I believe are vital guidelines about anger work:

1. If you have a history of violence, do not attempt expressive rage resolution work until you have consulted professionals and learned new skills to contain your present abusive behavior.
2. If you have a history of depression, suicidal ideation, dissociation, or psychosis, do not attempt rage resolution work without consulting knowledgeable physicians and psychotherapists.
3. **Do not** begin rage resolution work if you are currently using non-prescribed substances, including alcohol. All men that belong to my groups are asked to abstain from any non-prescribed substances during the period of time they are doing anger, fear, grief, and shame work in group. This rule serves several purposes. Substance use often alters a man's ability to feel and express feelings, even if he is not a substance abuser

or chemically dependent. Second, many men who do not see themselves as substance abusers find through a period of abstinence that they have been using alcohol or other drugs, to some extent, to cope with their pain. Finally, many men have discovered in attempting to follow this rule that they did have a problem that necessitated additional treatment (the beauty of this is that through sobriety many men find considerable improvement in their abilities to cope with anger).

4. If you are a newly sober addict (less than six months), approach this work with caution and a solid program of recovery (twelve-step meetings, a sponsor who understands anger and therapy, Rational Recovery). Some sources will tell you that you have no business working on these "other" issues until you have at least two years of sobriety. I have never been able to uncover the original source of this rule, and in my experience, this rule makes you vulnerable to several errors. If you have a history of repeated relapse, dealing with other issues, such as your rage, may be essential to establishing a successful recovery. Some of you also will find your anger so strong that you cannot wait to do this work; people are getting hurt. Many of you will find sobriety brings an improvement in your anger management skills, but this will not be true for every man. If you are newly sober and need this work, find a therapist and a group that understands your addiction, be it chemicals, sex, food, or gambling. Maybe your addiction is rage!

5. Expressive anger work must always end with your return to the present. If you are prone to dissociation, intense anxiety or depression, this work can be extremely helpful in your recovery. It can also be very unproductive to go into the feelings in a setting where you are not safe or are not in the company of clinicians skilled at assisting you in re-stabilizing after an anger process.

6. Be aware of what may arrive on the heels of your anger work. As I prepared to write today, I spoke with a man who has just completed his first major piece of rage resolution work. After several days of intense relief and joy, he has entered into deep sadness and more anger. For some of you, this work will come in waves, with significant breaks between. For others, this will be an opening of a door to intense emotion that will demand frequent and immediate attention. I was taught that each person has a self-monitoring mechanism that won't allow him to go any faster than he is ready to go; I no longer believe that is true of every man. Some of you have stronger boundaries and emotional defenses. Each of you must learn your style, your pace, your need for sup-

port. Most of us can't take a break from real life while doing our healing work. Gather your support. Be aware of how your work flows. Fit your healing work into your life.

7. This work is not simply about getting angry. It is about containing violence, releasing ancient rage, and making new decisions about how to live with less anger in your life.

Group Rules

I lead anger work in various settings: groups, retreats, men's initiation experiences. Each of these provides different opportunities and limitations for anger work. For many men, anger resolution needs to be more than a verbal and emotional experience. It must be physical. **The Number one rule of anger work is safety.** To insure the safety of the man working, the other men present and the staff leading the process, follow a few fundamental safety rules. As I am often heard to say, "I don't have very many rules for this work, but the ones I have are non-negotiable." In almost ten years of my leading work that can blast off the doors with power and pain, no man has ever been seriously injured, physically and each man has been emotionally nurtured. In part, the rules are dictated by the size of the physical space you have available. I often work in a large office or larger meeting room, which allows ample space for a group of men but is not safe for a great deal of movement. My general rules of safety are as follows:

1. Provide a carpet in the center of the room. The man working must remain on the carpet for the entirety of his work, unless given permission to leave by the facilitators.

2. When a man is planning anger work, he proceeds as follows: he sits on the carpet with a large pillow on his lap, and he asks another man to sit behind him and hold him loosely around the waist. (The pillow is for grounding and for something to hit if the man needs to express the anger physically; the Holder is for grounding, a reminder to the man to stay on the carpet and a reminder that he is not alone in his work.) Following these guidelines necessitates a man being ready to be touched by another man, certainly a big step for many men, often a huge step for men who have been physically and sexually abused.

3. This leads us to the all important rule about touch. No One touches you unless you say it's OK. If you are not ready to be touched, it is not your time to do anger work. Take as much time as you need to work on trust and safety issues, only moving into anger work when there are men available that feel safe to you.

85

4. Before beginning his work, the man repeats the safety rules: "I will remain sitting no matter how angry I get; I will not hurt myself or anyone else; if I want to hit I can only hit the pillow; I can say anything I want, at any volume I want, for as long as I want."

5. Any man can call a halt to a piece of work if he believes the safety rules are at risk of violation, consciously or by accident. This is best done by catching the attention of the facilitator, but the group may need more immediate intervention by a man in the circle if the leader is otherwise occupied.

6. Anger work, like any feelings work, can "hook" other men—the intensity of the work triggers another man's pain. I encourage men in the circle to take care of themselves by bringing another man close for support during someone's work, writing in their journals during the process, physically moving slightly farther back from the man on the carpet (we always process these hooks to maintain a safe container for each man, usually at the end of the work).

I will describe various methods to express the anger verbally and physically. I will also note exceptions I occasionally make to the rules of staying on the carpet and on the floor, exceptions that are consistent with maintaining the safety of all men. Remember, getting the work done is secondary to maintaining the safety; better said, the work doesn't get done without safety. When you safely complete your first piece of anger work you will better understand the immense relief at finding a method of releasing old pain that doesn't result in harm to you or anyone else.

> After his first piece of anger work Len explained, "This is the first time I've seen strong anger expressed that somebody didn't get beat up. I didn't believe there was a way."

Final Note: The rules, as described, are essential in any expressive healing work. As you move through the material and prepare to heal your fear, shame, and grief, return to review the rules. A safe container, with expectations and commitments that apply to each man, is vital to the cardinal rule of healing, "Do no harm."

The Anger Container

> Paul came to therapy stating, "I heard you do anger work with men, and I need to get a lot of anger out." Paul had numerous incidents of violence against others in his history, was frequently verbally abusive, and had also

threatened violence against himself (suicide) with serious intent on several occasions. He had heard about expressive anger work and hoped that by ventilating his rage in therapy he would release his tendency toward violence. Even as Paul talked about his anger in the early sessions, however, the group began to respond with fear to him . . . "I don't feel safe with you." Before Paul could safely express and release his historical rage, he would need to secure a new set of rules to guide his anger in his day-to-day life. Without these rules, his anger in group, no matter how productive, would spill over outside of session and escalate into abusive behavior.

The Anger Continuum

My experience with men has included a curious phenomena: hundreds of men who define anger as one of two states of being:

"I'm either not angry or I'm in a rage, there's no in between."

(Laughing ironically) "Is there anger other than yelling and throwing stuff?"

"I never lose my temper, so I really don't get angry."

Many of us have aged with a very rigid, childlike belief system of anger—I'm either raging or I have no anger. For some men this means a lifetime of going straight from no emotion to rage, a terrifying experience for the people around them. For others this means little or no direct expression of anger, or in many cases, denial that what comes out of you is anger:

"I don't get angry. My wife and I never fight."

"No, I'm not angry. I'm frustrated."

The Anger Continuum is a simple exercise to assist either the underreactor or the overreactor in beginning to understand anger as a wide range of mental, emotional, and behavioral choices, rather than a leap from numbness to fury.

Take out your journal. Draw a line at the top of the page that delineates a continuum from 0 percent to 100 percent:

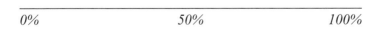

0%   *50%*   *100%*

Under 0 put No Anger; under 100 write Rage. On the page below the continuum, start a list of all the words your culture uses to identify some level of anger. If this is difficult, try these options. Go to the library, find a dictionary and a thesaurus and look up the words *anger* and *rage*. Ask friends and family what words they have that identify some level of anger. Take time to recognize slang terms that are commonly used (such as miffed, peeved, ticked, pissed). Give yourself several days to make the most inclusive list possible.

Take each word and assign it a value from 0 percent Angry to 100 percent Angry, whatever amount of anger you believe this word indicates. Place each word at the appropriate place on the continuum. Take time to review what you've learned up to this point. Become aware of the wide range of choices you have in describing your anger, the wide range of choices these words give you in the depth and intensity of your anger. From here, you can use this process in several ways:

If You Have Rage

For the next week, two weeks, or month keep a list of each situation in which you become angry. In each situation, note in your journal the level of anger you had for the incident or person. For each situation, assume that the level was out of proportion, an overreaction. (Even if this is not literally true, lowering your defenses will help make a powerful change.) Having made this assumption, pick a word other than rage that better identifies an appropriate amount of anger for the situation and note the more appropriate percentage of anger. In your journal, write how the situation might have been resolved differently if you had given it the revised amount of anger. Begin to practice this process behaviorally:

> When you are angry, stop.
> Assume you are about ready to overreact.
> Revise your assumption of the amount of appropriate anger.
> Change your behavior accordingly.

If your level of overreaction puts you or others in danger, practice the exercise by stopping, leaving the situation, revising your assumption, and preparing for how you will use this information at your next opportunity (rather than trying to return to correct the current conflict, which will often simply result in a return to rage, regardless of your best intentions). Take what you have learned to your therapist or group; take your questions and confusion, too.

If You Don't Recognize When You Are Angry

Begin by spending a week, two weeks, or a month listening to other people's expressions of anger. Pay attention to the words others use and to the behaviors that they engage in that match their words. Answer these questions:

What words go with what behaviors?

What behaviors are consistent with what words? (A person says he's irritated and he grimaces and walks out of the room.)

What behaviors are inconsistent with what words? (A man says he's not angry, he's just trying to get you to listen. He backs you into a corner, shakes his fist at you, and calls you an idiot.)

After you have taken time to note the words and behaviors of others, begin to notice the times you use words that may connote some level of anger (hurt, irritated, frustrated) and how you behave in these feelings. Using your journal, imagine using the word *anger* in each of these situations. How do you feel about this? How do you imagine others respond? If you believe you are totally without words for anger, imagine that when you use the words *tired, exhausted, numb, depressed, burned-out,* or *confused* that there is some anger in these states of being for you. Again, I ask that you assume this even if you are in doubt or denial. If you are ready, begin to substitute the word *anger* for the words you have typically used. You may return to the other words at a later date. This exercise is simply a way to practice being in tune and honest about your feelings. This is not designed to create a monster where there was previously a kind, gentle man. It is designed to add to your repertoire, to help you be more real, and give you opportunities to resolve previously hidden or misdirected emotion. Take what you have learned to your therapist or group, and take your doubt and denial, too.

If You Are Any Man

Using the new vocabulary you have discovered for your anger, open your journal and beside each word, list the following: physical, thinking, verbal, emotional. Under each heading make note of how you believe a man looks (physical), thinks (thinking), talks (verbal), and feels (emotional) when utilizing this level of anger in his life:

Example

Frustrated . . . (fill in the blanks with your own perceptions)
Physical . . . frown, furrowed brow, animated but not threatening
Thinking . . . distracted or focused, blaming self or others (will stay frustrated), thinking about his part in creating and solving the problem (more productive)
Verbal . . . agitated voice tone, loud but not yelling
Emotional . . . also feeling scared

In successfully completing this process, you have a much broader picture of what anger is and how to express yourself. A benchmark of maturity is flexibility, expanding your options. This exercise is a first step for some of you in accomplishing that essential life task in relation to your anger.

Ownership

Owning destructive forms of anger is an essential part of facing your Shadow and developing a new emotional structure. This ownership must take place on several levels to facilitate lasting change. The following exercise is recommended for any man who has been violent toward himself or others. The process has several stages and takes several weeks, even months, to complete. You may need to return to segments of the activity at various stages in your journey. This is especially true if you are also doing expressive anger work on early trauma—work that can repeatedly stir up previously practiced dysfunctional techniques for communicating feelings. If you fulfill the intent of the entire exercise you will feel significant remorse and perhaps other pain. Because of the shear amount of writing and the pain, some of you will be tempted to take shortcuts, to abandon the work before you move through all stages. I entreat you to dig deeply and push through. As with any portion of this book, if you are overwhelmed at any point, stop, access your support system, and return to the work at a later date, but as soon as possible.

A note about shame. These processes are not designed to shame you. They are designed to connect you with appropriate guilt for your actions and to surface shame that you may already have, in ways that give you opportunities for transformation and healing. If you touch your shame, **don't bury it again.** Shame about your past behaviors only feeds the next outburst. Men who are ashamed of themselves do not heal their rage, they stuff it only deep enough that it can be dredged back up in the next situation of hurt, fear, and other pain. When you feel your shame, find your therapist, group, or other trusted person; declare your shame and realize that the work you are doing is what will truly alleviate it.

A note about remorse. Remorse replaces shame and allows healing of past transgressions. Remorse is the heartfelt expression of regret and sorrow. It is far beyond, "I'm sorry" because first you must understand and feel the damage you have done, only then expressing this understanding in a way that says, "I know what I have done, I know I am fully responsible, this is my sorrow for how I have harmed you, and this is what I am doing to change that behavior." Remember, "I'm sorry" is only useful to the other person the first time you commit the act. After that it is simply a hope that you can avoid responsibility and still be forgiven. Remorse is a commitment to change. Capture your remorse as you move through the activities below.

Finally, if you are not sure your behavior falls into the category of violence, do the exercise. If you are telling yourself, "I only did . . . once (or occasionally)," do the exercise. If you are offended by the terminology I use to describe the anger process and believe it does not apply to you, do the exercise.

> *Dale came to therapy on the recommendation of his wife, who was ready to leave him if he did not change how he expressed his anger. Upon joining group, Dale immediately began to react to the terminology used by several of the men to describe their anger, stating, "I am not violent and I don't have rage. Sure, I throw things, I yell sometimes, I've pushed the kids down. But, I've never beat my wife like my dad beat me." In his description, Dale made two thinking errors common among men with rage issues. He was continuing to deny any incidents of physical violence that count, and he was minimizing the seriousness of his rage by likening it to the more extreme rage of someone in his past. Dale never did fully own his behavior, and his wife did leave.*

Stage One

Take out your journal. Make a list, to the best of your memory and honesty, of all the times you have done any of the following:

Called someone a name in anger.
Yelled loud enough to scare another person.
Used your body to intimidate, control, or restrain another person who was not physically attacking you or someone else.
Hit a person in anger.
Thrown objects in anger.
Verbally threatened to hurt someone.
Verbally threatened to hurt yourself.
Punched walls, doors, counters, or other objects when angry.
Used any physical force to touch a person sexually.
Attempted suicide.
Used any object to cause physical harm to yourself.
Attacked anyone with a weapon.
Injured or killed anyone.

Stage Two

Go to your therapist, group, or some other person you trust and take the list of your angry behaviors with you. Share the entire list, incident by incident, allowing yourself to feel your feelings (sadness, remorse, shame, anger) but do not offer any explanations, justifications, or excuses for your behaviors. The role of the person you are sharing this with is simply to listen, to accept your truth, to support you through any feelings you express, and to ask clarifying questions. (It is not the role of the support persons to pass judgment, to rescue, or to interpret the information that is shared.) At the end of this stage, it will be useful to get feedback from the support persons as to the level of honesty they felt coming from you and any encouragement they have for you to continue what may, by this time, have become a very painful process.

Stage Three

Return to your journal. Take time to close your eyes and return to two places in the past, a time when you were expressing intense anger toward yourself or someone else, and a time immediately after you had expressed intense anger. As you concentrate, begin to see and hear how you explained this outburst, both inside of yourself and to the person(s) present. Now, go to another incident of anger and complete the same process. Take enough time to return to as many situations as you need to, until you begin to get a clear picture of how you explain your anger. When you have this portrayal of your internal and external messages, open your eyes and begin to write the statements that you have used to explain your rage. As you write, it is OK to stop and feel. You may experience sadness, shame, anger, confusion, clarity. Keep yourself safe while you move through the feelings.

Stage Four

At the end of stage three, go to the top of the page and title these messages, "My Justifications." If you are not already aware, begin to focus on the idea that using these messages feeds your rage process. Also, many of you will begin to understand that although you may have many explanations for your outbursts, you return to specific justifications. These are your Core Justifiers, the repetitive ways you defend against taking full responsibility for your anger, excuses that generally fall into four categories: denial, minimization, projection, and rationalization. Denial includes any of your beliefs that say, "No, I am not really angry," or "My anger is not out of control." Minimization is any way of saying, "I'm not as angry as you say I am," or "My anger is smaller than you say it is." Projection is blaming someone or something else for your outburst and feelings: "I wouldn't get this angry if . . . (you'd listen, I'd had a better day at work, Congress was running the country better, the stars and the moon were aligned correctly). You may use an actual problem in your life to project blame for your inappropriate anger: "I'm sorry I yelled at you. It wasn't really me. It was the . . . (alcohol, drugs, depression, anxiety)." My personal favorite is the men who are using their recovery to blame for their rage: "I was just in touch with my Inner Child," or "Those were just my ACA issues coming up," or "Chris said in group last week that it's OK to get angry." If you have issues beyond your anger, take responsibility for those, too—heal the whole person! Rationalization is a great catch-all term for any other defense you use against accepting responsibility for your anger, any excuse you use to explain it away. Perhaps the most extreme rationalizations are loss of memory and revenge. "I guess I'm sorry for hitting you, but I don't really remember doing it. When I get that angry, I just see red and I can't really remember what happens" (if this is really true, you need a complete medical evaluation) or "I don't get angry, I get even."

After you know the defenses against accepting responsibility return to the list of messages you use for your anger, and assign one of the four types of defenses to each of your messages. As you assign each message a category, be willing to accept your truth. Do you minimize, rationalize, and project as you try to accept responsibility for your denial, minimization, rationalization, and projection; or are you able to see how your explanations feed the anger? Imagine an answer to these questions:

If I give up my defenses, how will my expressions of anger change?
If I give up my defenses, what emotions will I feel that have been lying underneath my anger?

Stage Five

At this stage, stop and take inventory of what you have learned about your anger. Make sure you take time to share with a man what you have learned, and if you are prepared to listen, share with a woman that you trust (not men or women you have abused, unless agreed upon with the assistance of a skilled facilitator), if you have not already done so. Make sure you give this person an opportunity to give you feedback about your level of honesty and other suggestions about dark corners to look in for healing that you may have missed.

Return to My Justifications and pull out your Core Justifiers, listing them in a column on the left side of a clear page in your journal, leaving room to write next to each in the right column. Using what you have learned from your internal work and from the feedback you have solicited from other men and women, write a heading in the right column: My Truth. Under this heading, create an honest, safe message that counters each of the Core Justifiers that you have used.

Core Justifiers	My Truth
I don't yell. I'm just intense.	*I speak louder and louder when I'm not getting what I want from you, to try to control and intimidate you.*
I'm not violent. I've never hit you.	*I am violent. I throw things at you and often call you vulgar names.*

As you write your truth, let yourself stop and feel. This is not a process aimed at shaming you; however, you may feel shame. At this point, a productive feeling to strive for is remorse. Remember, in remorse is your ability to empathize with the pain you have caused others and yourself; in remorse is your understanding of the importance of change; in remorse is your core willingness to transform your rage.

After you complete the writing section of this stage, share your truth with your group or other trusted person. As you disclose, prepare a statement of your commitment to change. Write it down. Speak it to the person(s) you are with:

> *I have learned of the harm I cause with my anger. I have faced my excuses and admitted my truth. I now know that I must change in the following ways: I will begin this week by . . . (be concrete and specific). . . .*

If you have dug deep and moved through each stage of this piece, you are already well into your commitment to change. Stay with it, this will be a foundation for much of the work that will follow. By the way, I honor your willingness to go into these ashes. Men of courage are men who choose not to spend a lifetime in rage and revenge.

Extensions of Ownership

Several processes can be used as extensions of the exercise above, enhancements that may be utilized in a powerful way throughout this work.

Disclosure

This title refers to disclosing your truth, at various stages, to those closest to you, especially those who have been harmed by your anger. Obviously, sharing with those close to you is an activity that is recommended in association with almost any process. The importance of highlighting disclosure in this exercise is that you are offering a safe container to your loved ones to begin sharing the fear and anger they have been carrying. Be aware that while this activity is an essential part of the work, there are risks in telling the truth. (Contrary to what we were told growing up, the consequences are not always less severe if you tell the truth.) Prior to disclosing new learning about your anger to someone who has been deeply affected, discuss your plan with your therapist, group, or other support system. Make sure to consider:

> Is the other person ready to hear your truth, or is he or she still too angry, scared, confused?

> Are you prepared to handle the other person's reaction to your admissions of accountability? Early in healing you may disclose with the Shadow goal of getting validation and forgiveness, only to return to rage if this is not forthcoming.

> How will disclosure, at this point, assist both you and the other person(s) in the healing process? This is not just about your need to heal; it's time to deeply consider the needs of the person(s) you have harmed.

You may return to this piece multiple times within the stages of ownership, sharing growth as it occurs. In whatever fashion you use this activity, stay in contact with men who will identify your Shadow as you progress, and often stumble, through your truth.

I Am a Dangerous Man

I find three words to be especially authoritative in describing the rageful man: *Dangerous, Scary, Violent.* These words go right to the heart of the denial of angry men I have known, including myself.

> *Brad was able, from the first session, to say that he was angry. He was able to honestly admit to the various verbally and physically angry behaviors that had been reported by his lover. Within the same hour he also claimed, "It's not that I'm really violent or dangerous, though. I've always stopped before I really hurt him." When asked if his lover was afraid of him, Brad laughed.*

The impact of honestly admitting the Big Three is often amazing. I have seen immediate insight and empathy never before touched by many men with similar stories:

> Stan began to talk in detail, for the first time, about the behaviors he engaged in with his wife and kids when he was angry: yelling, backing them into corners, and on several occasions, punching them. All the while, Stan maintained he understood that his children were scared of him but believed his wife was overreacting. Stan was invited by the group to look deeper at this issue and agreed, "I really do want to do what it takes to keep my family together." Stan was asked to stand and to pick a man in group the size of his wife (the smallest man in group was selected). After reiterating the safety rules, I asked Stan how much bigger than his wife he was, "Oh, I'm a big guy, I'm a lot bigger." I asked Stan how much louder than his wife he got. "I get reeeeal loud!" I asked Stan how much stronger he was than his wife. "If I wanted to, I could do anything I wanted." As I continued to ask Stan questions about what he was "capable" of doing when angry and what the likelihood was that his wife could easily stop him, he said, "OK, I get it," as he began to tear up. I asked Stan if he was ready to take the next step and he said, without question, "Yes." "Then, stand in the center of the carpet. Men, circle Stan standing. Stan, in whatever order you choose, face each man in the circle and state: 'I am a Dangerous, Scary, Violent Man. I scare my children. I scare my wife.' " As Stan came to me, he said, "I scare myself. I don't want to scare my family anymore," and he wept. From that point forward, Stan was more receptive to developing concrete skills to listen instead of controlling, to face his feelings other than anger, to look deeper at the origins of his rage, and to create specific alternatives to his abusive behaviors. This was not easy in light of the fact that as Stan became a safer man, he began to hear more of the buried anger and resentment held toward him by the members of his family, but he persisted and it worked.

My Anger, My Body

This process can be completed as an extension of the exercise above, Stage Five of ownership, or it can stand on its own as a useful ritual for men who struggle with anger. This exercise addresses how a man's body feels on the inside and how he acts, looks, and sounds on the outside when angry. You are in the minority if you claim your anger, and if you are aware how your anger feels physically and looks to others. A common response when I ask men to describe their internal experience as they get angrier and angrier is, "I don't know." The prevailing reply when I ask men how they look when angry is, "I never thought about it." Another response has often been, "I'm afraid to look. I'm sure I look ugly." For many of us, anger is about two things that prevent more cogent answers to these questions: denial and altered states of awareness.

Those of you who dug into the previous exercise, ownership, have become well acquainted with your denial and how to confront it. In terms of your physical self, denial works something like this. "Anger, or at least how I express my anger, is bad. I should never get angry, or not admit it when I am, or at least not admit how big my anger is. If I can't admit my anger to you, I can't admit my anger to myself. I have to begin disconnecting from the signals my body gives me that I am becoming angry and the signals about how angry I am." By altered states of awareness, I mean the heightened state of physical and emotional arousal that some men experience when angry; the high of rage. Most compulsive behaviors, perhaps all compulsive behaviors, have a cycle of pleasure and pain/shame. A behavior that feels incredibly good may simultaneously, and especially later, feel incredibly bad. The desire for the pleasure and the power of the compulsive behavior to temporarily alter the pain become potent catalysts for staying in the cycle. As difficult as some men and women may find it, acknowledging that anger is a different kind of drug, an extremely intoxicating drug, is essential in identifying and taming the beast.

Now, if you found this description obtuse, let's move on to the concrete identification of your physical anger signals.

Take your journal out. List the following categories on the page, giving yourself room to write, then follow the instructions on the right side of this page:

External and Internal Signals

External
  Voice
  Facial Expression
  Body Position
  Hands

(To the best of your knowledge, describe how your voice, facial expression, body position, hand movement changes as you become angry. Be aware that there may be several progressive steps as your anger builds.)

Internal
  Body Heat
  Physical Pleasure/Stimulation
  Body Pain/Discomfort
  After-effects

(To the best of your knowledge, describe how your internal physical state changes as you become angry. Does your face or body feel warmer or colder? Does the feeling in your hands and feet change? Do you feel any sense of increased energy, pleasure, or stimulation? Before or during your release of anger, do you feel pain or discomfort anywhere in your body? After you have released your anger, how does your body feel? Remember, there may be several stages as your anger builds.)

Without any other tools to assist you, the information you gathered above is your baseline of insight into the physical signals that your anger is coming, is building, and has been ventilated. Be aware of the amount of spontaneous insight you had into how your body experiences your anger. The information you gathered may be profound to you, or it may be very limited.

> *Zack brought his work on physical signals to group stating, "I never look at myself in the mirror, I've never thought about this stuff. All I know about the internal information is that whenever I plan to come to group to do anger work on the past, I feel real tense in my neck and I feel like I'm going to throw up."*

If, like Zack, you had difficulty making contact with the relationship between your emotional (anger) and physical (body) self, use any, or all, of the following processes to extend your understanding.

Choose A Scene

Close your eyes and use what you have learned about preparing for a guided imagery.

> *As you look from the present into the past, find a time when you became very angry, remembering that you are not going to relive the event, nor are you going to reconnect with any violence. You are simply going to be aware of how you felt inside, how you sounded, how your face looked, and how you used your body when you were angry. Be aware of how your body felt on the inside that day; remember any pain or discomfort as your anger built; remember any pain or plea-*

sure as you began to express and ventilate your ire, paying special attention to your stomach, neck and shoulders, head, muscles, and other parts of your body.

Step back and look at the external signs of anger that you were building, then expressing. How did your voice sound, in tone and in volume? What is your facial expression? How do you hold your body and hands , and does this change as you get angrier or as your anger begins to subside (do you sit, stand, get closer to the other person, get further away)? If you are experiencing any feelings during this work, be safe and let yourself feel.

Record the information you have gathered in your memory. If you believe that what you have just registered is an accurate account of your physical signals of anger, return to the present using the skills you have learned. If you are unsure, move to another scene and repeat this exercise until you begin to see a pattern in your body responses to your rage.

When you return from the imagery, open your journal and record what you have learned using External and Internal Signals.

Feedback

Seek out people who have been with you when you have expressed strong anger. Make sure that these are people that you trust, that will not shame you, and that you will not shame for being honest with you. Give each person the list of External Signals and ask for feedback on how you sound, look, and use your body when you are angry. If you solicit feedback from more than one person, what themes begin to emerge? Compare what you hear to your own perceptions. If what you hear is different from what you have believed, what does that teach you about the discrepancy between how you are seen and how you intend to be seen? I can tell you from personal experience that this can be one of the most eye-opening questions in a man's quest for healing, not just in terms of anger but especially in terms of anger. Record the feedback you receive.

The Mirror

If you do not own a large, portable mirror, buy one for your anger, grief, fear, and shame work. This is a tool to assist you in facing the one person who most needs to understand, confront, and accept you—you! Take the material you have gathered from your self-study and the feedback of others, and go to your mirror. Assume the body positions, the hand positions, and the facial expressions described in your data. Look closely, get familiar with the angry you, a disowned part of you that you need to keep in front of you if you intend to change. If looking is painful, look closer. Others have looked away too many times, you have looked away too many times.

If you are willing to take this work a step deeper, find a *voice mirror:* a tape-recorder or a live person who will mirror back to you how your voice sounds in anger. Tape your voice as you have described it in your data. Invite someone to use their voice at you the way he or she perceives you use it when angry (again, remember the importance of safety in these processes). If hearing is painful, listen again; don't let yourself forget how you intimidate others. Write what you learned on all levels in your journal.

My List

If all else fails, I now provide you with a cheat sheet, my less than all-inclusive list of External and Internal Signals.

External

Voice volume increases.
Voice becomes chillingly calm.
Voice tone becomes crisp, sarcastic, whiny.
Speech becomes more rapid, speaker more verbose.
Interrupting.
Finger pointing.
Fist shaking.
Standing over a person.
Body into a person's personal space with anger.
Hitting things.
Pacing.
Advancing on a person as he or she backs away.

Internal

Stomach hurts or burns.
Nausea.
Tingling extremities.
Increased body heat or body cold.
Muscle tension.
Head pain.
Chest pain.
Don't limit yourself, add to my lists.

How To Use This Wisdom

1. Never again say, "I don't know how I come across when I'm angry," or "I don't know why people are . . . (scared of, intimidated by, angry at) me."

2. Learn, and stay aware of, your escalation process: the early, more subtle signs that you are beginning to build your anger that, if redirected, move you away from intimidation, rage, and violence.

3. Acknowledge to yourself, to the men you do your healing work with, and to those other persons close to you, that raging is a conscious choice. You have hard evidence that while you may move from 0 to 100 percent in seconds or minutes, there are signals that you can become aware of to slow and reroute the eruption.

4. **My Alternatives.** Return to your External and Internal Signals. After each signal that fits into your pattern, list one to three alternatives to the external behavior, or one to three alternatives to your internal state.

Mick came to session with a new plan, "When I talked to my wife about anything serious this week, even if I didn't think I'd get angry, I sat down, made eye contact without staring her down, kept my hands on my legs, and made a decision to keep the volume control two notches lower than I would have in the past. Anytime I started to feel my face heat up and get red, I would stop talking, take three slow, deep breaths, and relax. I worked more on listening than on talking."

Start practicing a clear, concrete, and simple plan to adjust your behavior, and to slow down and relax your internal state.

5. **Volume Control.** I have a volume control in my head, and I suggest you install one in yours. I am, by habit, a loud guy; I seldom have a need for a microphone when leading workshops. Put my voice volume with my anger and you have . . . rock and roll. I have practiced listening to my own voice, the tone and the volume. When I am angry, I work for a strong, deep tone rather than an adolescent whine, and I typically go into my head, see a volume control from one to ten, and usually turn the volume down before I speak. I check the volume control to turn the noise down as the conflict proceeds. This is not to say that there is not a time to be loud. When I'm outdoors and playing, when I'm holding my ground in a safe confrontation with a man during our healing work, when my son is about ready to leap headfirst from the sofa. In general, I get more done with the voice of a powerful man than a rageful child in a man's body.

6. **Time Out.** A time-tested procedure for de-escalating rage is taking a time out, leaving the situation and person until you calm

down. The keys to taking a time out are to state the need to leave rather than storming out, to use the time away to journal and breathe and calm down, and to only re-initiate the conversation if there is truly a problem to be solved, not just a problem of your invention. Several adaptations of the time out that many men find useful in creating a safe distance for communication with lovers and spouses, writing and the telephone, are listed below.

7. **Writing.** Rather than trying to solve all issues verbally, try writing your thoughts and feelings back and forth with your loved one. There are several advantages to writing. You can edit, going back to re-read what you wrote and taking out incendiary language and blame. You have time to think instead of reacting impulsively. The person receiving the note has time to think instead of feeling backed into a corner, increasing the likelihood of a productive response. You're more likely to get to the point; it would take hours for some angry men to write what they can say in minutes. If you use this tool, I suggest several guidelines:

> share all feelings, not only anger
> don't blame
> take responsibility for your part in the conflict and ask
>   for what you need
> be concise

8. **The Phone.** A step farther down the road in risk, but safer than having a captive audience, is to process conflict by telephone. The rules of phone work are: set a time limit, no hanging up in anger, it is OK to hang up in fear (if the other person is getting abusive or out of control).

9. **My Anger Rules.** There are many excellent workbooks on anger management, each containing some guidelines for appropriate expression of feelings and thoughts when in conflict. As you complete the processes above, you may choose to seek out additional information and begin utilizing some of these guidelines. Great! There is, however, no replacement for your own commitment to your own guidelines. Return to your journal, and based on what you have learned to-date, make a list of ten Dos and ten Don'ts for yourself in expressing your anger. Share these rules with the men you work with. Get feedback from friends and family. Let people who care about you know your new rules. Hold yourself accountable to these new rules and let others hold you accountable.

Anger and Other Emotions

Anger is often driven by other feelings. Anger can co-exist with seemingly disparate emotions: sadness, fear, shame, even joy. How many of you have been angry at someone immediately after he or she scared you? (Think about the man who yells at his child for almost running into the street unattended.) Have you ever struck out in anger after someone embarrassed (shamed) you? This exercise, Anger and Other Emotions, is meaningful both for all of you who have difficulty in containing your rage and for you who experience the dilemma of identifying and touching your anger. Although the focus has been anger containment and redirection, I will offer variations for men who cover other emotions with anger and men whose other emotions cover their anger within this process.

Anger As a Cover

In chapter 2, I offered a simple exercise utilizing pillows to identify the layers of emotions that you may have lying in your heart. For many men, particularly those raised in the traditional Western male culture of rage, feelings other than anger were deemed unacceptable and weak. Some of you may feel as if you have two feeling states, numb and angry, and two emotional speeds, numb and high-velocity anger. In effect, all feelings other than anger are run through a filter and repackaged as some type of anger. Those close to us often assist in the masquerade by only looking as far as our behavior: He "acts" angry, thus he must "be" angry; I "act" angry, hence I must "be" angry. What goes virtually unnoticed in many boys and men are the wounds inside of the external rage, wounds that originate in fear, shame, and grief. A saying I have is: "Here is the story of many men . . . When we were angry we were taught to act angry. When we were sad we were taught to act angry. When we were scared we were taught to act angry. Heck, when we were happy we were taught to act angry (just look at the hostile aftermath of many sports championship games)." I believe that a crucial part of healing rage is establishing how much of your anger is actually anger, and how much of it is driven by other wounds, pain that in its original form was fear, shame, and sadness:

> *Wayne explained, "I decided real early that I wasn't going to cry when Dad hit me because he'd just hit harder. I remember thinking that I wouldn't show him I was scared, and that when I got big enough I would end the beatings, and I*

103

did. When I was seventeen, he came at me and I knocked him down. He never touched me again. I didn't even cry when he died. I remember later, when I'd get in fights, I wouldn't even feel the pain until afterwards."

The consequences of this predicament include a denial of other key feelings, leaving them to fester in your psyche, and the magnification of the anger. If someone hurts you in a way that calls for fear, or sadness or other expression of pain, only the anger is exhibited. Not only that, but the size of the fear, the size of the sadness, the size of all pain in addition to the legitimate anger, may get stirred into the anger pot and exponentially increase the expression of rage. Wayne did not only strike back in anger at his father. In his fist, he also collected all the unexpressed terror, grief, and shame of years of beatings, and he kept on striking back over decades of violence. And so, for those of you who know you are angry, and suspect you have other emotions, too, try the following process. Close your eyes and use the skills you have learned to enter a visualization.

As you relax, look inside of your body and find the place(s) where you keep your anger. I am going to ask you to imagine that for a little while you can gather all your anger in a pile and place it outside of you on the floor. How big is the pile of anger? How much does it weigh? Imagine the feeling of having to pick this load up every day, put it inside of you and carry it everywhere you go. Take time to feel. Now, imagine that a portion of this anger has gotten mislabeled. It has all been labeled as anger, but actually there are other feelings mixed in which take up some of the weight. As you look at the pile, you begin to see that some of the weight is made up of shame, perhaps times long ago, or more recently when you have been embarrassed or ashamed of yourself, times when someone else shamed you. As you look closely, divide out the portion that is shame and place it in another pile. Now you begin to see that there has been fear in your life, perhaps fear of people and events in the distant past, perhaps more recent fear. Take the portion of the pile that is your fear and place it in another heap next to, but separate from, your anger and shame. And now, let yourself see that there is sadness in this pile of emotion. How much sadness, how much grief, have you carried? Take the sadness and place it next to, but separate from, the anger, shame, and fear. Examine the heap of anger and determine whether you have buried any joy, any happiness, any passion under the

104

anger. Collect your joy and place it in a pile separate from all other feelings.

Look now at your anger. How much is left? Are you surprised at the size of your anger? As you look at the other piles of emotions, what did you learn about your fear, shame, and sadness? If you are ready, step back and see the full range of your emotions. Be aware that you are not here to heal all pain at once: you have time, you have help. Are you willing to keep your anger separate from your other feelings—using the anger to hide your other emotions—letting yourself begin to learn methods to express without rage your fear, shame, and sadness? So, look back into your heart and find a place in your heart for each feeling. Create a place for each feeling that is a safe corner in your heart, a space where that feeling will not leak or explode out, a space where you will determine when, where, and how much of each emotion is expressed. Place each feeling into your heart. Let yourself take whatever time you need to complete this task. Use whatever support you need from those around you. When you are ready, begin the protocol for returning to the present. When you open your eyes, write in your journal about what you have learned. Some of you will want to draw pictures of what you saw within the imagery.

Note of caution: Some of you will almost immediately begin to feel emotions other than anger as you move into this process. Often men touch sadness as soon as they become aware of the size and heaviness of the burden they shoulder each day. Others will connect with new, or new levels of, emotion as you bring your full range of emotions out of the anger. It is essential to do this activity with a support system in place. Touching your other emotions may seem overwhelming; the size of your other emotions may surprise, confound you. If the big picture is too much, access your support system, make sure to use those separate spaces in your heart to break this work down into tolerable amounts, and breathe a sigh of relief that you are not simply a constantly simmering cauldron of rage.

Anger Under Cover

I remember an old insult I have often heard about men, "He wouldn't know a feeling if it fell on him." (Oddly enough, if he's capable of feeling shame, that angry statement would most certainly bring it up.) Many men I know are in touch with feelings a great deal of the time.

They simply don't know what to name the feeling, believe they must disguise their feelings, and, as a result, turn their emotions into a myriad of stressors, addictions, and other masks. Not every boy is provided with the traditional male training of our culture at such an intensity as to cause him to translate all emotion into rage. For many of you, male and female, healing your anger wound is about breaking through the layers of other feelings that cover your true anger, anger that because of your masks is only expressed sideways (indirectly or manipulatively) or internally (against yourself in self-destructive ways).

> Kirk looked at me and said, "When the boss jumps me in front of the other guys, I really get scared. I'd like to stand up to him. I'm doing a good job, but he's too scary."

> Tony told the group, "When my lover tells me, in all the different ways that he tells me, that I'm a lousy partner, I feel so bad about myself that I just take it." Upon further discussion Tony admitted to rehearsing in his head what he would like to say to his lover, what he has never said, "I imagine telling him what an [expletive deleted] he is, seeing the look on his face that he's been devastated. I've even imagined hitting him, but I'd never do that!"

> Each time Wes began talking about his mother leaving him, and not returning, he began to cry. "I can't get angry at her (interestingly, no one in the workshop had suggested he should); it just hurts so bad that I never had a Mom, and that I've had four marriages trying to get a woman to take care of me."

As in the stories above, getting to your anger may be about developing skills to move through what I call your Lead Feeling. My Lead Feeling is the emotion that I have become the most familiar and comfortable with over the years. By comfortable I don't mean I feel good; rather, this is the emotion that I find the most acceptable to myself, the emotion that I somehow came to believe in childhood was the most acceptable to my significant others. For example, I have used fear as my lead feeling most of my life. I can get at least a little scared about almost anything: the truly scary event of a life-threatening emergency illness of one of my children all the way to feeling scared about getting my list of chores done on a day at home (a list of my own creation). I can even manage to get scared about good stuff like: will we really have fun on vacation, will my wife like her birthday present as much as I expect her to? I often say to men who lead with fear, "I understand from my own experience that you are able to kill the fun in the most joyous of events."

Returning briefly to the example in the Feelings Pillow exercise in chapter 2, many men also experience feelings in progression. It will often be difficult to reach your smoldering rage until you move through your Lead Feeling and any other emotions on top of it. On a deeper level, some of you have not even been aware of the anger you have buried because the Lead Feeling you've deemed acceptable to those around you (fear, sadness, shame, happiness) is the only emotion you have allowed yourself to feel on a consistent basis. What happens to these other emotions? Take out your journal. Write on a blank page any of the following words that apply to your life, past or present:

hurt	overwhelmed
depressed	shallow/superficial
confused	bad
exhausted	upset
frustrated	racing mind
used up	

If these words denote one of the following feelings in your life—mad, sad, glad, scared, ashamed—what feeling would it be? Note this feeling next to the word. As you read back through the information, make note of any other words or phrases that you use to designate feeling states without having to call the feeling what it really is. How does entering a . . . (depressed, confused, etc.) state of being, rather than owning and feeling the feeling, serve you? Who taught that it was more acceptable to stay . . . (bad, upset, etc.) than own the emotion? What does it cost you in your life to turn your emotions into these states of being, in your relationships, your job, your physical health, your emotional health, your sexuality, your self-esteem?

I believe that most men who spend considerable time in these states—confused, upset, tired, hurt, depressed, used up, overwhelmed, superficial, obsessive thought—are angry! If I experience my fear and don't move beyond it, to my anger and even beyond that, my state of being becomes obsessive thought and mental exhaustion. Anger that is denied, sublimated, and covered up is a quiet weight that you must hoist over your back every day, and it gets confusing, upsetting, tiring.

Me . . . And My Anger

If you are reading these words then I ask you to assume something with me—assume that you have unresolved anger inside of you and you are having difficulty in reaching and expressing it. Further, assume with me that one of the reasons that you are struggling is that you learned, probably early in life, to cover your anger with other states of being, other feelings, because someone or some life circumstance led you to believe that hiding your anger was important and necessary. Finally, assume that covering your anger no longer works in your life and that you are willing to become aware of methods by which you could safely touch, express, and let go of old anger. If you are willing to make these assumptions, close your eyes and simply be aware of the three decisions you just made:

I have unresolved anger.
I have learned to cover my anger well for myself and other people.
It is time for me to learn ways to safely heal my anger.

Having made these decisions, when you move into work about your anger here are several tools you can use within anger work.

I Feel

When you sit on the carpet to do work and begin to describe the issue, a common question that the facilitator will ask you is, "What are you feeling as you tell this story?" What will often come first, particularly early in your work will be your Lead Feeling. The next question, then, is, "So, you are feeling . . . (Lead Feeling) and . . . (what other feeling)?"

I Don't Know

If your answer to the questions above is, "I don't know," the next step is for the facilitator to respond with, "This is not school. Only you know the truth for yourself. So, if you did know . . . ." or "It's OK to guess."

I Still Don't Know

Choose someone to role-play and assign this man to be you. It is OK to see the role-player as an adult or child you, whichever would be most useful in helping you understand how you get frozen in attempts to reach your anger and emotions other than your Lead Feeling. Sit outside of yourself; look at the person being you. Have him retell the story; as an objective adult observer, what feelings would you expect him to have about this issue? "It makes sense that he would feel . . . and . . . and. . . ."

I Still Don't Know

This may not be your time to do this work; you may have other work to complete first. You may not be safe enough within yourself or in the environment to go this deep. Return to the beginning of this process and journal more on your Lead Feeling. Prepare yourself for more work on the events, relationships, and interpretations you made that led you toward covering your anger. (A mentor of mine often focuses on the importance of Adult Building, i.e., it is not safe to do deep rage, grief, shame, fear work until you have a sufficient foundation of new information and adult perspective.) Make a commitment to return to your anger work when you are ready. Remember, getting stuck doesn't have to be about quitting, or feeling ashamed, or resistance; it can be a clue to look elsewhere for the work that you need to be doing today!

But, I Didn't Hit Anger

The tools described above are not designed to move you only to your anger; they are provided to assist you in reaching whatever feeling or feelings are underneath your Lead Feeling. If you did not get to anger but are aware that you very likely have anger somewhere inside of you, continue to focus on the work in front of you and return to the processes above as needed. Having discovered my Lead Feeling of fear, having uncovered my other emotions, and having developed numerous skills for expression and release does not guarantee that I never return to old patterns. I revisit the process Me . . . And My Fear as often as I need to as I continue the work of growing up. And for me, the work is not complete. I am not whole until I move beyond my fear *and* my anger, through my shame, my grief, to my joy—my layers of emotion.

What Next?

The tools described above are offered to help you identify and connect with your anger. Later in the chapter we will focus on how to bring the anger up in ways to fully and safely express the intensity, along with methods to let it go. Before we go to that place, allow me to outline two additional exercises that can be useful in the Adult Building I mentioned, exercises that will better prepare some of you for the anger work ahead.

Naive, Cynic, Realist

This is an exercise that I began using with clients recently after using it on myself for years and realizing it might help other people. It is an uncomplicated way to see life as a range of choices, rather than what I call a series of "Either/Ors": either it must be this, or it must be that. This exercise utilizes a continuum of truths. Take out your journal and draw a line like the one below:

Naive	*Realistic*	*Cynical*

The line is a scale, a continuum of states of mind that many of us use to interpret the world: our work, our relationships, politics, the condition of our planet. These methods of interpretation affect the amount of anger you feel, best explained by describing each term.

Naive

"If I am as honest, hardworking, caring, and trustworthy as possible, other people will be, too." I find it hard to understand, even believe, when this doesn't work, so I usually just try harder. I may say things like, "I trust people. I give everyone a chance to hurt me once," and they often do—severely. We are all supposed to be naive, *as children,* but some of us simply decide not to grow up.

These types of people often hold a great deal of martyr anger, wondering why others don't appreciate them enough and wondering when they will be fully rewarded for their sacrifices and goodness. They often burn out on jobs, relationships, life, and eventually become cynics. Even as children, these people may be closet cynics; they stay naive children as an over-simplistic solution to not becoming the kind of adult they secretly despise (angry).

Cynical

"It's a dog eat dog world; you eat them or they eat you." I believe that people cannot be trusted, perhaps certain groups of people, perhaps no one. I justify my own untrustworthiness through my cynicism, "I wouldn't have to cheat on my taxes if the government wasn't so screwed up, and anyway, everybody does."

These folks have been angry for a long time, without adequate skills or appropriate outlets for their anger at the injustices in their world, so they generalize their anger to most or all of the world. They often believe that they are insulated against pain by their cynicism; this person is often seen in jobs where there is a daily onslaught of pain or injustice. I see more and more men like this as our corporate culture increasingly devalues such things as loyalty, longevity, experience, and quality. As children, these people often saw a very naive person get used and abused by a cynic, and they decided it was better to be the user than the usee. As men, cynics are not contributors— they are takers. Touching the inner cynic shows in men who gain job promotions in unethical ways, who learn to have ongoing extramarital affairs, who cheat in little and big ways with money, who live as a part of what has been called the "Me Generation" without regret and change. I find a great deal of cynicism in adolescents, who normally seek to blame the previous generation for the woes of their world, until some of them mature and begin to participate in making a positive contribution.

Both naives and cynics tend to believe in a one-dimensional world with over simplistic views of good and bad. Cynics are former naives who believe they've learned life's hard, true lessons. Neither style lends itself to positive individual or community change—both cause rigid anger. Many of us fall somewhere on the continuum, being somewhat naive or somewhat cynical, although there are a number of people at the extremes.

Realistic

This man is learning life's hard lessons, putting them to work to improve himself, and within the limits of his power, improving the world around him. He realizes that not everyone is as honest and forthright as he is. He realizes that *he* is not always as honest and forthright as he would like to be, and perhaps, sells others that he is. In the words of the Twelve-Step programs, he works for progress, not perfection. He has used The Trust Continuum and often makes solid judgments about how much to trust certain people—and he recovers from his anger when he makes poor judgments and is harmed through no fault of his own. The realist gets angry, then he chooses to take steps to resolve and utilize his anger for change—change in himself and change in the world around him. My realist mentors are Mahatma Gandi, Martin Luther King Jr., Jesus, Sheldon Kopp (a great author), Dr. Bob Brundage, and a sea of men that I have worked with as therapist and seeker of healing who have found the middle ground of optimism without rose-colored or one-way mirror glasses.

Now, pick several ages in your life, two or three childhood ages and two or three of your adult years. Place yourself along the continuum at various stages in your life. Where are you now? How did you get from where you were to where you are? Whose style, from the influences in your life, have you adopted? How well does your current style work in your life? How does your style relate to how often, and how intensely, you feel anger? What do you need to change about your style? What direction do you need to move in? What event(s) and person(s) do you need to do anger work on to resolve your naivete or cynicism? Will you commit to do this work: where, when, with whom?

The Crisis Continuum

This process is for those of you who are Catastrophizers, who go direct from OK or numb into extreme terror, rage, guilt, and shame.

Keith came to every session in some stage of panic, describing all of the things he "had" to get done that day and already focusing on what he "had" to get done in the next day, week, month, even years ahead. As he discussed his responsibilities, he was as intensely concerned about picking up the milk from the grocery store as he was the surgery that his wife was scheduled for. He described his completed tasks for the day in minute detail, as if he believed that getting the oil changed in the car was as significant as the flashback he had experienced about his father on the way to work.

This exercise is designed to assist you in de-escalating your immediate crisis response and in learning new skills to cope with any tendency to over-react, to Adult Build in preparation for the work on where, and from whom, you learned this Chicken Little response to crisis. Keep a copy of the following material close at hand while you are practicing this technique. Begin by reading the scale that has been designed to rank concerns, problems, and crisis in your life:

9–10	Life Threatening	Must repair or at least respond immediately.
7–8	Serious	Deal with as soon as possible, immediate response not required.
5–6	Significant	Reason for concern, make a plan to deal with the issue and a time frame to begin.
3–4	Non-priority	Non-essential, helpful and important to deal with when, and if, time allows.
1–2	So What?	OK if you never get to it.

Within each category can be a situation that occurs unexpectedly (illness), a situation that occurs regularly (job or family duties), and a situation that relates back to your early healing work (abuse issues resurfacing). Take the scale with you in a little notebook for two to four weeks and rank each situation that you consider a crisis in the following manner.

When the situation occurs or surfaces, rank the issue on the scale of 1–10. Unless the issue is a 9 or 10, immediately assume that you have ranked it *too high* on the crisis continuum and rerank it at a lower number, referring to the descriptions above. Continue this part of the exercise throughout the designated period of the assignment, searching for more and more realistic assessments of the crisis potential of events in your life. Begin to plan your responses to situations on the reranked, not the initial, reactions.

Be aware of several special circumstances as you search for a new response cycle. How often does your catastrophizing involve getting caught up in someone else's panic or agenda of priorities? How often do your anger, fear, and shame reactions result from catastrophizing? How often do you end up in emotional reactivity by combining multiple minor or nonemergent situations into one large emergency and mood disturbance? Begin to practice dealing with people and events one at a time, when possible. Begin to practice internally (without referring to the written scale) your new system of reranking your emotional responses. Begin to practice prioritizing your activities, duties, and relationships according to the new scale.

For those of you who are still deeply enmeshed with issues of your family of origin, this will assist you in making decisions like: "I promised I'd take the kids to the ball game tonight, but Mom just called in a panic and said someone had to get her prescription now because the pharmacy closes at 6 P.M., and she's only got three days of medicine left. If I don't go, she'll be mad and guilt me. Maybe the kids will understand. What should I do?"

This continuum can also be extremely useful in managing the pain that comes up from your early trauma. When you start digging into old history, one of the quickest ways to depression, anxiety, and decompensation in daily functioning is to react as if experiencing the pain in the *present* is worse than the *original* experience. Remember, you lived through the worst part already, and many of you lived through much of it with the intellectual and emotional development of a child. Use this scale to pace yourself, to plan your work, to determine realistically what needs to be worked on soon and what can wait. Use the scale to determine how to fit the priorities of your daily life with the priority of your healing work.

Finally, utilize this process to direct you toward specific interventions, methods of resolving concerns at their reranked level of importance. For instance, if you are working on serious childhood abuse issues, any time you rerank the situation and it is still above a 7, you plan to reach out to a support person. If you rank a situation as a 4 and someone else ranks it as an 8, you begin learning new skills for negotiation and assertiveness.

Underreactors

This exercise can be done completely in reverse if that fits your life. Some of you are underreactors; you find yourselves in serious crises because of your avoidance of a person or situation when resolution could have been achieved at 1-4. You may be what I call, scared backwards: you don't get very scared when you're in serious jeopardy because you're used to danger. Instead, you get scared of things like commitment, communication, and closeness. Our culture is full of guys who will get drunk and have unprotected sex while skydiving naked into a desert, but look like a deer caught in headlights if the idea of sharing feelings arises. Or you may avoid and underreact for the opposite reason, your level of fear results in potentially disastrous levels of procrastination. If you tend to use "So What" only to have things and people explode in your face later; if you tend to avoid until you have to respond; if you have difficulty knowing you are at the 7–10 level, even when other people suggest you need to be (a common occurrence for abuse survivors, chemical dependents, and other people who have lived in extreme chaos and danger), simply take this activity and practice it in reverse. Practice learning when to react to more strongly, earlier. Practice early response skills. Get feedback from people you see as relatively healthy about what constitutes a crisis.

Final Thoughts on the Anger Container

As you have begun to create a new, safer style of connecting with and expressing your anger in the present, many of the processes have also asked you to develop your understanding of your primary influences in developing this style. If you have found yourself falling toward either extreme end of the anger continuum, as a rage-aholic or as a man who has been unable to touch his anger when necessary, through the course of the chapter you may have felt anger at these people and institutions who influenced your style. Some of your anger work will be on the abuses and injustices you perceive have been perpetrated on you by other humans, and by life's events. At times, rather than being angered by a specific incident, your anger will be about relationships, the style of relating that taught you negative survival patterns. Perhaps most difficult for some of you will be owning your anger at people you love.

Michael came to session with a worried look on his face. "I never thought I was angry at Mom until this week. She was the one that was there for us. She was the one that always cleaned me up and held me after Dad beat me. I love her and I know she loved me. You can't be angry at Mom. She's too nice and she's married to that monster. Then, as I was working on my assignment, I realized that she taught me to be naive, to just keep hanging in there when people were abusing me. She acted like there was nothing else she could do, she taught me to take it." Later in therapy, an essential part of Michael's anger work was at his mother for staying with Dad, for inadvertently teaching him to stay a victim. Through this work, he was able to understand that a man can own his anger and love someone.

Others will struggle to own the love you feel toward someone that abused you, someone you carry massive fear and rage toward.

"I can't love him, I hate him," Al disclosed. Only through the resolution of his rage was he able to own the deep desire he had always felt to be close to his adoptive father and to accept the positive gifts he had received from the man.

You may have to direct your anger toward an institution (church, school, the adoption agency) or even an entity (God, an addiction, a disease). You may have rage toward another race, or gender. Be creative; work in a setting with a creative facilitator; go where your anger leads you.

In preparation to move on to the next chapter, answer the following questions: in your journal, by closing your eyes and seeing the answers in visualization, or by taking a large piece of paper out and drawing people and scenes in your life that depict your anger style. Answer these questions:

Looking back at childhood, which parent expressed anger the way you express yours?

Who else in your family, or other close relationships, expresses their anger similarly to you?

How do you remember feeling about how Dad expressed his anger?

How do you remember feeling about how Mom expressed her anger?

What other difficulties did you experience with your anger, or the anger of others, as you were growing up (school, peers, church . . .)?

What rules were you given about anger by parents, other family, school, church, the streets?

What did you decide about feeling and expressing your anger?

How have your rules of internal anger directed your life? How successfully are your rules working today?

5: Anger Resolution

he grieves the loss of his youth, his wife, his mother,
his father, the world, and most of all, himself.
he has lost himself.
the child is alone.
the child must heal,
the child (system) must die,
only loving men can kill this boy,
oh, the beauty of the funeral,
and the joy of the man.

exerpt, Tony Schanuel, 1994

As you begin your rage resolution work remember several messages. One, the key word is *resolution*. This work is not about feeling angry; it is about feeling angry as the first stage of releasing anger. If you have been doing this work for several months and you don't feel—and aren't behaving—less angry, you may be missing something at the letting go stage. Review the material in Chapter 4 before going any further. You may not have an adequate adult container, a core that allows you to do more than feel the pain, that allows you to let go and build new skills for expressing pain. Also, note how most of the processes in the next section end. Each activity will finish with some method of leaving a piece of anger behind. *The goal is to leave each piece of work less angry, able to call up powerful anger only when necessary to protect life and limb.*

Many of you do not feel in discrete categories. The next segment will focus a great deal on how your fear and shame often lies on top of your anger. Additionally, many of you will have feelings that immediately follow on the trail of your anger work, most commonly grief. If you are aware, or soon become aware, that you feel sad on the heels of your anger, read ahead into chapter 6. Look ahead to the information and other processes you need. Finally, if the pace you are moving is too fast, slow down. And, no matter what else you do, Breathe . . . slowly and deeply . . . Breathe.

Tools of Anger Resolution

Anger resolution is an emotional, intellectual, usually verbal, and often physical struggle.

> *I was making presentation about men's issues in Kansas City, and a woman in the audience, a crisis intervention worker in hospital emergency rooms, shared, "When men come in with a family member who dies, I often can't get them to share any feelings. They just want to rush around starting to call people and making arrangements. I can't even get most of them to sit down. How can I help them with this male b.s.?" (This was said not just with frustration and judgment, but with genuine concern for men in pain.) My response was, "First, you have to quit calling what these men do b.s.." I proceeded to describe, as I have earlier in the book, that men often do what men believe they must do, as do women, and that for men, this means getting busy. The common judgment is that this is how men stuff feelings. I suggested that this is also the best mode for men to feel their feelings. My advice to the therapist: "Follow him around and find out what he'll let you help him do. Talk to him as you work with him. Help him in the way he believes he needs help and, at some point, he may give you an opening to enter into his feelings with him."*

One of the keys to anger resolution is to search creatively for ways to use the same tools we have perfected for avoidance to get down to the pain. Many of the processes you will utilize in this section are about making noise, moving your body, seeing pictures of other trusted men who are there to help you move mountains of pain. You may employ talking, yelling, screaming, guttural noises. You may write, draw, scribble, tear, rip apart. You may hit a pillow, push someone away, kick your feet. You may pray. All of this will take place on the safety of the carpet.

The Carpet

I hope that most of you will utilize a support or therapy group to do this work. It is safer, more focused, and the feedback will assist you in getting started on a piece of work, getting unstuck in the middle of work, and being accountable for leaving a piece of work safely. However, some of you will try certain processes on your own, successfully. Others do not have access to a therapy group and are not yet sure of how you will find the men to create a support network. For all of you, here is the importance of The Carpet.

The Carpet is the Ritual Space, a symbolic, sacred place away from the daily world that insures the safety of the man working on his pain. The best learning environments are often ritual spaces: healthy churches, empowering classroom settings, brainstorming sessions on the job where everyone's input is valued, the place where Dad always reads his children the bedtime story. These are places of respect, honor, and meaning, away from people time, in touch with time immemorial.

When I lead workshops, I always utilize two carpets: the carpet we do rage, fear, grief, and shame work from and the Bill White Carpet. Bill was an old friend. In college, Bill bought a beautiful tapestry that he couldn't afford. Each time his parents, Bob and Dorothy, came to visit, the carpet became mine for the length of their stay. Over the years the ruse was maintained, even though Bob and Dorothy had long since caught on. On the day of my first wedding, Bill somewhat unexpectedly made it back to town for the ceremony. With a sense of great fun, and a deep feeling of being loved, I opened a large wedding gift from Bill—the newly cleaned carpet. Through the years and another wedding, the carpet has gone everywhere I have traveled. Two events, close together in time, made the carpet even more important in my life. First, Bill became ill and eventually died, a truly loving, giving man who was killed by his isolation, his shame, his unhealed anger. Second, I met my friend Jim and decided to begin leading men's workshops. As I considered issues of safety and sacredness for the first retreat with Jim, the tapestry became an essential part of my leadership plan. I always begin my first speaking piece at the beginning of a workshop from this carpet. Our music and imageries emanate from this carpet when we return for grounding at various points in our retreat. I love to tell and retell this story and I thank Bill every workshop for his anger, my grief, our love.

And so, get a carpet, whether you are doing this work in a group or on your own. Put that carpet in a space where you will consistently maintain the rules of safety, trust, and healing. Create your ritual space with artifacts of meaning to you and the men you work with. And always—Always—honor the pain and strength and healing of the men who have come before you!

The Big Pillow

As I have stated in the rules about anger (or other feelings) work, most of the work I facilitate is done sitting on the floor. This minimizes physical risks in rooms of limited space and also grounds men to the rules of safety. One of the most potent pieces of learning among men from violent backgrounds (as victims and perpetrators) is the expression of massive rage without any harm to others or destruction of objects. Still, many of us feel a deep need to give physical declaration to our anger, thus, The Big Pillow. A simple and effective tool for anger work is to create a pillow that is at least 4 feet by 4 feet, with a lot of stuffing. This pillow sits on the man's lap for grounding, and with the instructions, "If at any point you feel a need to hit, hit the pillow as hard and as many times as you desire." At times, I will have the man see in the pillow the person he is expressing anger at, and symbolically give the anger back. This is not about hurting anyone; however, it may be about expressing and letting go of the *desire* to hurt someone.

Other Tools for Anger Work

Other tools that may be used:

> a belt used in a tug-of-war with an abuser. (in role-play)
> a towel to twist and hit the pillow
> any object that represents a person or entity that engenders anger

Contracts

The philosophy under which I was trained states that a man will only complete the work he is committed to. Simply, you won't heal the anger *I believe* you need to heal; you will only finish what *you* choose to finish. In this manner, I encourage you to use contracts for anger, sad, fear, shame, guilt and joy work. The contract is a very simple concept. You simply state verbally and in writing to the group what you will heal in each piece of work, your intention for healing. Examples of contracts may include:

> I will release my anger at Mom for leaving.
> I will express my sadness at my brother's death.
> I will let go of my shame about the sexual abuse.
> I will get feedback about what is keeping me stuck in my rage.

It is important to understand that you will often be acutely aware of what your contract needs to be. If you stay in this work long enough, you will just as often be unclear of the who, what, when, where, and hows of your work. Work with the men in your circle to clarify the vague emotions, or sense of direction, before moving into deeper levels of feeling. This preparation reduces the likelihood of failure with frustration, offering you instead the perhaps exhausting, but satisfying, process of healing. "I will" is a statement of intention and personal responsibility for the work that you are about to initiate. I encourage men to decide on a contract that will take them just a little farther than they want to, or believe they can, go. A vague, undirected, frustrating piece of work often reflects a vague contract. A clear contract offers clear direction.

Common Pitfalls in Early Anger Work

Anger resolution is emotionally risky work, and most of us learned not to take many emotional risks. This can also be physically risky, and many of us learned to put our physical health at risk in a myriad of ways. It can be difficult to begin this work oriented toward trying to accomplish new goals by using old methods that are high in physical risk and low in emotional risk. I propose that men heal emotionally, not totally without peril to life and limb but with safeguards against reckless disregard for their bodies. Therefore, I offer warnings of traps that I have seen men fall into early in the journey:

Men begin to do anger work before they feel safe in the group and either stall or bail out.

The group allows a man to initiate anger work when members don't feel safe with him, or believe he will honor the safety rules, only to have him stall, have another member bail out, or have a conflict arise in the group that does not directly deal with the issue at hand.

A man tries to invent anger work before he is ready because he believes, or the group or therapist suggests, that this is "the real work" of healing, only to have him go into shame or anger at the group when the work in ineffective.

A man, who is ready but is scared, makes a passing attempt at anger work, saying "I can't" or "This is too hard," and the group does not challenge and assist him in going deeper.

A man is shamed by himself and others for needing to repeat what appears to be the same piece of work, overlooking the possibility that each repetition may take him to a deeper level of healing. (This does not preclude the need to evaluate whether you are repeating work because you have a resistance to letting go. It simply addresses the importance of not oversimplifying the process).

A man is shamed by himself and others for what appears to be a "small" piece of anger work, rather than supporting his early efforts and encouraging his plan to continue the work now that he has gotten his feet (and heart) wet.

A man tries to force anger work when he knows he needs first to go to his sadness, fear, or shame.

The group refuses to consider a new method for the work because "we've never done that before."

When a man has chosen a role-player who uses words that intensely hook the man to the person in his past he is angry at, a dialogue will often ensue. The result is an emotional, but intellectual, argument. Arguing is not anger work. The man must go inside of himself and bring up his emotional truth, regardless of the verbal barbs of the role-player.

Remember: This work is about being as physically safe as you can be, knowing there is risk—as emotionally risky as you can be—knowing there must be safety—and as creative as you can be—while making sure to use your head with your heart.

Getting To and Pushing Through the Anger

Many of the techniques that I will describe are not fully delineated processes. They are entry points into a specific piece of work that can be employed over and over, regardless of the event or person you are dealing with. Some of these tools will be best used in moving you beyond your fear, some with shame. I will highlight each as it applies.

If I Was Angry . . .

Pat sat on the carpet and described what little he knew about why his biological parents left him with relatives for months at a time as a child. "They were young and poor, with too many kids. I was the oldest and was shuffled around. They did the best they could, and now they're dead. I feel sad, but there's something else in me and I'm not sure what . . . " A man in the group asked Pat if he would finish the sentence, "If I was angry . . . " Pat started, "If I was angry . . . I'd tell Dad I don't care if he was poor, I was his kid and I needed him." Other man, "And. . . . " "I'd tell Mom that it wasn't my fault she and Dad kept having kids (his voice getting louder and stronger)." From this jumping off place, Pat chose to move into anger work at his dad for abandoning him, deciding to save his work on Mom for another time.

If you are looking at work that you intellectually believe merits anger, or someone you trust suggests anger fits, or you know there is a feeling that you aren't touching, try this tool. Of course, there are also, "If I was. . . (sad, scared, ashamed, glad)."

It's Not Happening Now

It is essential to remember that this work takes place from the present, through the looking glass of the age, size, and skills you have today. The goal is never to have you relive the past, which may be where you are already stuck with flashbacks, frozen emotions, and destructive behaviors. A simple statement that you can repeat to yourself, and others can repeat to you, "This is not happening now. Remember you are looking at the past from who you are today, with the feelings you still have." This message is equally applicable whether you are stuck in the fear, shame, and sadness that precedes your rage. A variation of this approach is a skill you have learned through safely entering the visualizations I have provided.

Each time Chuck began to shut down into his shame and fear he was asked, "Answer these questions. In 1996, how old are you? How tall are you? How big are you? How strong are you? Who is here to support you?" In repeating this data at several points in the work, Chuck was able to push forward with anger and intent.

The Rules . . . Again

I frequently repeat the safety rules for anger work as a man steps on the carpet, just as frequently asking the man to look me in the eyes and repeat them with authority, particularly if he is already deep in his pain. In workshops, someone states the rules when the carpet work begins and before every piece of work. While it may be irritating, this repetition is one of the reasons that no one has broken the rules on the carpets I have stood on.

Holding . . . Again

Throughout the book, I will refer to the support role of holding a man doing expressive work. Providing an anchor to a man who is doing anger work can free him to go all the way into his rage with the understanding that he and other group members will be safe. Let me offer several clues to those of you who will be chosen to hold a man during his work:

> Sit behind the man with your legs outside of his.
>
> Hold him loosely around the waist, clasping your hands.
>
> Let the man be aware of your presence.
>
> Do not hold the man so tight that you close off his feelings or his deep breathing.
>
> Sit with your back against something or someone; you'll get hot and tired during a tough piece of work.
>
> Keep your head to the side of the recipient's head so he doesn't rear back and bash you.
>
> Be available for the man to fall back into your arms if he needs to rest or hits his grief at the end of a piece of anger work.
>
> Take responsibility for saying no if you are asked to support a man and don't feel up to it. He needs the full presence of the holder.

Note For Facilitators: I seldom function as the holder for three reasons. I don't want men to become too reliant on me as their support person at the expense of getting safe with other men. More important, I don't want to restrict my movement by being in a place where I can't see the man's face, coach the role-players, facilitate the action. Professional boundaries dictate to me that therapist-client touch is not an essential part of healing and for many clients creates confusion about the very trust and safety issues with authority figures they are present to work on. I make some exceptions, for instance, when I know I can be in a man's ear and provide essential messages for his work, or at the end of a piece of anger work when a man feels the need to move into his grief and into the arms of a man who was present from the beginning. These exceptions are few.

You can know something about your intent and the level of your anger by whom you choose. If you choose the physically largest man, what does that tell you? If you choose a man that you trust deeply, what are you preparing for? If you choose a man you barely know, or do not truly trust, what is your intent? Whom you choose says something about how deep you plan to go and how successful you plan to be. One of my personal favorites, as a man with a history of being "vertically challenged" is when a physically large man chooses a much smaller man to hold him, stating, "I know you can hold me, I've seen how powerful your work is." This man is implicitly stating, "I trust you and you can trust me to honor the safety rules." Another favorite, and a common occurrence, is the man who picks a holder who recently completed work similar to the work this man intends to face on this day. We learn both how our work can look and whom we can trust by the work of the men who come before us.

Bringing Help: A Technique for Overcoming Fear

You may know going into your work that there is fear in front of your other feelings, or you may only hit the fear when you are on the carpet, attempting to reach the anger. Some of you will even experience the fear at the moment of truth, the symbolic contact with the person or event that brought you out on the carpet. Remember, you are working on old fear, and although it may not seem rational to still feel the fear this intensely, honor what you feel and then strategize on how to move beyond it. One of the best ways to empower yourself to move through the fear is to break the cycle of isolation you lived with as a child, and continue to practice as a man. If you want to be less scared of the monster, bring a team of big guys.

> *Oscar came to his men's meeting with the intention of confronting the priest that molested him. He chose a role-player, sat on the carpet with a support person and immediately went into what the group calls vapor lock; "I'm too scared to say anything. Except for the tingling in my hands, I feel numb." I asked Oscar to close his eyes and get a picture of the man he was today, the age, size, intellect, the power and growth he had accumulated in his recent work. "Are you able as you are today to go to this man and confront him?" "I'm stronger, but still too scared." "Who could you take with you that would make it safe for you to do this work?" "Dave, you, Debbie, and Mike, . . . can I take the whole group if I want to? OK, I just want to know that all you guys will be close by if I need you." "Sure!" I then moved to, "See, the support people that you are taking with you standing next to you? Remember, you must lead. They are there to keep you safe and support your work. When you are ready, open your eyes and confront this man." Oscar gathered his anger, opened his eyes and went right to his rage!*

In variations of this skill:

The man may choose to complete the confrontation in visualization, where he can maintain a picture of his support people .

The man may ask the group to physically move closer to him to feel the support.

The support people may be assigned roles like, "I need to visualize you standing in front of me so I can see him or her, but he or she can't get to me."

It is important, however, not to let the man put the support people in such powerful positions that they do the work for him—no risk, no gain.

Gathering My Anger

This process is an extension of the work on body pain (Chapter 3). Accessing and directing the anger where you feel it in your body is a powerful technique in learning to push through other feelings to give voice to your anger. The methods described below are preludes to anger work that need to be directed toward a specific person, event, or issue in your life. Several of the techniques involve going inside, with eyes closed, to access the anger. These methods can be utilized in either visualization or role-play work. You may remain with eyes closed as you begin to direct the anger, or open your eyes at the point of connection and direct your rage at the role-player.

As you prepare to work, sit on the floor and remember the safety rules of anger work. As you ready yourself, if you experience one of two difficulties—"I can't seem to find the anger. I'm numb," or "I feel the fear, shame, and sadness, but can't get to the anger"—then use one of the following methods:

Close your eyes and become aware of the feeling of numbness, fear, shame, or sadness. Where in your body do you feel this? If you feel this all over your body, is there someone in the group (or your therapist) to hold your numbness, fear, sadness, or shame until you have done your anger work? If so, gather the feelings (other than anger) inside of you, pause, and put them into your hands. When you have done that, place these feelings into the hands of the man you choose. Now, return to your body with your eyes closed and connect with the anger.

Close your eyes and become aware of the feeling of numbness, fear, shame, or sadness. Where in your body do you feel this? If you feel it in a specific place, let yourself see that just under this feeling is your anger. See the way in which your emotion (numbness, etc.) pushes to keep your anger down. See also the power of your anger. Make the decision whether you will push through your numbness, etc., today with that anger. And now, breathe down to the anger, and connecting your breathing with your anger, put air under it and breathe it up ... breathing ... breathing ... breathing. (If you are facilitating the work, be aware that if the man only breathes to his fear his breathing will become shallow, rapid, and ineffective).

Finding Your Voice

I utilize two techniques that combine accessing the anger in your body with giving your anger its voice. Anger work is often a very noisy process. These two methods can effectively be blended as the entry point to anger work. They are particularly useful if you are in contact with your anger, but have been unable to direct it in a healing way, or if you are experienced at anger work and need a simple tool to quickly reach the feeling. My description of these methods will be consistent with how men apply them in the group setting.

> *Close your eyes and go into your body to the place(s) where you keep your anger. Where are those places? (Honest disclosure at this point is a helpful risk in getting to the work.) Collect the anger from each place in your body, taking time to gather it even from those dark corners where you have hidden your feeling, and move your anger to your arms and to your hands. (If you are a support person in the man's work, at this point you will often see the muscles in his arms and hands begin to twitch; that is an indication that he has moved substantial anger to this place. If his feet are moving, he may be in touch with his fear, feeling "let's get out of here." It is OK to ask a man what he is feeling as you see the changes in his body. This will often help him verbalize when he is ready to express the anger, or it will help you connect with the man who is trying to go to his anger but is losing a battle with his fear or shame). Now, give yourself a sound or a phrase that expresses the full force of your anger. (It must be short; a long sentence will put the man into intellectualizing, and stop the anger). When you are ready, raise your arms straight over your head, and connecting fully with your anger, make the sound and bring your arms down on the pillow with power . . . again . . . again. (Encourage the man as he begins to direct and express his rage.)*

Reaching Anger Through the Voice of Fear and Shame

One of the simplest, and most potent, techniques for giving voice to your anger is as follows:

Sit on the floor and prepare yourself for anger work. Breathe. Close your eyes and connect with the fear or shame that has kept you from giving voice to your anger. And now, see the person or event you need to confront today. If you had not been so scared or ashamed, what would you have felt about the person or event? (Men most commonly connect with their anger at this point. If a man touches sadness, go to healing the feeling that is present.) Become aware of how angry you are that this person or event, scared or shamed you so deeply. Pause to let the anger build. When you are ready, look at this person or event and with all of your anger yell over and over, "You . . . (scared, shamed) Me."

Other Techniques

Some of you will simply not remember what it is like to get angry out loud. It's been too long. If this fits you, try one or more of the following:

Noise: Before you make angry noise you may simply need to make any noise. Get a drum, or pots and pans, and in privacy or with one of your kids, beat the noisemaker as loud and as long as you want. Enjoy the racket and the fact that no one can make you stop.

Vocal Noise: Now, go to that private place, again, and just start a low, quiet noise in your throat. As you slowly get louder, go down below your throat to your chest, to your guts, to your genitals, to your toes, getting louder and bigger. Yell the sound or sounds of your power for as long and loud as you want. (If you don't have a raspy voice later, you may not have gone deep enough.)

Breathing: Pick a man who is in touch with his anger and have him sit or stand in front of you. He will begin to breathe into his anger, not for his work, but to model for you. As he begins to breathe to his power, he will huff and puff and growl. Watch him. Begin to mirror him, going to your fierceness, breathing deeper, growling louder . . . and louder . . . and louder.

Your Face: Mirror the look of anger and fierceness that you see on the face of the man in front of you. Find your own face of anger.

Your Body: Mirror the man's body position, a position of strength, power, masculine energy. Find your own Wildman stance.

Freeze Your Body and Facial Expression: Immediately a man steps forward with a mirror to show you the look of your rage. Lock in that look; you will need it again. Process your immediate reaction to seeing yourself in your rage. This may give you clues about why you stuffed this feeling. ("I looked ugly," "I looked just like my father," "That's what my kids say I look like at home.")

Each of the techniques described in this section are designed to bring you to your anger. The direction you will follow is up to you and the men who are present to support you.

Saving My Kid with My Anger

Before confronting any abuser, or actually releasing and resolving old rage, you need to find within yourself the belief that we are now capable of stopping the events and people that once harmed us. Although the title of this exercise implies that this work is for the child you were, I want to emphasize that many of the processes in this section are utilized just as effectively for adolescent and adult trauma: war, sexual victimization, victims of other violence. The processes that I will describe build power and strength for the struggle ahead. They are separate activities, but one often leads immediately into the other.

Stop

This exercise is best utilized when you have a specific trauma memory that is unresolved. Choose a holder. Close your eyes and get a picture of yourself as you are today. You will be going into whatever memory, place, relationship as you are today to stop the abuse of the person you were. Are you able to go in alone, as you are today, and stop the abuse? If you need additional support, take all you need—anyone who is trustworthy and strong and will go with you (group members, friends, spouses, lovers). When you are ready go back to the place where and when the event took place and find the boy or man you were just before the event took place—and Stop it. (If coached properly, the man will go deep to his anger and yell, "Stop," often moving on to a confrontation of the person that harmed him.) If you need to, simply say Stop until you know that boy or man is safe. Get big for him.

Rescuing the Kid

Now, go to the kid or man. Pick him up or take him in hand and tell him you are going to take him out of this place to somewhere safe. Is there anything he must take with him? (In the case of child abuse, men will often visualize a need to clean and dress the child, perhaps give him liquids or food, perhaps take some treasured item with him.) Lead him out, making sure only the two of you and whatever men you brought as support leave that place. Slowly walk him to a safe place where he can stay. Reassure him that you will be back for him when he needs you. (At times, men may be ready to bring the child or man all the way back to the safety of the group. The risk is that this part of the man's experience is likely to integrate into his present consciousness and he may not be prepared for the flood of other emotions that may follow. If this is the case, this portion of his life can be left in the Safe Place and returned to for further work when he is ready.) Now, return to the safety of the present, to this place.

If you have many scenes, many times, many places, you may return to this piece on many occasions in your journey. Again, symbolically bringing parts of your past into your present can unlock deep, suppressed pain. Marshal your support system, use your journal, maintain your rules of safety, and know that it's OK to leave these parts in a new, symbolic Safe Place and integrate these moments later, as the ground begins to feel more solid below you.

Confronting the Anger Object

Most anger work comes down to basics, confronting the person, event, or entity that has engendered the rage and other emotions. The creativity is in how this confrontation will take place. I have provided methods to reach the anger. Now, let's move on to specific processes that will assist you in moving through.

Levels of Role-Play

For many years, I have aided men in designing role-play experiences on levels of intensity that match their needs and the degree of risk they are prepared to take. It was only recently that I seriously took the time to consider in a concrete way how I make the decisions; a step that I took due to my own fear and the feedback of colleagues, as I prepared to co-lead a women's workshop: that women might not feel safe getting into anger work in a workshop led by men. I decided to create levels of risk in how Jim and I would structure, and offer to lead, the carpet work. For about five minutes, I believed I had developed a new method for Jim and me, only to soon realize that I had simply put in written form what we had been offering men for six years. We brought in several women who had completed their own carpet work as "mentors" to assist us, and not only did women do anger work in a retreat led by men, but you could really feel the power of the feminine that day. Thanks to my fear and insecurity in facilitating work with women, I can render a clear delineation of three levels of anger work. The various stages will be described in the first person.

Level One

I step onto the carpet and state my intention to do my work. (One method we often use is to have the individual state, "I claim this space for my work," and follow with a statement of my contract). I choose not to use a role-player at this level. Level 1 is about taking the time to verbalize and feel my anger (and other feelings) without other men on the carpet to assist me in going to deeper levels. The exception to this is that I agree that the facilitator always has the option of stepping onto the carpet for the purposes of safety and support. I may choose to sit, kneel, or stand and "share my truth" at whatever depth I am prepared. This may include talking, yelling, crying, pacing, moving my body in any way that expresses my rage. The tools of anger work, such as the big pillow, are available. It is recommended that I have a contract about what I intend to resolve at this level. (For a man early in his work this may be simply the ablity to say he is angry, and at whom and what). If I get stuck or desire support, I am free to invite the facilitator and other men to offer feedback or ask questions. If in the course of my work, I decide to go beyond Level 1, I am free to request that the facilitator come onto the carpet and assist me in designing work to move deeper into my anger. It is essential that I not judge Level 1 as "therapy light." I have seen men move through incredible pain to great healing at this level; I have seen men who never need to go beyond this level to achieve the healing they seek. At the end of my Level 1 work, it is imperative that I state what I have gained from this risk, how my life will be different as a result of this work, and how I will practice these changes in my daily life. When I step off the carpet, my work is done for that day.

Level Two

I step onto the carpet and state my intention. I choose someone to role-play the person (such as Dad), the event (a group of kids that hurt me), an institution (white culture), or entity (my disease) that I am going to confront. The instructions for the role-player are to simply be a physical presence to challenge, without any verbal feedback. The addition of a person to represent the object of my anger will often intensify my fear and shame, and, I call for the facilitator to assist me in getting into my anger. At this point, my options are many, including verbalizing my anger directly, using The Big Pillow, pushing the object off the carpet—My Space . . . My Life—with my words, or pushing the object off my carpet with my hands. If in the course of my work I choose to move to a deeper level, I can call for assistance from the men in the container. I am free to move into other feelings at the end of my anger. Before leaving the carpet I will state what I have gained from these risks, what will be different in my life as a result of this work, and how I will practice these changes in my daily life.

Level Three

I step onto the carpet and state my intention. I choose one or more role-players to represent the work I have decided to complete. I instruct the role-players on what to do or say that will challenge me in this work, prodding me to go to a deeper level. (Often these are the shaming, threatening, denial responses that the man has heard, or interpreted as having heard, in the past. The role-player may also be coached to use certain facial expressions, gestures, and body positions, such as turning away from a man who is angry about being abandoned.) The facilitator will remain on the carpet for the entirety of my work to offer support and ideas at any stuck points. I have available to me any of the tools of anger work to assist me in emotional, verbal, and physical release of my rage. I am free to move into other feelings as I need them. At the end of this work, I will state what I have gained from these risks, what will be different in my life because of this work, and how I will practice my changes in my daily life.

A Note about Intention

In workshops I often work for the first time with men who are not familiar with the concept of contracts. Any man, even one experienced at this work, may need assistance in identifying the intention of his work, especially when moving into a new territory with a particularly painful person or event. It is the facilitator's responsibility to assist the man in clarifying what his work needs to be, who or what the true work is about, and at what level he is prepared to begin. You may step onto the carpet with a clear purpose; you may step onto the carpet with a rough idea or a raw emotion. Ask for what you need. Allow men to help you clarify what your contract is and offer ideas in how to set up the drama for healing. Think for yourself and invite the thoughts of others.

Techniques for Anger Resolution

The common denominator that I see in all expressive feelings work is the release of pain from the heart, mind, body, spirit. For anger work to be effective, I believe the goal that is the underpinning of the entire process must be a desire to become less angry, even for those of you who are just beginning to accept that you have anger in you. The following techniques are about releasing anger, and often include releasing shame and fear as a prescription for filling yourself with stability, joy, maturity. Each of these tools is designed to confront the shaming and frightening object with your power, to bring up the man inside who will fight for the boy's right to grow up safe and healthy.

Use Your Eyes

Upon arrival at the carpet, many of you will promptly shut down any eye contact, particularly with a role-player. Dropping your eyes sends the signal that you are in your shame and your fear. Eye contact is essential in moving beyond these emotions. In anger work, the shame and fear come from what was done and said to you, rather than what you have done and said, but the form of communicating the feelings will often be the same, an inability to look another person in the eye. Try this:

> *Pick one man in the circle that you feel the safest with Sit on the carpet and have him sit directly across from you. As you look him straight in the eyes, tell him what your contract is for this day and ask him for the support you need. Give this man a chance to respond to your request before going further into your work.*

Another more threatening, hence powerful, method is to choose the man you find the scariest, or most intimidating, in the circle and complete the exercise exactly as described above.

One more step along the scale of risk is as follows:

> *Sit on the carpet and set up your support system. Call out onto the carpet the role-player who will represent the object of your anger. Attempt to look him in the eyes, repeating to yourself, "I am angry at you because you . . . " (finish the sentence). Continue to repeat this message internally, looking more directly and deeply into the eyes of the other man and when you are ready, give voice loudly to the*

same words . . . louder. . . . louder . . . looking more directly and deeply into the eyes of the man. Speak your truth, push through the fear and shame, continue through the anger.

Clearing Your Carpet (Your Life)

In the initial stage of a contract, the carpet symbolizes the unhealthy space that the issue before you commands in your life. A healing metaphor is the act of clearing your carpet of the pain and the object of that pain. There are several techniques that may be used singly, or in combination, to accomplish this end.

A Note About Clearing People

A common concern among men is a reluctance to "finish" persons who are still in their lives. You may need to complete anger work on someone you love, someone at whom you are not angry in the present (for instance, an alcoholic parent who got sober and became a good friend), or someone who is now elderly and would be destroyed by the intensity of your anger if you expressed it directly to him or her. Remember three things. The work is more about your pain than it is about the other person, who is the symbol of the ongoing emotional block in your life. You are working on the person as he or she was, not necessarily how he or she is today; work through the legitimate anger based on the past, and the relationship will likely get better. Finally, we do this work symbolically so no one, *including* the person who engendered the original pain, gets hurt. The goal of this work *is not* to end the love you feel for this person. It is to hold him or her accountable for past behaviors and give you the opportunity to let go of rage and move on. In fact, the result of this work can be to discover the gifts given by people you believe brought you only pain. (I often say to men who believe they got nothing good from parents, "You got the gift of life and I'm glad you're here.")

Anger Work Foundation

What you are about to read is the foundation for much of the anger work I facilitate. Most anger work is primarily about learning a safe, effective process; the genius of this work is often found in its simplicity. If you learn how to find, collect, express, and release anger, any skilled and creative circle of men can create specific processes to deal with the huge variety of relationships, events, and traumas that men will bring forward to heal. The techniques that follow will be used to confront specific people and specific events: but they may just as readily confront states of being ("I want to stop being a victim"); internal traumas, such as anger at a disease; and relationship states ("my anger at men"). And so, follow closely.

More Eyes

Many of us view anger as an emotion that naturally involves noise and perhaps physical contact. Some of us also remember the stare of a parent that implied as much disapproval and anger as yelling; you know, the icy look when you made noise in church, in a restaurant, at a relative's house. In turn, you may be able to speak as much of your truth with your eyes as with your words when releasing anger. Try this:

> *With safety in place, ask a man to role-play someone you are angry with. Have the man sit in front of you. Close your eyes and get in touch with your anger, collect it and compact it, making sure to go to each corner of your body to gather all of it. Now, move the anger to your eyes. When you are ready, open your eyes and release the full force of your anger eye to eye with the person across from you, using no words, taking the words, the messages, the feelings you feel and sending them out of your body through your eyes. Communicate the full depth of your feelings. Feel the anger move out of you, out of your body. With your eyes, move him or her off your carpet—move the pain out of your life.*

Along with the power of their eyes, many men will need to give voice to the sound, the phrase, that truly identifies his pain.

Finding Your Voice

> *As you feel the anger begin to move out of your body, as you feel your strength, your courage, your power, find one sound—one word, one brief phrase—to say it all, to speak the full force of your pain. Breathe into the anger, and with your eyes, with your voice, tell this other person . . . Now.*

At this point in the work many men will feel a strong desire to put physical expression into their work.

Go To The Pillow

> *As you give voice to your anger, raise your arms straight above your head and hit the pillow with all your power . . . again . . . again . . . again. Sustain it with eyes up, hit, into the pillow . . . again . . . again . . . again. (It is extremely useful for some men to have their group offer encouragement and challenge to continue beyond the man's usual limits.) Keep sending the anger out and feel yourself releasing the pain from your head, your heart, your body, your spirit. Let it go and let the*

anger stay out of your body. Stay with it until you have him or her off your carpet. (Each time the man begins to give up or stops before he has truly let go, the role-player moves back onto the carpet; this will often renew the man's resolve to finish the work.) It's OK to rest. See that the object of your anger gets renewed power if you stop before you have finished. (Each man has the capacity to stop his work just before he gets to the place where he is free of that issue or person in his life. Encourage him when he slows down, shuts down, lowers his eyes. Men will often rest and then go even deeper.)

Common Pitfalls in Pillow Work

A man hits the pillow and grabs it simultaneously, an indication that he is in the middle of his emotional dilemma, trying to let go of and hold on to at the same time. This may mean his ambivalence about letting go of the anger and the trauma or relationship is being expressed physically. Ask the man to let go of the pillow, to hit it straight on. If he is unable, there are times to stop the work and ask him to give voice to his indecision (so he is aware) and to ask him to decide if he is ready for this work (so he knows he is in charge of his healing).

A man diminishes the power of his work by bringing his arms up and down in a more sideways motion. Encourage the man to, "get the anger out straight: arms up-and-down straight."

A man hits the pillow with closed fists or with his hands clenched together; I call this "the emotional recycling center." Encourage the man to hit the pillow with open palms, feeling the anger move out of his body, releasing his pain into the atmosphere.

A man stops short of his deepest work, excusing himself as tired, weak, or unable. There are three legitimate reasons for stopping a piece of anger work: a person does not feel safe; another feeling is coming up and the man needs to go to it; the man has gone as far with this work as he chooses to at this time. It is always OK to stop, but take responsibility for your choice.

A man stops and the group jumps in, assuming he is done. Let the man rest and offer him the choice of continuing when he is ready.

Alternative To The Pillow

I am not certain how some men know, internally, that hitting is not the way out of their anger, but they do. Statements like, "Get away from me," may indicate a man needs to push that event or person off his carpet. Some men will simply hit a stuck point and say, "I need to push" or "hitting a pillow doesn't work for me." For this man, the following technique will often accomplish the desired goal:

> *Sit, with your holder, on the floor or on your knees. Place your arms straight out with your palms facing out, toward the role-player. The role-player will sit or kneel and place his arms out in the same fashion. When you are ready, with eyes open or closed (whichever gives you the most power), place your palms against those of the role-player and push . . . harder . . . harder. Put your sound or words to the effort (often, "Get Away!" works for this man) and push harder. (Remember: this, too, must be safe. The man is instructed not to slap at, grab, or pull on the hands of the role-player. If this occurs, stop the work and ask the man to decide what this behavior means; ask him what his intention is in this work. The power is in the sustained effort, the man feeling himself push the pain away and out.) Keep pushing. Get this pain off your carpet, and out of your life.*
>
> *There is one possible exception to the rules. Through the process of pushing, the man may slowly move forward as he pushed the role-player off the carpet. It is vital for the holder to stay with his man and to stop the work at any point when anyone in the circle expresses concern about safety. Many men will be able to look inside of themselves as they close this type of work and see the pain or the person pushed out of their lives, out of their bodies.*

Closing The Work

Often anger work leads to a deep need for support, nurturing, and grief. Collapsing into the support of a Good Father or the company of a nurturing community of men is an essential closing piece for many men. Two responses to this need that I use over and over are below. (Additional closings will be offered in chapter 6.)

Good Father

Pick a man to be your Good Father. Have him hold you in whatever way feels right to you. Let the father tell you how he feels about your work, how he feels about you, and about how proud he is of you.

Take it in. Now, tell your father what you have always wanted him to know. The interchange goes on as long as each man desires. (As the good father, speak from your heart; tell the man what every son needs to hear. Each man often will go into joy and grief in this moment.)

Circle of Men

All men circle up with the man who just completed his work in the center. In turn, face each man in the outer circle and receive his gift of words and/or touch that come as a result of your courage in this work. This may be followed by a group hug in which the men close into a tight circle. This often reminds me of the huddles of athletes . . . the sweat, the smell of men, the energy, without the competition.

I believe that closing work in Adult is essential. It returns us to the more concrete foundation that allows us to get home after group without driving into a ditch. Several questions that assist this process I have highlighted throughout the book are the following:

> What percentage of your anger do you believe you released tonight? This is a request for the man to go inside of himself and make an arbitrary judgment about his progress, take credit for the work he completed, and take stock of what is left. Some men are able to immediately answer the question; some look at me quizzically and then close their eyes, go to the places where they carry their anger, and judge the amount that is missing.

> How will your life be different having done this work? Be specific.

> How will you practice these changes in your life, and to whom will you report them?

A man answering these questions knows the expectation is to carry the progress into daily life, which is the purpose of the work, and to be accountable to someone who is aware of his commitment to change.

Techniques for Releasing the Anger

We have located your anger, along with giving methods for bringing it to the surface and confronting the object of your anger. These steps call for enormous courage, leading to what may be the supreme act of fortitude—letting go of the pain. Releasing the anger means many things to many men: stepping into a void; discovering how to fill the empty space that has for all time been filled with rage and self-loathing; stepping into the most hated of all emotions, sadness; moving toward an action a man may have promised he could or would never take, forgiveness. The healing to your mind, body, soul, and spirit is only complete upon releasing the anger from your life, at a minimum upon reaching acceptance of the trauma, the person(s) who engendered the anger, and of yourself.

Drawing

It is not unusual that I will use drawing in working a specific piece of anger with a man. I may ask him to draw the trauma memory that he is angry about, complete with the people, places, feelings, and decisions he made in that situation that still affect him today. I may ask him to draw the representation of his dilemma.

> *Kris verbalized his anger that his mom had called him, again, to complain about his stepfather, "I'm angry that she put me in the middle, again, and I'm angry that I fell for it, again." He was asked to draw his anger and created a picture of a large female and a large male without ears, with a small boy placed in the middle with "rays of anger" coming toward him. This picture described how he had spent a lifetime internalizing his mother's anger at men and his view of both genders as not listening. At this point, Kris selected role-players for Mom and Step-dad, moving to his confrontation of Mom for dumping her pain on him, then to his anger at Dad for passively letting this happen, by not stepping forward to deal with Mom's concerns. As Kris reached the apex of his anger he stated to both, "No more. I won't listen to you complain about him any more! **You Deal with Her!. She's Your Wife, Not Mine!"** As he hit this point of releasing the anger and making a new decision for his life, Kris began ripping up the drawing and throwing pieces at the role-players. Dad picked the pieces up and kept attempting to toss them back to Kris stating, "I don't want her anger. You take care of her" (a great technique to get to the bottom of the anger—to solidify the man's decision to let go and, as you will see, to send him the message about the limits of his power). As each piece came back, Kris entered a throwing match with his dad, getting deeper into his rage and more resolute in his decision. Suddenly, he stopped pushing the pieces of paper (his*

lifetime of both taking Mom's anger in, but also trying to get his Dad to take action) off the carpet and entered his grief. "I'm not going to get him to change; all I can do is quit doing his job." Over several months Kris reported opportunities to set his new boundary with his mother. She continued to test him, reacted with some anger and guilt messages, but the terrible falling out that he had always believed would take place did not happen. She still loved him and survived his breaking of the triangle quite well. It did appear that Dad was catching a little more of the heat directly, but he, too, continued on much as before. Kris's joy was stated as, "I feel stronger; no one fell apart, and I'm just not very angry at them anymore."

Kris is arriving at what I believe to be a powerful place in a man's life, to offer to his parents what he has always wanted from them: acceptance, perhaps even unconditional love.

The technique described by case example can be used in confronting and letting go all manner of trauma, particular drawings that depict abuse, triangles, losses, internal states of shame and pain. We are only limited by the walls placed around our creativity.

The Messages

Often, what men are releasing through anger work are messages that were received or perceived about self and life. In a previous chapter, I provided exercises that assisted you in gaining clarity to what you learned in your childhood from others. Clearing the messages that don't work in your life today can be accomplished in a concrete fashion, once again best illuminated by a man's story.

Grant was in another rubber-band relationship. When the woman wanted him, he cruelly pushed her away, and when she went away, he rekindled the contact. When initially asked who taught him how to treat women, he responded, "I was always close to Mom and was the stereotypical good boy. She taught me to respect women and I think my problem is that I'm a good codependent. I rescue women in trouble like I took care of Mom. I realize I'm angry at Mom." Over a period of months Grant did substantial healing work around his relationship with his mom. He reaped many emotional rewards; however, significantly improving his romantic relationships was not one of these. As his frustration and shame grew, his defenses diminished and Grant opened up to the other side of the equation, how the men in his family treated women. In this work, Grant touched and owned a deeper, and more shaming, part of his Shadow, a part I recommend all "good sons" look at: the basic contempt he had for women as taught to him by his grandfather who was loved by all in the community but frequently treated his family with disdain, and by his father, a rageful alcoholic, and by his church, which saw women as less than men.

Asked to journal on the messages he was explictedly given and the ones he surmised from actions of men and women around him, Grant returned ready to confront his father. As he confronted the role-player with each of the messages (such as, "women are good for sex and not much else"), going deeper into his anger, each message was written on a small piece of paper by a group member and given to the father. As Grant worked, the father simply restated each message and tossed it back to Grant. A pitcher's duel ensued with Grant going deeper and more physical with each throw. At the bottom of his anger, Grant hit his self-generated shame about the many times he had practiced these messages in his life at the expense of women and himself. Reaching this understanding, he knew the messages were his to release, not his to return to his father and grandfather. He designed a burning ceremony where he stated the release of each message to the fire and made a statement of the new decision he would use to replace each old commandment.

Utilizing physical movement in this fashion gives voice on another level propelling old messages, old rage, old lies, old beliefs about self and others out of your mind, body, and psyche.

Killing The Pain

There are men whose rage and other pain is deep enough that they have felt, in their deepest Shadow, their Killer. This is the part of a man, perhaps any man, that knows he could destroy to protect himself and the ones he loves, or to gain what he believes to be just revenge. If you have touched this part of yourself, you may have felt a primal energy that gets parceled out in smaller doses at people around you. In our current culture, the misdirected Killer is a daily reality. A day does not pass in the community where I work in which a man, woman, or child is not murdered by someone who chooses to kill a person—instead of their pain. I understand revenge, but it simply doesn't work in healing rage.

In place of violence, some of us are offered the opportunity through men's work to access the Killer symbolically, to kill the pain, the abusive messages, the part of the abuser that still lives in our hearts.

This is not always an exercise in putting to death any connection you have with the person you are angry at; it is about killing the part of the pain that keeps you from being fully alive yourself. The rage generated by this process often brings out a period of intense grief, followed by the freedom to fill a place in your heart, body, mind, and spirit—previously occupied by rage, fear, and shame—with.light, love, and peace. (Refer to page 174 for a powerful addition to the end of this process.)

Jack came to the group with the intention of "finishing the pain of my abuse." He spoke of years of fantasies of finding the clergyman that molested him as a boy and shooting him dead. "I have actually looked into hiring a private investigator to locate him." The message given to Jack was that he did not need a group to exact revenge; however, we were present to help him let go of his pain and move on with his life. Over several weeks, Jack's work stimulated discussions on revenge, the righteous desire for payback that so many victims feel and perhaps deserve. I offered Jack my perspective from years of meeting men who had waited for, and some whom had sought out, vengeance. They simply stayed bonded to their past pain forever. Jack's choice, ultimately, was to kill the pain the abuser had left inside of him.

On the evening of this work, Jack chose his man to function as holder and selected the man to role-play the abuser. He visualized the man he was today, the man angry and powerful enough to fantasize about revenge, standing as a shield for the boy who had been exploited by the abuser. He looked inside his body to find the anger and located his heart, pounding and filled with the color red. As Jack reached his anger, he put forth how he had been hurt and betrayed by this trusted elder, moving deeper to his rage with "get out of my head . . . get out of my heart," moving to "Die" with a volume, power, and repetition that compelled the role-player to move back and lie down. Jack was coached to stay with his release of the pain, periodically doing body checks to determine whether he was holding back, saving a little trauma to use against himself at a later date.

A common struggle for many of us is to be willing to let go of all of the pain; victimization can teach a deep, often unconscious resistance to being OK. An excellent technique for facilitators when a man is truly in his power, but seems to stop short of complete release, is to ask the man to look into all the corners of his body for any residual rage. If the man says he is fatigued and doubts his ability to reach the bottom, the group's supporting his right to stop and live with the remaining pain challenges him to close the work without shame, if he has given his maximum effort for that moment, or challenges him to clear all of the pain.

Jack focused his energy and "killed" the pain until the role-player was laying on the carpet with his eyes closed, and Jack's heart was free of the anger. He was then given permission to stand with a stack of pillows and the following encouragement, "It is time to bury the past. With each pillow, give back a message that you have lived with as a result of the abuse. Bury each message with him." As Jack covered the role-player with pillows, he returned to the abuser the shame, the blame of God for what happened, his sexual insecurity, and more. He then returned to the arms of the men, was asked to look into his heart where the anger used to be and fill it with any color that created what he wanted to feel. In the weeks that followed Jack reported a sense of peace and well-being that he had only been able to create before for brief moments. Each time he experienced unease caused by the usual events of his present day life, he would return to the new sensations in his heart, and he was able to meet these new challenges with calm, direct action.

In this work, I have witnessed men heal physical, verbal, racial, and sexual abuse; rape; childhood abandonment, and a multitude of other shame-based life experiences. This is not work for the faint of heart. It helps to remember that we are not warming men up to kill those that have hurt them; we are killing the pain of the experience that lives inside of the man. Time, experience, and courage do not always prepare me fully for the depth of hate that lives in the hearts of some men, or the depth of healing that comes from giving men a safe container to release and heal this hate. Each time I participate in this work with a man, I come away with the belief that someone will live longer because of it; perhaps the actual person who delivered the initial blow, more often some other person who has become the recipient of the man's misdirected rage, most often the man himself, who has lived in addictions, suicidal ideation, self-destructiveness, and the prospect of early death by broken heart.

Working a Scene

Although there is a great deal of focus in my profession on repressed memories these days and a significant number of men reach me with, at best, sketchy pictures of childhood events, it is just as common in my experience that men have vivid auditory, visual, and visceral recollections of traumatic incidents. Even men with vague memories are, through non-directive techniques, often a short distance from clearer illustrations of times past. For many of you, anger work will be a simple, although strenuous, pilgrimage; pick a scene which represents key trauma in your life and push through it. Review the following illustration as representative of how you may proceed:

> Van reported great confusion about his fear of his father, and concomitant fear of males throughout his life. In reviewing history he remembered physical abuse of his siblings, but had no memory of his father using any physical discipline with him. At one point in his work he decided that he wanted to work on his feelings of fear and anger about how Dad mistreated his sister. He selected a scene in which his sister had received a particularly severe beating in front of him. With his support system in place and a man to role-play Dad, he entered the scene through visualization. As he watched the scene evolve, moving through his fear to his anger, Van froze . . . "I'm next." In his anger he was able to see what he had pushed away a long time ago, that he was watching the beating because he had been ordered by Dad to wait his turn. With the support of the group, Van moved through this next level of terror back to his rage, using the Stop and Rescuing the Kid exercises to begin to work on his own abuse. In the weeks that followed, Van remembered several incidents of being physically abused by his father, each occasion including Dad's ritual of having him watch and wait his turn. Van discovered that his memory had been neutralized by the terror of standing in line for his beating. He had simply shut down. From the point of this breakthrough, Van progressed rapidly in his work, finding new power in his life, new trust of himself and the good men around him.

Because you work with the memories you have, where you start is not where you will end! I cannot overemphasize how many men have simply confronted scene after scene in their journey, until reaching the joy. This technique is most assuredly the one that I return to most often in facilitating carpet work. From it comes anger, grief, shame, fear, and joy work that both keeps it simple and allows for a maximum in creativity.

Rejection

One type of anger comes from an entirely different direction but ultimately leads us back to the journey as described throughout the chapter—Rejection of Your Child. Self-blame and self-recrimination is a common response to childhood trauma of divorce, abandonment, neglect, and abuse. The most profound example in recent memory is from a female client, but I could recount many similar tales. This particular woman had spent years denying her painful, abusive childhood history. One night, upon uncovering a painful memory, she threw her doll out of the car window as she drove home on the highway at full speed. Her explanation was the anger she felt at the doll, the symbol of the truth of her victimization. It is essential to address this issue in your healing with adequate adult information, with support from your group, with a redirection of responsibility onto the adults. For sexual abuse survivors, there is an abundance of literature on the issue of self-blame. (My first book, *Double Jeopardy,* has several excellent worksheets on the topic.) For all men, I find this issue is dealt with effectively by placing yourself in the shoes of that child in one of the following ways.

Role-play

Have a skilled and nurturing man take your doll, place him on his lap, and role-play the child. Give your child the negative messages you have been telling him internally for years (probably messages he recorded from the abuse he received). The role-player will feed back to you how it feels to have you treat him the way he was treated in the original trauma. Take in how it costs you to keep replaying the trauma tapes against yourself.

Picture a Child

This version is especially effective for loving fathers who have labored to nurture their own children. Picture your son or daughter. Try to imagine blaming or hating or punishing him or her as you have punished yourself. Now imagine your response to someone who tried to blame your son or daughter in the ways you have blamed yourself. Why wouldn't you blame your son or daughter? Why would you need to blame yourself for what you would not blame your son or daughter? What must you face if you stop this process of self anger?

The Abuser Has Him

This can be an effective, but extremely painful, method of letting go of self-blame, of facing an issue you have been running away from, and of abruptly catching your anger's attention.

J.R. was adamant that he should have been able to stop the abuse at his age. He also recounted that he had forgiven his mom years before. "I prayed, let go of my resentments. I realized that she had a terrible childhood, too." In spite of these beliefs, he found himself depressed and unable to reach more than a couple of months sober time in SA (Sexaholics Anonymous). With trust for the group, he agreed to consider the relationship between these problems. He chose a holder and someone to role-play Mom. I asked for his doll (which he readily relinquished), and I gave him to Mom. As she began to give the kid the same abusive messages she had given years before, J.R. offered, "I don't like her treating him that way." He was encouraged to see that his discomfort was of little consequence when he treated the kid no better than Mom. As the role-player escalated in his messages, J.R. began to touch his anger at her behavior. Ultimately he demanded the child back and considered forgiving himself for being a child during the abuse, for being unable to stop Mom, for being angry at Mom even though he intellectually understood her pain.

Final Thoughts

I have devoted more pages in this text to anger work than any other subject; yet, I could fill another chapter with stories and processes for anger resolution. As a leader and participant, I have countless stories of the renewal found through anger containment and rage resolution. Men are reincarnated emotionally in this work. Anger is killing our world. It is at the core of child abuse, domestic violence, crime, addictions, disease, war, gangs, poverty, racism, sexism, ecological disaster, homophobia.

Anger is understandable, even justifiable. It can also be healed.

6: Grief Work

As a younger man I often expressed anger at the feminists who blamed men, all men, about the status of women in our culture. Didn't they know I was a modern man: gentle, loving, capable of cooking, cleaning, **and** ironing! As time has moved on, I have discovered deep levels of shame about the numerous men in my extended family who have mistreated women, about my own barely hidden rage that lurked underneath my soft exterior. My defensiveness in the past now suggests to me that I carry an even deeper Gender Shame that must be mourned. My grief for the women, children, **and,** men who have been violated by my gender is a key to modeling and creating a life-giving masculinity. In this process I do not seek to become the soft male who carries blame for those who simply look to avoid their own accountability; rather I recognize the power of myself as a man of sadness joining with the sadness of my brothers, creating a new understanding of the power of the feminine, and a respect for it.

Chris Frey, 1994
Presentation: Men in Therapy

The sadness that men feel takes many forms. One man needs to mourn the loss of a parent, another a lost childhood through incest or abandonment. Men may grieve specific incidents and memories in their lives, or experience the pain of pre-verbal and preconscious trauma. Many of us will not focus on specific events of life trauma, but must grieve a deep, often vague, ache in our psyche, an ache that has been called Father Hunger and The Father Wound, the grief of a father physically or emotionally absent. On another level, many of us must simply grieve the traps of masculinity that we step in—sexism, violence against ourselves and others, racism—the origins of which go to places in our history well beneath our known family. In short, this work is for every man that doubts himself, his masculine identity, his passion for life. You may read a story below and say, "This is not my work, my pain is . . . (less or more, dependent on how you run)," but your heart will know,

"Every man carries sadness. Grief is not an aberration. It is a fact of the human condition that binds us all together."

On any level, grief work presents a challenge to many men greater than skydiving, war, fistfighting, facing loss of life and limb. For to truly grieve is to let a part of you die: the fantasy that Dad will come back, that Mom will get sober, that the abuse *didn't* happen, that the past can be rewritten by denial and hope. And to truly grieve in the masculine way is to break all the rules, to fall into the arms of safe men and women and do what big boys were told not to do: cry. Big boys may not cry but big men do!

Now for even better news. On the other side of this sorrow is the joy, the passion, the connection with your higher self.

> *Phil came to group to mourn. In an hour's time he faced his truth. For twenty years he had lived in fear, resentment and shame over the deaths of both parents. He had literally believed that he, not Dad, should have died. He lived the life of the walking dead: drinking, working, yelling, running. Words cannot fully describe the power of his work that night, burying Dad and Mom with anger, sadness, and love, finally surrendering to the sadness. The following week, several men who had missed Phil's work greeted him as they entered the group room: "You look different, more relaxed. What did you work on last week?" At some point in the evening Phil's response was, "I want to Live."*

An important note as you prepare for this work, and look forward to the joy: let go of the expectation of the *when*. There is no formula for when, how, or how much the joy will appear in each man's voyage. Some of you will experience immediate and lasting relief from certain work. Others will rapidly move from the resolution of one wound into another, stopping only momentarily at the joy. Many of you will resolve a deep trauma, only to be transported to an issue that you were not aware needed to be addressed. Approach your healing as a commitment to the long haul, with detours and lots of potholes. This does not mean you cannot feel the joy until all the work is done; the male perspective that you cannot feel good until *all* the tough stuff is finished may be one faulty belief you work through to reach the joy. If you have done significant grief work and have never found the passion or the pleasure, try skipping to The Feelings Container toward the end of the chapter before returning to additional grief work processes.

As you get ready to move into the grief work exercises in this chapter, let me offer a personal note. Each time I bring my grief to the healing circle of men and move through what faces me, I further embrace life, accepting the realities of my past and working to create a powerful future. Perhaps most important to me, I accept that my time as Chris Frey appears to be limited, and rather than fearing death, I must live this moment!

Entering My Grief

For many of you, consciously planning the methods you will use to enter into your sadness will be a fruitless intellectual adventure. You will not be able to conjure up your grief. Instead, the sadness will erupt as you travel through a portion of your anger, particularly if you are in an environment of support and masculine love. Grief may enter immediately after anger, or it may simmer under the surface of resistance after a piece of anger work, leaking out over time or allowing you to actively pick your moment to express the sadness that has replaced the rage. If you have recently completed a significant piece of anger work without expressing sadness, be aware of the possible signals that your sadness is lying close to the surface: low energy, fatigue, poor concentration, feeling "numb," and any physical pains that you may have discovered through the body work in chapter 3. These pains are indicators of repressed feelings. For example, my warning signs of a need to do sadness work are fatigue and a sense of heaviness in my eyes, almost as if they are filled with tears that I am holding back. Be aware, and give yourself permission to feel.

When you are consciously deciding to do grief work, several tools will be helpful in providing a safe environment and assisting you in progressing through your resistance. The first and second tools are methods to locate and take charge of expressing your pain, tools three and four are methods to utilize the support of other men in expressing the feelings.

Where I Hold My Sadness

This information is an extension of your work on locating pain in your body:

> As you prepare to work on your sadness, close your eyes. Where in your body do you see or feel your sadness? If you are not sure, where in your body do you feel heavy, tired, strange? There may be more than one place. Review your entire body and connect with each space. As you connect with this grief, collect it all in one place inside of you and move it

to a place that will enable you to express the sadness. As you have gathered all of your sadness, give it a sound—words, or only a noise. Make the sound of your grief.

This portion of the exercise may be a practice session to learn how to feel and give voice to your sadness. Having done this much, you may choose to feel sad without any focus on specific grief work and then return from this piece using the protocol for imageries. As you become closer to your sadness, you may use this segment as a method to initiate a particular piece of grief work, opening the door for you to openly direct your sadness toward a person or event in your past.

The Balloon

As I have stressed throughout this text, breathing into and through the emotions is perhaps the simplest and most important tool in this work. In your efforts to bring up and out the sadness you feel, the following adaptation of deep breathing can be useful:

Walt came to group and offered the contract, "I will grieve my denial of my love for my father." He sat on the floor, asked Jerry to sit with him for support, closed his eyes to access the sadness he had been in touch with every day since our last session, and stated, "I'm numb, I can't feel it." As he said this, Walt rubbed his hand on his chest. When asked to stay in his body, rather than disconnecting from the feeling, he stated, "I feel like it's in my chest, and there's something keeping it down." Walt was asked what "it" was. He smiled and said, "I'll own it. It's not an it, it's my sadness." Walt was then asked to determine his readiness to commit to his contract. "I'm scared, but I'm ready to feel this sadness." (Remember: owning the fear of the work and reaffirming a commitment to do the work will often be the encouragement you need.) At this point, the instructions were: "Walt, go down to the place in your body where your sadness lies. Put a balloon of air, your air, powerful, healing air, under the sadness and begin to breathe. As you breathe, see and feel the balloon of air pushing your sadness up, pushing into the sound of your sadness, the sadness that you have spent a lifetime denying your father, your love for your father, the connection between your pain and your love. Make that sound." From Walt came what can only be described as a primitive, guttural noise, turning to deep sobbing, turning eventually to words of grief and love.

An image such as a balloon may shift your focus from the fear, from your natural defenses, into a method to reach the emotion. Try it!

Hold Me

I believe that physical support from a trusted, safe man can be the critical triggering element for some men to enter their sadness, particularly men who have followed this rule: "Don't cry, and if you do, make sure you do it alone." Allow me to describe this technique from the standpoint of a man's work:

> Stan came to confront his mother, who had committed suicide when he was an adolescent. He chose Dale to hold him, stating that he first needed to express his deep rage at her for leaving him, fully expecting to move into sadness at some point in the work. As is usually done in group, Stan sat on the floor with a big pillow on his lap; Dale sat behind him and held him loosely around the waist for safety and grounding. As Stan moved through his anger, he sat up straight, leaned forward, hit the pillow at times, and gave full voice to his rage. At the peak of his anger, Stan touched his grief at being abandoned by his mother, left to his own devices in coping with the depression he also struggled with, and he began to cry. Almost immediately, his body became rigid and he started to shut down his sadness, responding to old messages about boys not crying and to the strange feeling of being held by a man that was not angry at him, or desiring sex from him. The instructions at this point were simply, "It's OK to feel the sadness. Let yourself fall into Dale's arms. Let another man hold you in your pain." As Stan relaxed into Dale's arms the sadness came in waves, with Dale whispering permission to feel and expressing his love for Stan each time his grief receded. As Stan relaxed deeper into the safety of Dale, he released long-buried pain, while simultaneously realizing that he did not have to sink into the abyss of his mother's depression that he had feared for so long.

In this work the holder will play many roles for the man doing his work: friend, safety valve, the rock the man will stand on to keep from falling into the pit. As will be discussed further on when we look at father-son work, the holder will often become the role-player for the Ideal Father. *Note:* At times, a whole group will hold a man in his grief; use your imagination.

Role-Play

In this section I offer several ways that the use of roles can assist a man in locating his sadness. A key question when using a role-player for sadness work is, "What is the role-player doing, saying, not doing, not saying that is sad?" Often, physical movement by the role-player will elicit feelings, such as beginning to leave the room when the man is working on a person who abandoned him, or turning away when the work is about being ignored. Remember: the role-player must be willing to see actions he takes within his role that cause his friend's pain as his loving effort to help the man heal his pain; this is not being mean, it is not about being soft, it is about listening to the man's need and being strong enough to assist him in his process! These are just a few examples of how the role-player can be a catalyst; be creative.

The Funeral Fantasy

I have many gut-wrenching stories of using this exercise: The healing of the man who lost both parents to cancer as an adolescent, the man who saw his brother killed in a car accident, the man who found his father in the kitchen where he had committed suicide, the veteran who listened to his friend die over the walkie-talkie while on patrol. This process is a cornerstone for many people in moving on, reclaiming a part of themselves that is trapped in the past. The goal of this exercise is to grieve the entire person, event, or relationship, honoring the best memories, letting go of the pain, *not the person,* saying good-bye to the past, reclaiming your right to continue on. I have often seen people stay stuck in a loss not only by resisting their grief, but by only being willing to grieve a portion of their experience. For example, "I'm sad about Uncle Harry's death. He was the kind of guy that would give you the shirt off his back." (Uncle Harry also beat his kids, but no one mentions that.) Or "Good riddance. Harry was a real jerk to me that time I needed money, and he was a drunk," when Uncle Harry also gave that family member a job and had three years of sobriety when he died. Recognizing only the positive perceptions, or only the negative, leaves the grief work incomplete. So, the intent of this exercise is not to forget—it is to heal the wound, and I have seen grief wounds heal that men truly believed would last forever.

This exercise can be effective as a journaling tool or on a more intense level as a guided imagery. It is a useful process in letting go of someone important who has died, left, or refused to change in a way desired by the man, even the "death" of a key relationship through separation or divorce. The example below will focus on using imagery to mourn the death of an important person. The key to this exercise is moving through it with the assistance of someone you trust who will help you stop and express your pain at essential points. There is a tendency in deep pain work to keep talking to stuff the hurt when silence will bring catharsis, to stop breathing or breathe shallowly when breathing into the pain will release it, to cry silently when letting your grief be heard initiates new, healthier rules about your sadness. Let someone be present for you to facilitate this work.

Begin by breathing, filling your lungs in and slowly releasing. Be aware of your breathing throughout the exercise. Know that when you hold your breath or breathe short and quick you may be preventing the release of the tears, the pain. See yourself as the adult you are today. You will be doing this work as an adult feeling the pain of a younger self. Now, see a picture of the person who has died. Perhaps you are walking back into the funeral home where you last saw him or her, perhaps you must create a picture of how this person looked the last time you saw him or her, possibly you must create your image of a person you are grieving that you do not remember. For a little while, imagine that for the last time this person can hear you as you speak but will not speak back until you are ready. First, tell this person out loud what you got from him or her that you will keep and use in your life: knowledge, personal qualities, gifts of love, essential moments, important physical qualities, meaningful memories. Pause with time to speak and to feel. (Often, sadness will be expressed about the many or few things to be kept. With parents who died early in life, who were extremely abusive, gave the man up for adoption, or abandoned him, the man is coached to remember even this parent gave him the most precious gift of all—Life.)

Next, tell this person what he or she gave you that you are giving back. Depending on the relationship, this could be specified as the messages, pain, abuse, shame, or neglect. A man may return specific events, parts of the relationship, certain aspects of the person's Shadow that the man has carried for him or her. (The man may be coached to say, "I give back to you the. . ..") Now, tell this person what you have imitated in his or her behaviors and are letting go of. Examples of this are many and often involve the avoidance of responsibilities to care for oneself and to treat others with love and respect. See yourself literally lifting all of the pain you are giving back and placing it on this person, whose burdens you carried much too long. As you release this pain, do you see any part of yourself that you left with him or her so that you could carry his or her burdens, or so you could carry the hope that this other person would return and give you the rest of what you wanted? (Particularly with men familiar with the "Inner Child" concept, the man will see himself as a child, literally in a casket with the deceased.) As you see the part that has been missing from you, pick that part of you up, hold him close. It's OK to feel. Now, take the time to tell the person anything else you have needed to say; say it with your feelings. And now it is time to say good-bye. Are you ready to leave the past, keeping with the knowledge of this person, the good stuff he or she gave you, leaving the pain behind? (At this point in the imagery there are many variations. One variation is to see the person in the casket, making sure the man buries no part of himself, seeing the casket go to the grave, saying good-bye and returning to the present. Another is to see the person going over to the care of the man's view of Higher Power, especially helpful in the loss of a child or other strong positive relationship. In group or a workshop, the man may have someone role-play the person and cover them up with pillows or blankets, symbolically burying the pain. Whatever the method, it is important to design some type of closing ritual that leaves the pain in the past and returns the man to the present.)

Having said good-bye, see yourself walking back to the present, growing yourself to your strongest, oldest self as you move. As you near the present, you see people in the distance, familiar people. These are the men, women, and children that love you in today's world. How are you more able to bring them close as a result of your work? How do you feel more free to be who you need to be? Return to the present, to this room, to the arms of those who love and accept you. As you are ready, open your eyes.

At the end of this piece of work, men will often benefit from being held, stroked, spoken to in soft, loving tones. Each man is different. Some of you will want to discuss the work, some will want to journal immediately, some will simply process in silence. One key bit of information at the end of the work is to be alert to the possibility that you may return to sadness over the next several days. It is essential to feel, journal, and reach out to your established support system. Over the days following the work, journal the specific changes you will practice in your life as a result of this work. I reiterate that this work will not cause you to forget the person or the events of your relationship with the deceased. What will change is that someone could ask you about the person or the memories and you could acknowledge them without feeling jerked back into the pain of the past.

I close this section with a story. This is a story about a woman, but it is truly a story about and for men *and* women.

Sylvia came to my office after several years of serious depression escalated to almost unbearable depression. She told the story of recently becoming pregnant and finding herself increasingly less interested in her husband, her other children, and especially in her unborn child. She cried much of the time. Sylvia knew that this pain was directly related to the death of her first child, the son who had been born with serious birth defects and had finally succumbed to his illnesses at the age of six. Sylvia spoke of her devotion to him, that his care had been her first priority, especially after the boy's father, her first husband, had abandoned them. She spoke so eloquently of what a special child her son was, I could envision a little angel in heaven as she spoke. She shared her guilt that although she was a religious person with a lifelong relationship with God, she found no solace for her grief and wondered why God chose her family for this pain. Over the course of several sessions, several things became apparent to me about Sylvia: she was intensely motivated to work on her pain, she had a strong fear that she could never significantly recover from her loss, she had intense guilt about closing out the very loving man who had become her second husband, and she easily built trust with me. When offered the idea of The Funeral Fantasy, she took very little time to verbalize her fear and said, "OK." As we moved through an extended session, Sylvia demonstrated her creative self in the imagery, visualizing a God that she could give the care of her son over to, speaking to God not only as a universal being but as somebody that better take proper care of her son! Perhaps the pivotal moment in her work was when she began to honestly give back what she did not want from the relationship with her son: the ways her fear and guilt had trained him to be tyrannical in his expectations of her caretaking, his tantrums, her exhaustion as a testimony of her love, her depression as a testimony of her love. She al-

lowed her son to talk at one point and imaged hearing from him that he was OK now and that he wanted her to never forget him and to always love him, but to move on and take care of herself and the people she loved who were still alive.

Over the course of several months, a large part of Sylvia's depression lifted quickly. She gradually felt more positive, more involved with her family and pregnancy, more at peace with her son.

Grieving My Addiction

Danny was angry, "I'm tired of sitting in SA meetings and hearing about how grateful people are for recovery. This one (expletive deleted) even said we should consider ourselves fortunate to be addicts, because nonaddicts don't have a place to focus their healing that guarantees a better life. I have five years of recovery, and I still get scared I'll relapse."

In the section on body pain, I offered an exercise for grieving an illness. The process described below is directed toward many of you who struggle with what I believe to be a potentially terminal subset of diseases, addictions. If you consider yourself addicted to alcohol, drugs, food, sex, work, gambling, consider this. Before an addiction begins to steal a man's life, it may have been his lifeline, providing solace from loneliness, abandonment, child abuse, or simple growing pains. Many of us have experienced our addictions as our best friends long before they became our path to self-destruction. In deciding to recover, men often need to grieve the loss of this powerful coping strategy, facing the unfairness (anger) of being an addict, the fear that there will be nothing to replace the power of this survival tool, the shame and sadness of how the self and others have been damaged by this loyal, ever present, deceptive, cruel friend. Those of you who may interpret this exercise as an opportunity to arrive at, "I grieved my addiction, I let it go, I'm not an addict anymore, I'm cured," be warned: that is not the intent of this piece. Rather, this addresses a part of recovery that I believe may be missed: Honoring the original need for the addiction, how it hurt you, but also how it *served* you. This piece is not simply about deciding to recover; I have seen powerful healing through this process for men who have years of sobriety. This is about owning and releasing the emotional Shadow of the addiction, the friendship, the anger at being "given" an addiction, the fear and sadness of facing the world without the Addict in front.

Take a sheet of large unlined paper and markers. Draw your addiction. If you are doing this work on your own, place the drawing across the room and sit facing your addiction. The exercise will often be more powerful if it is an interactive process; if done in group, select a man to role-play your addiction (someone who understands addictions). Begin by deciding how you feel about being an addict. Tell your addiction how you feel about him (I use "him" because your addiction is not just a thing, it is a living, breathing, cunning part of you). Begin letting the addiction hear the feelings with the full power of your anger, sadness, fear, shame, gratitude, and whatever you feel. As you work, reflect on these questions:

> As a young person I needed you because. . . .
> You helped me when. . . .
> I came to rely on you for. . . .
> What I still don't want to admit about you is. . . .
> I used you to replace. . . .
> You began to turn against me when. . . .
> What makes me the . . . (angriest, saddest, most afraid) about you is. . . .
> The worst part of letting you go will be. . . .
> The scariest part of letting you go will be. . . .
> The best part of letting you go will be. . . .

Close your eyes. See what being addicted has cost you physically, emotionally, and spiritually, in your relationships, in your dreams. Speak these truths to your addiction. It is time to decide—will you step into the place of uncertainty and say good-bye to this lethal friend? If your decision is yes, make this be known and state how your life will be different as a result. If your decision is no, state what work you must do to move on. Let yourself feel as you decide whether you need this addiction in your life today. Open your eyes, journal, and receive feedback from those who care about you.

Using a role-player for this work offers several advantages. A man knowledgeable in the ways of the addict can hear hidden pain, passive resistance to letting go, and denial of the loss of the pleasurable aspects of the addiction. (Although they may be well in the past, one must only listen to male addicts competing with the "war stories" of their addictions to understand that many men miss the pleasure, the freedom, the spontaneity that came before the pain, the captivity, the impulsivity.) The role-player can challenge, cajole, and even try to seduce, just as addictions do.

Having done this work, men will often report a renewed interest in a more active recovery program, rekindled empathy for persons who are struggling in early recovery, feeling less separate from the "normies" (non-addicts), greater acceptance of the "little boy" (who is, after all, the original addict for most of us), all of which facilitates the rest of the journey.

Leaving My House

The two years in which I wrote this book held several especially significant losses and renewals in my life, each of which related to the processes I will now describe. After six years in private practice with good friends and an essential female mentor in my life, I made the decision to move down the road and put my name on my practice. The reasons for this change are less important than the process of preparing and recovering from this loss. The second greatest change to date is taking place as I write. My friend, my partner in five years of mens workshops, a man who has been an integral part of my healing work for six years, and my mentor, leaves town for a new career opportunity. Intellectually, I am aware that leaving my old territory and staking out new space to work was a positive choice, a direct result of "growing up" in my career. Intellectually, I am aware that Jim is making a positive move, motivated by something I love about him, the best interests of his family. Emotionally, I face a time of intense sadness. The sense of loss experienced in moving on can encompass the pain of leaving familiar, safe physical surroundings; familiar, safe people; even the pain of choosing to leave behind a past fraught with danger, abuse, and neglect.

Leaving My House may be utilized as a process within itself or as a component of numerous other pieces of healing imageries. The concept is to emotionally leave the place and people that are associated with your pain, taking with you your Child and any belongings that are valuable to him. Each time you use this exercise you have the opportunity to reclaim another part of yourself, aspects of your experience stuck at various ages. The image of the house is used in my title, and I will give an example below that will highlight getting your Child out of a house he grew up in. However, this process can be used to remove yourself symbolically from many other physical locations where a part of you became frozen in time—a school or church setting where you were mistreated; the house of a friend, neighbor, other family member where you were abused; a playhouse, the woods— literally any space where you were traumatized. Don't be limited by what I don't say in this text; utilize the ritual in the manner that best fits your healing. I will offer several variations of the exercise, discussing them in a progression of intensity that I have often seen among men.

Rescuing My Child

When men describe childhood neglect and abuse, they often speak as if a part of them is still stuck in the place where the trauma happened. Many men moving from fear and shame into anger and grief work experience the power of rescuing the little boy from the environment in which he got emotionally stuck. You cannot change the past, you cannot literally erase the past in any healthy way, but you can reclaim your head, heart and soul from those dangerous places.

Close your eyes and begin the protocol that you have learned for guided imageries. As you breathe, see a picture of yourself as the man you are today, a man with the intention to save a boy in peril. If you hesitate, ask yourself this question, "If I saw a child in a burning house and could save him, would I?" If you still hesitate, ask yourself this question, "What children have a right to a safe life, only kids I like or should all kids be safe?" These questions are offered because many men are ashamed of their childhood, hence their Child, and have essentially decided to neglect, abuse, and abandon themselves just as others did. Healing does not take place without a decision on your part to give this Child another chance. This means rescuing him whether you like him or not, facing him—facing the pain of the past. Denying him will not save you. It will only push the pain deeper into your Shadow to be released in secret, destructive ways another day. As you make the commitment to save this boy, be aware that he is trapped, or is hiding, in the place where he was . . . (abused, neglected, abandoned, lost). Will you go in and bring him out? Today is not the day to work on what happened to him in this place. This is the day to find him, save him, and reconnect.

As you prepare to go in, remember the adult you are today. Do you feel ready to go in on your own to get this boy? This is not a macho exercise—use whatever support you need to feel safe. If you need help, pick anyone you believe can and will help you save that boy (a therapist, men in group, other friends, family). Make sure the people you pick are men and women you know have power, and even anger, in place to protect a child who is in need.

When ready, enter the place where it makes sense to you. As you go to find the boy, see your support people with you, say out loud where you are, what you see, what is going on. If you find someone in the house that is unsafe, coach your support people. What do you need from them to assist you in carrying out your mission, such as stand between the man and the unsafe person? (This moment is often one of revelation and discovery for men, along with one of powerful grief.) As you find your Child, you will often find him in the early stages of coping behaviors that later become serious concerns in his life: compulsive masturbation, isolation, fantasy, silent pain, hiding, drug use. Let yourself feel this. The healing is in grieving the discovery, getting the boy out, and beginning to give him new options in his life.

Go to the boy. If he is hiding, do not scare him, simply let him know you are a safe person and are going to take him away from this place. He may resist; take your time helping him believe he can trust you. What age is he? When he is ready, take his hand or pick him up (this is a good time for someone to hand the man his doll to hold), making sure he is dressed properly, and take him out the way that makes sense to you. If you meet any resistance from people in your past, rely on the support people you brought in. As you leave this place, make sure the boy is with you, shut the door and make sure no one leaves except you, the boy, and your support people. (In the life of a man who carries great fear of this place of abuse and danger, he may imagine his support people guarding a door, holding back the abusive person, leading the way as he takes the boy out.) As you walk away, bring the boy back to this safe place, hold him gently, tell him you will keep him safe with you. If he is ashamed of where he was and what he was doing, it is your responsibility to let him feel that pain, to promise him you will not abandon him in his shame. If a feeling of safety overcomes him, tell him it's OK to feel, scared boys often cry when they are finally safe. Now, begin the protocol for ending imageries that you have learned, and when you are ready, open your eyes. Having opened your eyes, there may be something you want to tell this boy. Tell him now.

In being introduced to this exercise, many of you will begin to grieve how long you have been scared and felt unsafe. As you become accustomed to using this process, you will find extensions of this piece that will take you through fear, anger, and grief. *Note:* Many therapists will ask you to "place the child in your heart" as part of this imagery. Be cautious, early in your work you may need some emotional distance from this wounded child. Premature intergration of past and present experience can be overwhelming, especially if you experience dissociation. Take your time. Parent the child, don't become him.

Confronting the Grief

As you become safer and stronger in your work, you may use this process for a greater intention than simply removing your Child to a safer place. You may single out specific memories and relationships for which you carry sadness and choose to confront this pain within the imagery. Feelings other than sadness will often surface and be expressed within this work. My purpose here is not to imply that you draw some artificial line between feelings, but simply to highlight the use of this exercise as a grief process. This part of the process enters in after you have found the boy:

> . . . . As you hold his hand or pick him up, you decide it is time to confront the pain that has left this boy stuck in the past. Who or what will you confront for this boy today? Go to the place in the house where you find . . . (Mom, Dad, the abuser, the empty house). Today you are this boy's champion. You will speak for him, express his pain. Share what you are sad about. How do you feel, having been left unattended in this place for so long? Share what pain you have been experiencing and hiding in this house. Are you willing to leave this boy with it again today? If not, decide that you are taking him away and you will no longer wait for anyone else to take care of him. Feel this decision. As you prepare to leave, go to the place in the house where you will tell whoever waits there that it is time for you to take this boy, to take care of him, and that you will not be leaving him in the care of anyone in this house any longer. Feel this decision, and be aware of the response of the person you inform. Share your feelings about their responses. Make sure you have said everything you need to say. Are you ready to leave with your Child? If so, take him from the house and bring him back to this safe place. If you are hesitant to leave, what holds you back? At this point you may connect up with another piece of work that you need to complete; if you are ready, go for it. However, it is OK to stop at this point, to take your Child out with this piece done, and to return to work another day.
>
> Having healed this part of your pain, I want to introduce you to a powerful way to bring closure to a step in your work, a method that you will return to in your journey. As you begin to bring the Child back to this safe place, as you walk

in peace with him, look at him and grow him up as big as you can. How much has he grown as a result of your efforts today? At whatever age he stops growing, you will simply know there is more work for another day. And now, take this boy and see your Adult self blending with him, as you place the boy into your heart (again, seeking guidance on when it is safe to begin this integration process). After all, you are not in parts—you are one man and that boy is a symbol of your history and your healing. As you place this boy into your heart, know that you are giving yourself access to an element of yourself that has healed: elements of your creativity, energy, spontaneity, genius, strength. You are also gaining access to elements of impulsivity, orneriness, and Shadow that you are responsible for Parenting. Feel what you have reclaimed, own it. Now, return to this place.

Leaving My Siblings

Henry had moved through the imagery to the place where he found and reclaimed his Child. As he got ready to take his Child from the house, his face froze, "I can't leave my brother and sisters there. I took care of them."

Henry faced the dilemma common to men who are working through childhood and were not the only child. Children are often sworn to take care of a parent forever when the other parent leaves or dies. Children become substitute caretakers for younger siblings in families where parents are absent due to illness, addictions, death, work. Children place themselves in the line of fire for physical and sexual abuse in hopes of saving their siblings. Children are trapped in neighborhoods bereft with physical and sexual violence among their friends and siblings. In many cases, these children grow into adults who unknowingly accept emotional servitude to the other damaged children in their lives. In the words common to Twelve-Step recovery, the exercise Leaving My Siblings is a process in establishing loving detachment, the art of continuing to love and be available to siblings and friends in healthy ways while deciding to move on from the interminable responsibilities that keep us in the quagmire of the past. Complete this piece when you know that the pain of other kids in your past is keeping you stuck, and you have decided you are ready to feel the grief of leaving them behind. You **do not** abandon people that you still love in the present but get unstuck from inappropriate past accountabilities. This work can be completed in imagery, in role-play, or in combination. I will delineate the combination of both.

Select the role-players to be the children you are leaving behind. Position them across from you as you see them, give each role-player a name and an age. Close your eyes and begin the protocol for imageries. When you are ready, it is time to go to the place where you will find each of these children and to gather them together. Only you and the children are present. As you gather, see the other children that you care for, perhaps children you have taken care of. Look at your Child. Be aware of the sacrifices that you had to make to care for and about these other kids. Be aware of what your sense of responsibility, real or perceived, cost you then and still costs you today. Remember: even if you did not physically care for these kids, you may still carry the weight of some shame or sense of emotional responsibility for them. As you look back and forth between your Child and the others, you become aware that it is time to choose; you realize that you cannot save everyone. You must choose between taking care of your Child and taking care of the others; to choose to stay stuck in this place in the past or bring your Child into the present, leaving the others to make their own decisions about getting out. Let yourself feel the struggle of this decision.

When you are ready, it is time to speak to the others; you may choose to speak to them singly or collectively. (The role-players will have been instructed at the beginning of the work whether to respond and what the responses need to be. Often the messages of the other kids are, "I understand" or "I need you to stay.") It is important to tell the others how you feel about them, what you have tried to do to save them from their pain, how you have succeeded, how you have failed. It is important to tell them that you have decided to leave this place and you cannot take them with you. Feel this decision. Let yourself know, and tell them, the responsibility that you took for each of them that was not really yours to take— you were just another kid who was struggling too. Let yourself and the others know who was really responsible for their care and their pain. Be aware that each of them will decide how he or she will cope and proceed through life (this may be particularly difficult if the sibling has died previous to this work). Feel this. Say anything else that is important to you in this moment, then say good-bye. Making sure to pick up your Child, looking back for the last time, leave this place alone and close the exit behind you.

As you walk back to this safe place, let yourself feel the sadness and the relief. When you are ready, begin the protocol to return to this safe place. Upon opening your eyes, reaffirm two things with this boy. One, honor him for all his efforts to care for the other children; even with the limitations of a child he may have helped them mightily. Two, secure within him the knowledge that his job is done and you will now take care of him. If you are the father of your own children, affirm with yourself that your responsibilities are yourself and your children (at times the order of importance is your children and then yourself), others that you care about, and the children of the world, in that order.

Many men have returned to a session after this work feeling a great lifting, of responsibility for children that should have been cared for by someone else, of pain caused by others to those children that the man had no power to prevent, and a new freedom to carry on more adult, equal relationships with those other children who are still in his life (and who probably aren't children any longer either).

I close this section with a personal example of how this piece can work in your life. I have had the opportunity to do this healing both symbolically and in the live version. For years I carried guilt about both my brother and sister because I was the good boy of my family. In my own journey, I chose to do work to release the guilt for my sister's long-standing conflicts with family and my brother's role as the kid who could never quite measure up to his big brother. This work was stimulated by my emotional resignation from the job as the perfect son, which came quite painfully, but easily, on the heels of my divorce. I was struck by the realization that I no longer needed to feel guilty about Lisa's relationships; she managed to stay married through her trials. I realized that I was no longer Kevin's big brother. We were both men, who had both succeeded and failed in life's tests, and that it wasn't my fault that some of his weaknesses were in my areas of strength. The final beauty was that I was able to communicate these messages directly to my sister, my brother, and my parents. I remember when Lisa admitted how angry she had been at me for most of our lives and then was able to hear that being the golden boy had its downside, too. Today, in no small part due to that conversation, I count her as one of my best friends.

I remember writing my brother and resigning as "Big Brother." Although we have not communicated in the same depth as I have with my sister, I took a freedom from responsibility for his issues, past, present and future, from our contact and sent forth a hope, not a need, that Kevin also found some use in the process. This work, as much as any I have done, has helped me clarify who I am responsible *for* (my children . . . our children), who I am responsible *to* (my wife, my friends, my other family, my clients), and who I am responsible *with* (the other adults on this planet . . . You).

All My Children

There comes a time in the journey to collect the child you were from all the places he is symbolically stuck, making sure that all of him—all of you—is reclaimed from the house(s) in your past. When you are ready, follow the imagery below:

It is time to enter the house you grew up in (or the place you were hurt in), for a final moment, to claim all of your Child and to bring with him all that is valuable to him.

Prepare yourself to enter the imagery as the man you are today, ready and willing to bring this boy fully into your present life. Gather your support people, the men and women who have gone in with you in the past and assisted you in rescuing this boy. Tell them that this time you must lead the way. You may have them follow you into the house, or you may ask them to wait for you outside as you go to meet this challenge. And now, enter the house and go to the first place you find the boy. Pick him up. What does he need from this place? This could be something emotional, like the knowledge that he is a good boy, or something tangible like his clothes or an important stuffed animal. As the boy looks down, he sees that you brought a Treasure Chest with you, and you put in it all of his treasures from this room. Now, what does the boy need to leave in this room? Again, this may be emotional, the shame and pain of that place, or something tangible, such as, the belt he was beaten with. You decide to leave these things in a strongbox that will remain in the room. As you place these items of your past in the box, let yourself feel whatever comes up. Make any final statements you need to make before you leave this place, and when you are ready, go to the next room and find the boy. Where do you find him? The process continues in each room in the house, including closets, basements, or garages if nec-

essary, until the man has removed the Child from every loca-
tion in the house. The Adult brings the Treasure Chest into
every room. The man takes time in each room to grieve and let
go of remaining pain before he leaves. Leave this place in the
past for the last time as you bring your Child to the exit with
his Treasure Chest. Gather anyone who has been in that place
that you will say good-bye to. Tell each of them about your de-
cision to take this boy with you, to no longer leave him in their
custody, to no longer leave him to take care of them. Let your-
self feel the feelings that come up. Making sure to bring both
the boy and his Treasure Chest, turn and leave this place, clos-
ing the exit behind you, knowing that you can only take the boy
with you this day. As you walk away, let yourself feel any emo-
tion that comes up. And now, it is time to return to this moment
with the boy and all the people that love him in the present. As
you begin to walk back into this safe place, grow the boy up as
big as you can. Having done this, blend him into your Adult
self, placing him into your heart. Knowing that you are not in
parts, the boy is a symbol of your past, a part of your healing
that you can keep in your heart. Now, come back to the present
according to the protocol you have learned.

You've now recovered a major portion of your past. You may have done this without ever recovering many of the specific memories of your past. Now, it's time to *Celebrate!*

The Celebration of the New

The beginning of the new is always preceded by the death of the old—there is no birth without death. In the work above, just as you rescued a boy from ancient entrapments (new birth), you laid rest to much of your fantasy childhood. For the man to be truly born, some of the boy must die. In the ritual death, you left antiquated beliefs, outdated messages, old pain, and you begin to catch a glimpse of the celebration of bringing the boy of your past into the man of your present. The following process is a ritual that has been adapted in group many times, a ceremony to welcome a man into the wonderful and frightening possibilities of today. This exercise may be completed as it's own piece, but it also fits beautifully when blended into a process such as, All My Children. I offer this exercise in a form that most men will find useful at some point, and then I extend it to men who have gone away to war.

Making sure to bring both the boy and his Treasure Chest, turn and leave this place, closing the exit behind you, knowing that you can only take the boy with you this day. As you walk away, let yourself feel any emotion that comes up. And now, as you walk away, look into the distance and see that someone, maybe more that one, is waiting for you. As you approach, you see that these are the people who have been there for you through your healing, those who love you and are proud of you for the work you have done. Oddly enough, some of the people may be different incarnations of the people you left behind. For instance, you may leave behind a family member who was an active chemical dependent whom you needed to confront and leave, but you may re-connect with that person in the present, when he or she is sober. As you gather with these loved ones, you realize that this is a celebration, of your growth, your life—of you. (If this work is done in group, this is a great time to have everyone verbally express their love and celebration.) Let these people know out loud where you have been, what you have been through, what you have changed and healed. Hear from them how they feel about you (in group this is out loud and can be in unison or individually), their joy at your return, their knowledge of your travels and exploits. When you are ready, open your eyes (again, if in group), stand, and take in the love that is yours today.

My personal favorite at this time is to have the group circle the man, have him look in the eyes of each man and see the love, the respect, the reflection of his courage, then have the group close in on him with arms linked so he receives a hug from the entire circle simultaneously.

A Soldier's Welcome

In my twenty years as a therapist, I have been honored to serve veterans of World War II, the Korean War, the Vietnam War, and the Gulf War. Anyone reading these words is probably aware, and has his or her own feelings, about how our nation reacted to the men and women who served us in Vietnam. Most veterans of this war were not only not welcomed home—many were ignored and even ridiculed. Of those I met early in my career that had been welcomed home, it was only by each other, occasionally by some family, rarely even by vets of other conflicts. The devastation of combining war with the shame of returning home to these responses is well documented. I offer a perspective that is of little political value but goes to the heart of how soldiering impacted many of the men I have had the opportunity to accompany on part of their masculine adventure. I gained this **not** from a combat vet but from a survivor of family violence who went to the service, became a soldier, was shipped away to Germany, never spent a moment in combat, and re-experienced the abandonment of his family without ever firing a shot.

Dean grew up in a family of severe physical and sexual violence, and alcoholism. Like many troubled young men of his era, his first opportunity to escape this environment was to enlist. As he spoke in group of this time in his life, he recalled the hopes: that his family would express fear and sadness at his leaving, that within the service he would find the direction from "fatherly" men that he had lacked from his own father, that upon his "triumphant" return as a man in uniform his family would be proud and joyful. With tears, he also recalled that none of these dreams came to pass. Instead, he spoke of the silent fear he re-experienced in boot camp, much as he had lived with his entire childhood. He did whatever he had to do to survive, including progressing from a fledgling drinker to the early stages of his own disease. Over several sessions, Dean's work focused on the guilt and shame he accumulated while serving his tours of duty; alcohol fueled sexual acting out and violence. As he moved through ritual time in his work, Dean arrived at the day he returned home . . . and no one was there to greet him. From this sad moment was created the gold of "A Soldier's Welcome."

Close your eyes and begin the protocol for imageries. When you are ready, return to the day that you came home from the service. Remember how you arrived in the place you called "home." Go back to that . . . (plane, boat, train, car) and see yourself as you were. What hopes did you have about your arrival? Feel the anticipation of a young man who hopes to be greeted, perhaps as a hero, perhaps simply as a loved one who has been missed. As you arrive, you see several people in the distance. You realize that these people have come for you. As you get closer you see that they are the men of your group, men who have always been waiting for you, men who welcome you with open arms. As you step . . . (from the plane, etc.), you receive a greeting you have waited years for: the men welcome you with the words that are in their hearts. The men gather about you, concerned to hear about your experiences, your well-being. But this is not your time to speak, it is your time to take in the love . . . time to feel. One of the men takes your bags; he wants to help you carry your load, and the group leads you through time, moving ahead to a place of safety. As you walk in, you see all the people that you call friends and loving family. You may notice that there are people missing that you have long waited to welcome you home. It is OK to feel this. You notice that everyone present is there just for you—this is a celebration of your homecoming. There will be time to deal with where you have been, but right now everyone is simply glad that you are back. (At this point in the process the man is brought back from the imagery, after feeling whatever he needs to, and he sees the group circled around him with hugs, handshakes, food, tokens of love and honoring. At this point, I have seen men go to their shame, not feeling worthy, and move to their grief and joy when the shame is overwhelmed by the honoring of the group).

Since my the inaugural voyage of this process, I have utilized it with combat and noncombat vets, in group with combat and noncombat vets alongside of men who never served in the military. In this exercise I have learned several key things about the men I work with:

Many of the combat veterans who were the most skilled at surviving in war were kids who had already been in combat with their families, creating a powerful system of survival, emotional defenses, and layers of pain.

The end of the draft created a great chasm between many men in our culture, those who have served and those who have not. The guilt of some men who have not served is significant; the guilt of men who fought and came back is often catastrophic; the guilt of men who served in times of war and did not see combat is notable; and the symbolic act of welcoming within this process provides every man with a mirror for his pain during these tragic episodes in our lives.

My limited experience with combat vets teaches me that I can never become so jaded, even after twenty years of stories of horrendous abuse, that I believe I have heard or seen it all.

And so, this process is founded on the words of a Native American elder I heard speak once at a pow-wow. As he introduced a dance that would feature veterans and family members of deceased veterans he said, "We don't honor war. We honor warriors."

Rebirth

Here comes the ultimate in leaving, symbolically leaving at birth. I frequently work with men who have difficulty consciously remembering early enough in life to feel: "I was a good kid" . . . "I was wanted and loved" . . . "Someone took good care of me" . . . and (perhaps most crucial for some of you) "It's OK that I'm a boy/a man." If you are one of these men, you may have done a great deal of powerful work yet feel stuck. You may feel that you do a significant piece of grief work, have a few hours or days of relief, and then it seems as if the progress you made is water that you are trying to hold in your hand: it simply trickles through. When men are working hard and running in place I typically look at three things. The man may have an active addiction, or he is doing great work of the heart in my office, but isn't doing the head, hands, legs, and heart work in the real world (he isn't putting his emotional changes into concrete action). Or, he does not have in him what I call an adequate Holding Place, my metaphor for a symbolic space in a man's psyche where he "holds" emotional changes that counter what he received from his early environment. There are innumerable theoretical explanations, and labels, for what I just described. The understanding that gives me the most to work with is that some of you experienced a level of pain before conscious memory, perhaps pre-verbally, even prenatally, that is not adequately attacked by work on specific memories, or on ages of your Child after infancy. In that light, I extend two processes that are structured to provide you with a foundation for a fresh start, introducing new possibilities about this boy as he was, even as he arrived in all his naked glory.

Claiming the Original Child

This exercise is designed to take you back to the origins of your life, to give you the opportunity to claim your life from the moment of physical arrival, and to make a decision about your original "goodness." Perhaps most important for some of you, within this exercise is an opportunity to claim your maleness, to decide that being a boy, and becoming a man, is a gift, not an affliction.

> *Close your eyes and begin the protocol for imageries. Today, you will be returning to an early time in your life, returning as you are in the present to reclaim your original strengths, your right to live, **your maleness**. If you have a picture of the hospital or other place you were born, see that place in your mind's eye. If you do not consciously remember the place, recreate it in your imagination. The man you are today is returning to this place; see yourself approaching the*

entrance to the maternity ward.

As you enter, you are aware of old feelings. Let yourself feel, then proceed to the delivery area. You are drawn to a specific place, and when you enter, you see that your mother is in the room. (If you have no conscious memory of Mom, recreate her in your mind's eye.) You see that she is nearing the time to deliver a child. You have a decision to make on this day: will you participate in the birth of this child? As you decide to be present, you become aware of Mom's feelings about this pregnancy, this child. How does she feel about the child? Herself? The father of the child? Is she ready to parent this baby? Let yourself feel the answers to these questions. Now, the time to deliver the child has come. You place yourself in the position to receive the child into the world. (Regardless of how smoothly your actual birth was, the exercise proceeds with the child slowly appearing.) You begin to see the child's head appear—describe the process of the birth to yourself as the child slowly begins to emerge—face . . . shoulders . . . torso. The child is into this world, into your hands, and you see that he's a boy and his name is . . . (your name)!

As you hold him, be aware of how he looks—check his body parts, his toes, hands, eyes, everything to make sure he is OK—making sure that if he has any struggles, you give him over to the proper care of the doctor, and wait with him until he is OK. As you look at him, what comes to your heart? (Often you will see a boy who is OK just the way he is, untouched by most of the trauma of life.) Take him to a corner of the room, clean him up, clothe him in something soft and warm, hold him close to you and feel the connection. Decide now that you will claim this boy, that you will parent him from this day forward. Know that this commitment includes loving this boy in spite of any pain, handicap, or limitation he arrived with. Be aware, perhaps for the first time, that whatever pain is going to occur in his life is not because he arrived bad or defective. You have in your arms a beautiful, vibrant boy, open to many possibilities—whatever limitations he has are simply part of who he is and who he is capable of being.

As you decide this, you become aware that you have neglected one part of the birth process, the umbilical cord's still attached to his mom. It is time to cut the cord. You are aware of the considerable strength of this cord; it represents the strength of the bond you have maintained with your mother.

*Select whatever mechanism necessary to cut a cord this powerful, and when you are ready . . . **cut the cord (pause to feel this).** When you are ready, face your mother as she was. This may mean seeing a mom who died at the birth and doing that grief work; letting go of a mom that you never really got to know because of adoption; facing a mom who was not in a place to properly parent the boy, or simply a Mom who has done her part and is no longer responsible for the child. Let her know that you will no longer leave this boy in her care. Tell her how you feel about her as a mother for this boy. Thank her for giving him life. Reaffirm to her that he is OK and that it is good he is a boy. Tell her it is time for you to leave, that the boy cannot stay to be taken care of or to take care of her. See her feelings as you decide to leave. Now, making sure you have the boy, say good-bye to Mom, turn, and leave this place. As you move toward the door, be aware of anyone else that you must speak to and leave at that place (Dad or in the case of an adopted child, perhaps a social worker or adoptive parent that carried him away from his Mom). Share your feelings and intentions with these people, just as you did with Mom. And now, it is time to leave, making sure you have the infant with you. As you walk out and away, let yourself feel.*

*As you return to the present, become aware of what this boy will need from you to grow. What are his limitations; physically, intellectually? Are you willing to care for him knowing that seeing him as OK **does not mean** he will always feel OK, do OK, or be without struggles. (This is a key element for men who were born with some disability or other limitation that has been seen as a curse.) What does properly caring for him mean? Are you willing to let him grow up, not leaving him to live in eternal childhood? What does growing up mean in his life? Now, having made these decisions, it is time to return to this safe place. As you do this, grow the boy up as big as you can get him, and when you have done that, if you are ready, blend him in with the Adult you because you are not in parts; you are one person. This process is about accepting yourself as you were from birth—this is your life! When you are ready, begin the protocol for returning from imageries.*

Let me reinforce several aspects of this piece that will necessitate additional work for many men. If you lost your mom at birth or early infancy due to death, adoption, or abandonment, this visualization may open doors to that work. Accepting that this loss was not caused because you were defective or bad may or may not resolve other anger and sadness about the loss. In fact, closure of this piece may unlock deeper levels of feelings about Mom. Because this work is a long journey for some of you, don't lament the appearance of new work to replace the old; pick your time to move to the next stage. Second, if you were born with some illness, or disability, that affected how you were loved, and loved yourself, then you will probably encounter additional work from this process, work that may incorporate aspects of shame, anger, fear and grief. Finally, some of you will determine that accepting yourself at birth is insufficient; you felt or were even told that you were unwanted from the beginning of conception.

> *Cal came from what he described as, "The family that put the capital D in dysfunction." His mother told him when he was a little boy that she had attempted to have him aborted, but was not able to. Further, he heard stories about how his abusive father had kicked Mom in the stomach during a fight. "I didn't feel that it wasn't OK to be a boy; I felt it wasn't OK to be alive." Cal had lived this out through a lifelong series of dangerous, self-abusive behaviors.*

For those of you in this situation, simply move further back in time to begin the imagery. Find your mother at conception and begin to parent this boy into birth. Remember: You were born . . . you are supposed to be here . . . you were supposed to be a boy and arrive in the manner you arrived, however crazy the method. Be creative, find that boy as early in his existence as you need to. Don't take my word for his beauty—go find him yourself. Within this work you will find great pain. You cannot recreate the real past; the work we do in this imagery is in ritual time. What happened to Cal in utero happened. He could only be present in his feelings to complete the rage work at his mother and father, to grieve the pain he experienced before even seeing the outside world, to learn to love and accept the boy who wouldn't give up. And so, the work may look something like this:

> *As you see the boy conceived, watch his growth within his mother. Visualize the trauma he experiences before his birth. Feel the pain that you cannot save him from. Feel the joy, the pride, the love that he will withstand this pain and still arrive in the world. Follow him throughout the pregnancy, seeing him grow, seeing the strength of a child who will fight even then for his right to live.*

The Feelings Container (My Holding Place for Love)

This is an excellent follow-up to Claiming the Original Child or any other process that discharges pain.

> *Take out your journal, a large sheet of unlined paper and several markers. Close your eyes for a moment. Visualize the place inside of you, a place that has been in you since birth, a container where you hold all the "good stuff"—the love you are capable of giving, the love you have received, your self-esteem, your belief that you are a good man and that you know, feel, and do good things. For years, this is where you have filed away compliments, hugs, accomplishments, intimate relationships, and healthy expressions of sadness, anger, fear, guilt, and joy. Can you find this place in your body? How big is it? How full is it with good stuff? How much room do you have for more? Is the container made to allow the good stuff in? Is it made to hold on to the good stuff that is offered? If you have difficulty finding a place inside where you carry this love, what does that mean? Is the place too small? Is the place too empty? Is the container made of materials that will not hold the love? Give yourself time to feel what you are learning about the holding place for love in your body.*

When you are ready, open your eyes. Answer the following questions in your journal:

> Who gave you positive input for what you did as a child and adolescent?
>
> Who gave you positive input for who you were (I love you simply because you're here)?
>
> As you were doing the visualization, did you find a container of sufficient size? Empty, full, partially full?

Now, take out your large sheet of paper. If you found a container in your mind's eye that is old (as old as you), that is made of solid material, that allows you to let the love in and store it, you are done with this process. Through the remainder of your journey of healing, take time on occasion to look inside and make sure you are feeding the new "good stuff" into your body, your heart, your soul. Many of you found one of two other possibilities. You found some form of container inside of you, but found it to be too small or with too little of the good stuff, or you found no holding place for the love you have received or could receive in your life. Within either of these struggles, you may have connected with one other hazard (one that your Shadow will be reluctant to admit), that you have a hole in your container. Whenever someone, including you, tries to put good stuff in, your sense of worthlessness tells you that you don't deserve it and you simply let it flow through, **or** your insatiable dependence and neediness has caused you to create a container so big that it can never be filled (but you encourage people, especially those closest to you to keep trying). If any of these conflicts fits in your life, don't kick yourself. This simply means that your Holding Place, your Feelings Container, was damaged at some point in life and needs to be repaired, or even recreated.

*Take out the paper and markers, selecting a color of marker that is for you a color of power and strength. Close your eyes again and go into your imagination. Picture a boy, a beautiful, energetic, curious, creative, little boy. Imagine that this boy is open to all the possibilities of life. He is eager to learn, and he is eager for feedback about that process from those around him. You are aware that to be successful in his explorations, this boy will need encouragement, safety rules, knowledge about feelings, a great deal of information, and considerable love. The first task in this process is giving him the initial message that will allow him to create a holding place for all of this good stuff. Look at the boy and say out loud, "I love you simply because you are my child and I will help you in every way I can." See his enthusiasm grow; see the holding place for your love (soon to be his love for himself) begin to develop. As you get a picture of the container inside this boy—the place where he will hold his sense of worth— open your eyes and draw the container. Draw the size, the shape, the colors. Be aware of the material that the container is made of, and note that somewhere on the paper. Can you see through the container, or can it only be seen in certain ways, at certain times, by certain people? Note the answers. Create some method of opening the container to let the good stuff in, a secret method that is known only to you. Make sure that there are no leaks in the container—no secret methods for the good stuff to escape. And now, take another marker, a color that signifies love. Within the container, begin to make two lists, "Doing Strokes," and "Being Strokes." Under the first heading list the talents of this boy. What does he "do" well. List these abilities that he has as he develops through boyhood and adolescence, and becomes the man **you** are today. Under the second heading, list what you like about "who" this boy is, characteristics of him that are not about* *tasks but are validation of his character, skills as he grows from childhood to adolescence to become the man you are today. Finally, close your eyes again. As you breathe and relax, visualize yourself placing this container inside of your body, give it room in your heart for love and affirmation and feelings and safety. Relax, understanding that putting the "good stuff" into this space is the reward for the hard work you have done and the work you are yet to do. Live in this bliss for as long as you wish, returning to the present when you are ready.*

As you continue through your work, return to your Feelings Container, on paper or in your visualizations. Add to the "good stuff." Record your progress on paper, in your heart, and by telling stories of your journey to those who care. **Give new birth to your self-worth!**

Other Losses

There are several other losses that stand alone in my work with men, losses that I have been educated about through specific men who have touched and enlightened my life.

Meeting My Original Parent

My maternal grandfather was adopted after the death of his father. He never spoke of this in my presence, and in a life filled with losses, hardships, irresponsibility, and avoidance, I can only guess at the impact on his life of this particular loss. I have worked with many men and boys who were adopted due to the death of a parent or due to being relinquished by parents after birth. I have been close to men who were abandoned or removed from the biological parents' home due to neglect or abuse, who spent their childhood in foster care, the home of another family member, or group care, never to be adopted. A common view for many of these men has been, "I never knew my biological parents, so they really had no effect on me." Often as the work progresses, the men will come in contact with the impact of abandonment on their lives, how they act out some unseen pain in their adult relationships. Other times, a man will connect with characteristics and idiosyncrasies that he did not share with his adoptive family, or physical traits that could only come from a biological parent, and begin to ponder the impact of his original parents. Some men have struggled for years with their images and feelings about these people and seek healing specifically for this pain.

Some males had a significant amount of information about their biological parents, some had almost no information. Some were raised by loving caregivers who courageously parented a child that they did not give birth to, but some were adopted or placed into neglectful, even abusive families.

If you are this man, you may have sought to learn more about your biological parents (or as we have named them, "bio-dad and bio-mom"); have located and made contact with bio-parents; or have decided that adoptive parents are "mom and dad" and have no desire to look further. In some situations, despite the best efforts, there are simply no adequate records available to inform a man about his origins. If you are adopted, or grew up in foster care or group care, you may have made your peace with your origins. You may have decided that the people who assumed responsibility for you were your "real" parents, and feel no pain with regard to your original parents. For others, there is a critical loss to be grieved, a loss that may have occurred before you have any conscious memory of Mom or Dad.

> *Bret had focused for months in group on his critical father and passive mother, who had adopted him several days after birth. In spite of this work, he continued to feel "different." His ethnic background was different than his adoptive parents, coming from his bio-mom. He had some sketchy information about his mom, almost none about his dad. When asked to focus on his bio-parents, a whole range of information and feelings came to light: the fantasy picture Bret had created of his bio-mom from the limited information available, his questions about who his bio-parents were and why they relinquished him at birth, the direct connection between his vague, ill-defined representation of manhood and his vacuous image of who his bio-dad was. In the months to come, as Bret confronted these images of the biological parents, his grief was immense. As we forged ahead, on the other side of this grief was his acceptance of the gift of life given to him by these young, ill-prepared parents, an embracing of his ethnic origin, and a decision to develop his own sense of masculinity beyond the limitations of his biological **and** adoptive fathers.*

Such is the work undertaken concerning this issue. Rather than describing a specific exercise for this work, I will provide several steps that may be utilized separately, or in combination. The example I will provide will be directed toward an adopted child. It is equally applicable to anyone who was removed from the care of biological parents; simply change the words of adoption to those that fit your life (foster care, children's home, extended family member).

My Questions

Unless you have unusually enlightened adoptive parents who were themselves given adequate information (I honor them if you do), you have carried, perhaps unknowingly, questions regarding your adoption. These questions often fall into several categories: Why did you give me up? Who are you? Who am I? A powerful place to start this piece is by finding your questions. Begin by imagining an opportunity to meet with your bio-parent one time. You may choose to do this by drawing an image of each parent on large paper or by closing your eyes and seeing the picture you have created in your mind's eye. Imagine that this is your chance to ask all the questions of these people that you need to ask; as you think of the questions, simply open your eyes and write them in your journal. Write down any question, no query too small or unanswerable at this time. Over the course of the next several days, return to the exercise to add other questions. Be aware that the act of simply finding your questions may bring up feelings, and seek out support. Express the feelings. Let this work be part of your healing.

Having found the questions, you may proceed in several directions. Some of you will choose the challenge of locating records of your adoption and seeking answers. You may find substantial, partial, or minimal information in your quest; in any event, this effort will facilitate your grief process. You will need to share, process, and grieve what you learned, and what you don't learn. Some of you will choose to do all of your work symbolically, using your questions to enter into your grief in a manner that may be similar to my description below.

> *Greg came to group with his questions in hand, "It's time that I face my parents with my feelings about giving me away. I'll do them one at a time because some of my questions for Mom are different than my questions for Dad." Greg chose to draw a picture of his mom on this night, based on the little he knew about her and what he had imagined her to be when he was a boy. A role-player sat with the picture in front of his face; his role was to reinforce what Greg intellectually knew, but had not confronted—that most of his questions would never be answered by this woman. As Greg began to ask his question "Why did you leave me?", he entered into the full range of emotion he had carried for nearly forty years: his anger, sadness, and shame at being abandoned. He confronted, raged, begged, wept, and began to let go. As he worked, Greg gave up the su-*

perficial forgiveness he had always had for his mother—"I heard she was really young and couldn't take care of me"—for his deeper pain—"I don't care why! I wanted my mom!"—for a deeper level of acceptance, "I know you aren't coming back. It's too late for you to take care of me anyway." Through the weeks that followed, Greg faced his mother several more times with his pain and, ultimately, with a new level of forgiveness. At one point in his work, he adapted The Funeral Fantasy exercise to reclaim what he did get from Mom and to let go of his childhood need for her to finish parenting him. And, in time, Greg gave Dad his day.

My Answers

Each man may choose to claim his birthright, that some of his innate physical, intellectual, and emotional characteristics come from his biological parents. And each man may choose to answer the questions that will never be answered by these parents, or by anyone else.

At some point in this stage of your journey, you will begin to answer the questions you have lived with. After each piece of work in confronting your pain, return to the questions and provide yourself with the answers you have found. Be aware that some of the answers have always been there, but you have been unwilling or unable to accept them. Some of the answers may be "I'll never know," "That's the answer I never wanted to accept," "That's what my adoptive parents told me and I resented them for it." Some of the answers will be catalysts for your anger, your grief, your acceptance of yourself, your biological parents, and your adoptive parents.

Grieving My Abandoned Child

This is an exercise in accountability. For many years I have worked with men and women grieving a decision to give a child up for adoption or to abort a child. When a person is in my office working on these issues, there is no room for the politics of these decisions—I am faced with people who are in pain even if they intellectually believe they made the necessary choice. Over time, I began to realize my sexist attitude had prevented me from seeing that our culture discounts the pain of men in these decisions. Men and boys who conceive and abandon a child are seen as either insignificant in the process, or as ne'er-do-wells who deserve no consideration. I have one man and one woman to thank for being the catalysts of my awakening.

Ben and Cindy were teenagers when they became parents for the first time. In the shame-based response common for

179

those times, Cindy was bundled off to another state, and the couple was separated for some time. The child was given up for adoption. The couple later reunited, married, and parented several more children. Many years later, coming to therapy for seemingly unrelated issues, the couple rekindled the pain of their adolescent loss, and the toll these unresolved feelings had taken on them individually and together. Working with each of them in separate groups, I began to see the deep bond of shame, anger, and sadness that they shared, how their separation during the pregnancy and the loss of their first child had permeated their relationship and become a metaphor for decades of distance. I let myself see, for the first time, that Ben's pain, although different from Cindy's, was just as deep.

I wonder if some of you are reacting to my use of the word *abandonment* when discussing a person's choice to abort or give a child to adoption. Again, this is not a political statement nor a moral judgment. I consciously use this word to validate what I believe many of you who have made these decisions have felt—the pain of making a choice that forever prevents the child from knowing the parent. I use the word *child* in the exercise because I believe that many of you, regardless of political and moral stance, live with the emotion that you abandoned a person, and you have punished yourself based on this belief. Whatever the moral climate of your culture, you made a difficult, painful choice, perhaps under horrendous pressures and circumstances. It's time to heal and move on. If you are a man reading this, still saying, "I don't get it," I say, you lost a chance to father a golden child. You were too young, too poor, too naive, too impulsive. Your pain may not know that yet.

The process for these losses is similar to the example I provided in The Funeral Fantasy. The goals of this work are to release the shame and sadness of the loss, and to release the vision of the child that you carry. (If you are utilizing this exercise you probably have an emotional, perhaps even visual, picture of the child that might have been, or exists in some other place.) The work may be completed in journaling or through visualization. I will describe a letter format. Remember, it's OK to feel as you write, it's OK to stop writing to feel.

Take out your journal. You are preparing to write a letter to the child who never was, the loss you experienced when you conceived a child you did not parent. Give the letter the title you feel. Greet the child with the greeting that seems right to you (you may or may not have a name for the child). In whatever order feels right, make sure to tell the child the following:

Why I let you go.

How I have imagined you would have looked, acted, been.

How I imagine you are today.

My feelings about you.

My feelings about myself for choosing to let you go.

My hopes for your life or after-life.

How losing you has affected my life.

In the case of an adoption, it is time to relinquish care of the child to someone else, to say good-bye, to share any love you feel, to feel the pain of leaving, and to let go: "I give you over to the care of. . . ."

For an abortion I recommend at this point returning to the example in The Funeral Fantasy, and turning the unborn child over to the care of a Higher Power. For some of you, this will be a prelude to seeking self-forgiveness through the grief and through the love of your Higher Power.

For both, remember, it is not the child's responsibility to forgive you for your choice. You must seek this on the other side of your grief, with the support of people you trust who do not condemn you for your decision, and with the support of your Higher Power.

The final stage of this process is to share this work with at least one other person, someone you trust, someone who will be present for you in your grief: your group, your partner, your therapist, your best friend. Let go of your secrets.

There are two issues that I am aware of that affect some of you and need to be addressed within this part of your journey. Many of you did not have a choice in proceeding with an adoption or abortion. Some of you were not even told that you were a prospective father until late in the process. Many of you were young and subject to the influence, perhaps even shaming and coercion, of caregivers when deciding your future. For you, there may be anger work on the people who manipulated you into making decisions that you regret. Perhaps you don't regret the decision but harbor anger about the methods of those who were involved with you through the process: parents, social workers, medical personnel. Return to the previous chapters on anger and prepare yourself to release your anger. Second, you have work to finish with the prospective mother. Look back, did you stand by her through the ordeal? Did you tell her of your pain and listen to hers? How did the relationship end? Did it end? Journal, take a look at this relationship. If you find remorse, sadness, shame, anger, bring it to another man, to your group, to share. Bring a role-player out onto the carpet. Tell this girl or woman what is in your heart. Feel it, let it go. You won't forget, but you can forgive.

I Did Everything I Could

The issue I am about to discuss is fresh in my mind, and in my heart:

Jeff came to his first session recently, concerned about a lack of energy, a lack of motivation, and difficulty concentrating. Upon further questioning, he also described disturbing nightmares and intrusive thoughts during the work day. He told the story of his work as a scuba diver in rescue teams at sport boating events. Several years ago, during a race, he was called away to a nearby swimming area where a young boy had gone under and not come up. He dived, found that the boy had hit his head on a rock, pulled him out under extreme conditions, gave the boy a chance, but the hospital was unsuccessful in their attempt to revive the boy. Since that time, Jeff had relived the rescue in his dreams, night and day.

Some of you may recognize the symptoms often labeled Post-Traumatic Stress Disorder, a disturbance of functioning common to individuals in situations of extreme, life threatening crisis: war, natural disaster, extreme torture, and abuse. This exercise is not intended to resolve PTSD, but directed toward letting go of the self-blame that often accompanies extraordinary efforts in the face of adversity, efforts the person may be out of touch with. Using journaling, visualization, drawing, and any other available tool, the man is directed toward expressing the shame, anger, sadness; the grief.

Through the course of his therapy, Jeff was asked to record his day, and night, dreams. Several themes began to emerge: a deep sense of regret at not being able to tell the boy, or anyone close to him of his efforts to save the child, and an unfocused anger and sadness that the boy had been unsupervised in a dangerous swimming area. Jeff found it difficult to express these feelings, not only because of their depth, but because his training had taught him to cope unemotionally with catastrophe (both as a man and as a rescue worker). Over time he realized that this was not just any rescue, that this accident, this child, had changed his life. We moved from discussion, to writing in session, to writing between sessions. The work culminating in two letters, one to the boy and one to his parents. The letter to the child expressed Jeff's deep sadness that the boy had died, his assurances to the boy (and himself) that he had completed a highly skilled rescue and had done everything within his power to save the boy, and his hope that the boy had gone to a place (Higher Power) of safety. After this letter, Jeff reported a significant decrease in his dreams, a decrease in intrusive thoughts about the accident, and an improvement in his general mood and concentration. The second letter expressed his anger at the parents for leaving the boy unsupervised and his sadness at their loss. After this letter, Jeff reported being able to think about the rescue as a serious incident in his past, rather than feeling as if he was still in the experience.

Your story may be significantly different from Jeff's. Perhaps you struggle with a powerful survivor's guilt from your experience, perhaps you feel you were less courageous than he. Your trauma may have been days, months, years in length, rather than a single occurrence. In any event, it is essential to face your grief with a recognition of the tools you had at the time of the trauma, then heal your shame, sadness, rage, and fear from the perspective of your efforts to survive and your efforts on the behalf of others.

Other Words on Grief Work

Much of my grief work with men is designed on the spot with the brilliance of a man determined to heal, using the expertise I have gathered from mentors, clients, my own experiences, and the benefit of a Higher Power. When I am at my best in using my gifts, I have access to my previous experiences but am not bound by them. Each workshop is designed to move me beyond my limitations. Group after group, men invent unique twists to our labors of love. The sweat is always the same, but each man's style is his own. In this light, I offer a few final guidelines.

Grieving a Life Scene

As you proceed through your work, I believe most of you will arrive at specific memories, or scenes, in your life that stir sadness in your heart. Through the use of techniques already described, it is possible to work through many occurrences that you need to let go of; yes, even those that have plagued you for years, that you have "learned to live with." At times, you will work on the same scene multiple times, reaching and healing deeper levels of pain as you move forward. When you encounter a period or event in your life that brings you sadness, an effective method to set the work up is as follows:

Close your eyes and begin the protocol for imageries. As you are secure in the picture of yourself as an adult, imagine that you are going to come upon the scene from the past that touches your sadness. You will be an observer, at first, seeing the boy or man you were, experiencing the loss in his life. Approach this boy (man), connect with him, and tell us his story out loud.

You may continue within the imagery, or simply connect with the support people who are present, as you move into the sadness. Often, it is extremely helpful to have someone there who will merely reflect your pain and let you know he understands and cares. Tap into your artistic genius; create your own versions of this process.

I Realize That. . . .

I have found that a lot of grief work comes on the heals of confusion. First, I have several favorite responses when a man answers a question about his pain with, "I don't know." These responses are "This is not a test, it's OK to guess," "And if you did know?," "I want you to imagine that you do know." Many of us learned to fall back on "I don't know" responses to avoid our feelings. As you proceed, ask those close to you to challenge your confusion in this way; you will find that underneath this puzzlement lies knowledge and emotion, often sadness. Second, men who are willing to wander around in their discomfort will walk right into their truth, and touch their grief.

Ralph came to work on his rage at his father's sexual acting out. He confronted Dad; he literally beat the pillow up. As his anger subsided, he became confused by a heavy feeling in his throat, something that was "choking" off what he believed was more rage. I moved close to him and said, "You've always been comfortable being angry at Dad?" "Yes." "If what you're choking down is more than anger, what are the words you need to say to Dad?" "I don't know." "And if you did know?" Ralph hesitated and said, "I'm so confused. I've been angry and blamed you for ruining my life, . . . and I did the same things you did." On the heels of this disclosure, Ralph fell back into the arms of the man holding him and wept. Between deep moans of sadness he admitted his sexual acting out, the promises he made to himself as a young man that he would never be like his father (he had convinced himself that he was not because his sexual behavior had been with men), and finally, his deep desire for his father's love and attention.

As he closed this piece of work, Ralph shared, "I realized that
I love my dad. I wanted to believe he loved me, and ultimately,
the sex seemed like the only connection we had."

I'm Not a Child Anymore

"Inner Child" work can get stuck in the Child, a focus on healing and nurturing the young child we were without growing that child up and healing adolescent and adult traumas. Pain does not stop at puberty; for some of us, it intensified. My first job as a social worker was, at twenty-one, in a state institution on a locked unit with adolescent boys and girls. I was still an adolescent! I am grateful to these kids and my colleagues for many things, but especially for several essential particles of information about adolescence:

> Our culture teaches parents to intensely dislike, envy, and be terrified of their adolescents.
>
> Many helping professionals, even with their training, dislike, envy and are terrified of adolescents.
>
> Points one and two are the result of very few of us having resolved our adolescent trauma and very few of us being properly initiated into adulthood by elders. Adolescence is the coalescing of unfulfilled childhood need and the random attack of the physical, social, emotional, and cultural aspects of puberty.

Adolescence

I offer no additional exercises to focus on the adolescent stage of your life, many of the processes already described will fit well at any stage of your journey. I simply propose that as you utilize the processes in this chapter, you not forget the pain of your adolescence. I do not refer only to specific traumas that some of you will recall from that time, such as a continuation of family abuse. I am also pointing to resolution of adolescence as the beginning of full blown acting out of your earlier trauma (adolescence is when most addictions begin to flower). I am also referring to this stage of life in and of itself. In preteenage and teenage years, most of us were introduced to the Shadow Initiation rituals that would replace the lack of true masculine initiation in our lives: alcohol, drugs, sex, gangs.

A vital step in my personal healing work was the ages of fourteen and fifteen. The most serious external trauma at this point had been moving to another state after my sophomore year. Frankly, we had moved before and on the pain scale, although it was a challenging experience, it was far from a life-threatening psychological event. My work was not primarily about these life events or significant others but about my internal response to the external me. I, along with my friend, Mike, was the shortest kid in school, again. Along with this perceived disability, I had the dubious distinction for a boy in a small, rural community of being very smart. To my knowledge, I was the last boy in my class to reach puberty, and I was already more than a little obsessed with the female body. At this age, with these struggles, I first turned to alcohol, to various types of obsessive thinking, and to what I later came to see as a chronic, low-level depression masked by my intelligence, wit, and All-American Boy act. Some of my most beneficial work has been on this boy. I have grieved my intense anger at that part of myself (my shame). I have marveled at his (my) energy, courage, persistence. I have forgiven my body. Most important, this work allowed me to look in the mirror and see that I am no longer that boy—I am a man. It's a strange feeling to admire my crow's-feet, to realize that I grew to five foot ten inches, that I'm hairy, that rather than scrawny, I could stand to lose a couple of pounds. In this work, I have also found much of my sexual recovery.

I often find men who are stuck again after completing major work on themselves. More and more I am aware of these men having moved up to, but not through, their adolescent issues. Unlike our media suggest, I don't believe most of our lovers, spouses, and friends are hungering for another terminally adolescent male in their lives. **Don't neglect this stage of your journey.**

Adulthood

Several of the examples I have already given are about blows to the adult, not child, psyche. The processes that are described throughout this text are as available to your adult grief as to your little boy. The work you are doing in healing past trauma gives you a road map for dealing with the distress that will continue to press upon you at other times in your life. I have been close to men who have utilized most of these processes to concentrate on healing the inner man, not the inner child: war experiences; loss of a son, daughter, spouse, lover; death of a friend being physically or sexually assaulted; retirement; and catastrophic loss. I have used these skills over and over, to heal my fear after my wife, DiAnne, suffered a life-threatening illness, to grieve the near loss of DiAnne in her heroic and life-threatening delivery of our son, to grieve the day of separation from my first wife and my beautiful daughters.

My Remorse

A part of letting go of past pain and living a life of integrity is grief work on the choices we have made as an adult, the choices that have damaged others, the ways we have damaged ourselves. In the introduction of the book I provided the term, "self-generated shame." I developed this term in response to a paradox I have often seen and heard in my work with men and women. The paradox sounds something like this, "I'm angry, sad, hurt, scared, and ashamed because of what my parents did to me. They are responsible for hurting me and choosing not to change!" At some point later in therapy, the same person often verbalizes, "It's not my fault I hurt (whomever); I wasn't given what I needed growing up to be a better . . . (father, husband, lover, man)." This becomes a convenient, allegedly therapeutic, loop: my parents are responsible for their behaviors, regardless of their childhood journeys, but I am not responsible for my behaviors **because** of my childhood journey. A second, equally popular, paradox is, "I've already forgiven my parents. They both had a rough childhood and did the best that they could with what they had." This is often followed soon afterward by, "I don't know why . . . (whomever) can't just get over what happened. I did. I've done my work on this. I haven't done it again, and I'm ready to move on. If he or she isn't, then that's their problem."

In response to these, I offer an alternative to truly dislodge the pain of your hurtful and abusive choices, an alternative to superficial forgiveness work, an alternative to superficial amends work to people you have hurt. It is a part of the journey that is designed to heal the self-generated shame, what I call remorse work. Remorse work is the part of grieving that allows me to look at how I took the information I was taught as a child and adolescent, interpreted it, and put it to work in my life, often with positive and often with disastrous results. This grief moves me beyond being a victim of my childhood. It moves me into knowing that I am an intelligent, intuitive, breathing being who took information in, made choices about the information, and acted those decisions out over and over in my life, with varying levels of success for myself and others. This is grief work about *accountability, responsibility, and integrity,* three words that must be in the vocabulary and behavior of every successful man.

The Twelve-Steps of recovery with which many of you are quite familiar include taking a fearless moral inventory and making amends, directly to people where this is safe and appropriate, and symbolically when otherwise necessary. For many men, this is remorse work, the healing of shame and pain associated with damaging others through the expression of regret. The work I am describing is an extension of that process, taking the work to the deepest level of emotion possible in an effort to heal the external damage and the internal wounds to your mind, heart, and spirit. This process may be utilized in letters, visualization, role-play—and for some men, meeting the person that sustained the damage of your behavior. In describing this work, I take literary license and combine the stories of several men, each of whom used pieces of this process, and who, in combination, provide a comprehensive view of healing the inner adult.

Jay began to talk in group about a different kind of pain. "I have worked on my father's violence, my mother's neglect, the molesting by the neighbor boy, and I'm really hurting about something else. I'm looking around and seeing for the first time the destruction I've left in my path: how I've hurt my wife, my kids, and people whose names I don't even remember. Sure, I've apologized to as many of these people as I can, and I've changed a lot, but there's something missing." As the work proceeded, Jay decided the "something" that was missing wasn't missing at all. There was something still sitting in his body, a pain that came up not when he thought of his parents, but when he thought of his verbal abuse of others, his extramarital affairs, his workaholism. Even as he identified the nature of the pain, Jay closed his eyes, found it in his body and began to cry "It's like a dark hole in my heart that I can't fill." When challenged to put the love of the men into the hole Jay responded, "I can't. I don't deserve it." For Jay, teaching the little boy inside of him that he was a good kid did not heal the damage inflicted on himself, and others, by himself since childhood.

From this pain came a new decision. It was time for Jay to do the work of accountability and self-forgiveness for his adult years. In the course of the next several months, Jay utilized a number of processes to heal, beginning with a letter to his wife.

This letter contained several components:

These are the things I know I have done that harmed you.
*These are the words I have to accept responsibility for my
    actions (complete with an admission of how I have tried to
    justify and avoid accountability in the past).*
These are my feelings of sadness and remorse.
*This is what I have done and will do to insure that I will not
    repeat these mistakes.*
*From the letter flowed additional work for Jay. He read the
    letter in group to a man who role-played his wife.* **He** *role-*

played his wife and listened to the letter as read by a man who role-played him. Finally, he had the opportunity to read the final letter directly to his wife and hear her response. Each step of this exercise brought tears, new levels of insight, and changes in the letter.

Jay repeated the process of expressing his remorse with each of his children, all of whom were now adults. He even adapted the exercise to own how he had mistreated his mother in her old age as "payback" for his childhood by reading a letter to his mother as she lay in bed in a nursing home, unable to respond. At each point in the work, Jay was taken back to the hole in his heart and encouraged to release the grief, filling the hole with the colors of acceptance, accountability, and love.

One evening, as he checked out of the group, Jay shared, "I realize there's one more piece, and I'm not sure how to finish it. I feel like I owe an amends to the women of the world . . . the ones I used in my attempt to feel better, and the one's I would have used if I hadn't changed. I don't even remember the names of all the women I've been with. I'm not sure where to go with this." Jay agreed, that in some ways he had dishonored the Feminine, and that by dishonoring so many women, he had ultimately dishonored himself. Jay was assigned to finish the sentence, "Women are . . . " in as many ways as he could, from the perspective of his Shadow, and return to group. Upon his return, he was asked to trust the group process and enter into work to heal the gender shame he had lived with and passed on in his relationships. He was instructed to select group members to role-play several of the specific women he had used and manipulated, with the remaining members (except one man to hold Jay) role-playing Woman, the gender. Each Shadow message about women that Jay had written in his journal he then owned in the symbolic presence of the women he had harmed. As he spoke, the rage, the shame, the blame of his childhood messages about women was replaced by the remorse and deep sadness that he felt as he reviewed his treatment of the Feminine in the presence of other men. (When this work takes place in any men's group, there are a lot of heads nodding the affirmative. Many of us must do this man's work to fully heal.) Finally, he was asked to feel the reality that the impact he had had on many of these women could only be healed symbolically; the pain he had caused could not be repaired directly. Through

189

this aspect of the process, Jay touched an awareness that is often a cornerstone of healing adult pain. **Those I harmed are often out of my life. I can only heal my shame and change my life. I will live knowing little about my ongoing impact on the lives of those people that I no longer have contact with.**

Jay chose several processes to bring closure to this portion of his healing. In much the way as he had written letters to his family, he wrote a letter to himself, a letter that spoke of the loss in his life due to his disrespect of the Feminine and of his continuing commitment to change. In group, this letter was read to him by another man, role-playing his Shadow self, and as he wept, he sank into the arms of a Good Father who told him it was time to let go, to heal, to love the best parts of the Feminine in women and in himself. In a final gesture of release, Jay requested time to complete a ceremony the following week. As we stood in the backyard at my office, Jay instructed us to circle around a small fire. He produced the Shadow messages he had written, each on a separate piece of paper. Stepping to the fire, he spoke each message a final time, releasing each to the fire and to his Higher Power, and speaking one sentence of new awareness that he now chose to live.

As I wrote this piece, I wondered if someone would read and say, "Come on, that's a lot of hoops to jump through for this issue." Yes, it is. And many men have done so. This example is made up of the work of several men not to artificially add steps to the process, but because the stories of so many men flashed in my mind as I prepared to write this section. Each man within this story took months and completed numerous tasks to heal his pain. In this example is held all the essential elements of grief work: a safe container of other pilgrims, ownership of the behaviors and feelings, significant emotional and at times physical labor expended to expose the wound, and positive, loving ritual healing.

If this work speaks to you, I offer several cautions. You may find it difficult to successfully complete this part of your endeavor without first doing the work that holds accountable those who have harmed you. This work can contain powerful risk among a group of men. I have often said to men, "As shaming as it can be to share your stories of being victimized with other men, some of you will find even greater shame in sharing how you have victimized others." In this work, men will disclose sexual abuse of others, other violence against others, illegal activities, past offenses that often run counter to the image the man has created in the eyes of the other men. I have heard stories of embezzlement, gay bashing, date rape, murder, war violence, and all manner of sexual acting out. The sweat of men in remorse work can truly test the mettle of a support or therapy group. There must be a place for this work. A man who heals what was done to him and does not heal what he has done to others is half the man he can become.

No More Secrets

Secrets are shame-based. To release secrets is to grieve your hidden self, to face, accept, and move beyond your Shadow. This is a simple process. Take out your journal. Make a list of all the secrets that you have about yourself and your life that you have not shared, or have shared in such a way that a part of you still feels as if the information is a secret. You may choose to divide the secrets into categories: sexual, childhood, adulthood, family, financial, whatever feels right to you. Go to a mirror, look yourself in the eyes, and state, "Before I leave (therapy, my mens group, the retreat this weekend, this relationship, etc.) I will disclose this from my secret list." Make a commitment to yourself to disclose all secrets to some person or persons you trust before your life's journey is complete. Beware of not only keeping secrets, but what I call "Secret Piecemealing," giving bits and pieces of your secrets (our shame) to many people, but letting no one know all. I encourage each of you to have at least one man and one woman who knows you as you really are, who knows your story as you know it. Unconditional friendship is a mighty sword in shame killing. Through the course of your work, try going to the mirror with your list of secrets. Look yourself in the eyes and say, "The truth about my secrets is . . . " and read each of the secrets out loud to yourself. Own them as yours, feel the pain, express your grief.

As you proceed through your work, return to the list occasionally. Are there secrets you neglected to write? What secrets have you disclosed and healed? Cross them off the list.

When you have done the work that crosses every secret off your list, design a closure ceremony in the presence of trusted others, to release all secrets to the universe, to Mother Earth, to Father Sky, to God, to whomever or whatever you see fit. Many men have found sending the secrets down river or burning and burying the ashes to be useful parts of their ceremony.

More About Adult Trauma

Pain, tragedy, and even victimization does not necessarily stop at childhood. Do not discount the adaptability of many of the grief processes you have used for childhood pain to the traumas of adulthood:

deaths; illnesses; family tragedies; physical, emotional, and sexual upheaval in your adult years. Within the safe container of my therapy and my own support groups, men have healed divorce, deaths of family and friends, the pain of sexual dysfunction, career turbulence, and the myriad of trials that many of us face, even as initiated, mature men of spirit. I refer you to the many rituals already described in healing your adult pain, many of which are adaptable to any age and developmental stage. Having developed advanced healing skills from work on early life trauma, many of you have discovered a vital tenet for future recovery: *If I give myself permission to feel and heal as I move through a life trauma, I will not create another hidden reservoir of pain.*

A fitting close to this section is a story of a man who changed my life several summers ago in the space of twenty-four hours. In 1993 I received a request to go to Kansas City to speak on male grief at a conference for an organization devoted to family members of murder and suicide victims. My personal life has been closely touched twice by suicides, and numerous times in my professional work by murders and near-suicide. But the most intriguing, and frightening, aspect of the request was that I would make my presentation with a gentleman I did not know, a man who was the father of a murder victim who presented a very personal perspective on a man and his grief. I arranged to meet my co-presenter the evening before our workshop. Upon my arrival, we expressed our mutual doubts and fears about working together, which did little to alleviate my concerns, and we briefly reviewed the content of our respective speeches. I went to bed with great unrest, totally unprepared for what the next day would bring.

In the morning I was greeted warmly by seventy-five Moms, Dads, crisis counselors, and social workers, hungry for information and discussion on the struggles of men in pain. As Don began to speak, I heard the story of Everyman: a man, a father who had worked and provided for his family, a man who avoided his feelings, a man who knew the feeling of anger well and found most other emotions strangers. As he pressed forward, I learned of one event and one quality that made this man different from many men his age (over 50). He was a man who had to face the totally unexpected, the murder of his daughter. He then used this enormous tragedy as an opportunity to read every book on men's issues—to find his fear, sadness, shame, humor, and hope—to commit his time and energy to a mission of helping other men to see how unprepared we are as a gender for the tremendous adult calamities that often befall us.

Through the day, I met some of the most amazing people, and I received the gift of watching and hearing about the best parts of the masculine grief process. I spoke with men whose grief was a call to action: visits to emergency rooms and funeral homes, phone lines in their homes dedicated to crisis intervention, hours and hours of court watch. And I watched Don, a man who had learned to blend his traditional sense of manhood with the teachings of a new way, a healing road of tears, touch, rage and tenderness. Together, we faced our fears and insecurities and gave one powerful workshop that day!

Good Grief

I have been reminded by the recent move of a friend that the intensity of my sadness is in direct proportion to the intensity of my love for this man. As I revisit my passion for life and people through the work I am describing in these pages, I am brought to tears of joy and sadness when: my friends go away, when my son sings in his first pre-school program, when my daughters give me a beautiful picture of their growth in their annual dance recital, when watching my wife reminds me of the illness that might have taken her away. These are the tears that come not from the pain of abuse, neglect or absence, but the tears that come from having *loved*. Like many of the traumas you will work through, this grief is in the memory of what was, and may not be again. A men's retreat leader helped me see this gift. I have heard him say more than once that he is both joyful and sad at the end of a retreat because this group of men will never again exist in exactly this configuration. In Good Grief, we have memories to hold on to.

Take your journal out. Close your eyes for a moment. As you prepare for this exercise, go into your heart. Assume the stance of a man in touch with whatever feelings become available to you. This is a time to cry, to smile, to remember. Review in your mind's eye the past year of your life. Select one memory from this year, one positive memory. If this has been a particularly difficult year, one with seemingly no positive memories, dig deeper for a memory, maybe a moment. Continue this process. Go to last year and recall a positive event, situation, person, moment in your life. As you recall last year, open your eyes. On the left side of a page in your journal, write the age you are this year and on the right side make a note of the memory. Below this, write your age last year and on the right side, the memory. Continue this process in the fashion that feels right to you, going back one year at a time and recapturing a positive memory for each year, as far back as your consciousness will take you. You may choose to go all the way to your first memory before writing more, or you may choose to alternate remembering and writing. The key is not to make an exact written record but to locate the memories. As you reach periods fraught with trauma, concentrate, look closely for the moment, the event, the person, that brings you a positive feeling in that time of strife. (Many of you focused so deeply on the trauma that you have become unaware of wonderful events and people in your life during these times.) Let yourself feel the emotions that come up as you review. If you begin to connect with other positive memories from a certain year, go with it, remember them all. If you begin to reconnect with trauma about that year, or that person, let it flow through you and refocus on the positive. Take as much time as you need to complete this process. A few days after this process, take this work to someone you trust and share the Good Grief and make a commitment to yourself to periodically review what's good in your life.

For many men, tears will accompany this assignment. These tears of joy and sadness have come from the man who reconnected with the memory of the neighbor who took time with him when his father wouldn't, the tears of the man who remembered moving away from his childhood neighborhood of safety and fun, the literally hundreds of men who recaptured loving memories about parents whom they had recently only remembered as abusive or absent. We will talk again about Good Grief in the chapter on the father-child relationship. You may or may not find tears in these chapters, but at the very least, I hope you find smiles and laughter. As we say in group, "We do joy here, too!"

A Few Final Words on Grief

I have struggled to complete this chapter in the midst of some of my own grief work and in the midst of my combined desire to tell all I know with the reality that I find new possibilities in grief work almost daily. I remind myself that offering just one more process is not the key to this text. My hope is that you have found within these pages an understanding of *masculine* grief and that, through some of the exercises, you have created for yourself a road map for healing sadness. Return to this chapter time and again, reuse the same processes, reinvent new versions of those that speak to you, and share what you find with others.

7: More on Fathering, Sexuality, and Honoring

Playing "guys"
Wrestling
Superheroes
Water slide

Juice boxes
Ice cream
Oranges, peeled
Not sliced

Turtle
Piranha
T-Rex
Great White Shark

Weigh-ins
Vitamins
Races
Kid in flight

You're a better man than me
He said

I didn't want to be better . . .
OK . . . a lie . . . I did
But . . .
First, I wanted to be you
Then, better than
Now . . .
Part of you

Part of me
Part of he
Or she
Each to their own
Each better than before

"Thant shue dad"

"The Grateful Child"
Chris Frey, 1996

The topics of fathering and sexuality have been addressed at length throughout this book, and many of the processes for healing wounds have been adapted to these issues. In this chapter, I will briefly offer several other healing activities specific to these essentials of life. Although I do not include all available processes on these issues, these are activities directed toward your transition from healing past trauma into the practice of that healing in your life today. As you move through these exercises, prepare yourself for the final chapter that will ask you to focus on bringing your new perspective into the lives of children, partners, friends, and other family. In the section on fathering, I offer a detailed process for honoring of the father energy. The section on sexuality provides exercises that I often use to open honest, healing discussion about healthy sexuality. I will close with a brief section on group discussion, and finally about how the best parts of our past can become our future, the honoring of Elders and Mentors.

Real Dad, Ideal Dad

This process can be utilized at many levels in your work, uncovering wounds, identifying specific pieces of healing work, stimulating grief, fear, anger and shame, even as an honoring of fathers and their sons. This is a process with multiple steps. The Ideal Dad component can be completed individually; the Real Dad component necessitates having access to at least two other men. In workshops we often lead the completion of the entire module; however, you will see that each section may be used on its own. This process works in men's and women's workshops with equal power. As always, use what fits and adapt the rest.

Ideal Dad

Close your eyes and prepare yourself for visualization as you have learned . . . breath and relax. See a picture of yourself as you are today, walking to a place, a safe place of your creation. This may be a place that actually exists in your memory, a meadow, a mountain, the water, or it may be a place that exists in your imagination. See the colors, smell the air, feel the sensations offered by this safe space. As you walk into this place, you see another person in the distance. As you draw closer you see that the person is a man, a man you sense is wise, kind, loving, strong, and powerful. As you approach him, stopping at the distance you feel safe, you see that he is the Ideal Father, the man who has what you have always needed, a man who knows the answers to your questions. He asks you to sit with him. As you look at him, you become aware of the teaching he offers. He begins to share what he knows; what you have always needed to know. What does the Ideal Father teach you about:

- *Men*
- *Women*
- *Children*
- *Love*
- *Work*
- *Play*
- *Sex*

- *Courage*
- *Alcohol and Drugs*
- *Anger*
- *Fear*
- *Sadness*
- *Shame*
- *Marriage*

- *Honesty*
- *Family*
- *Success*
- *Money*
- *Fathering*
- *Closeness*
- *Belonging*

What does the Ideal Father want you to know about yourself? What are his hopes and dreams for your life, for the development of your manhood?

Now, you hear the Ideal Father begin to tell you about his knowledge of your strengths, the best parts of who you are and what you can do. Listen and take in what he gives you. The Ideal Father also is here to challenge you. With love, he begins to tell you of your Shadow. What does he teach you about your dark side, what you must face and grow beyond to move closer to who you need to be?

It is your time to talk (take as much time in this portion of the process as you need). You ask all the questions you always wanted to ask a father but did not. Ask him now and hear his answers.

Finally, it is time to go. As you prepare to leave, become aware of everything you have learned today, of the love and blessing you have received. You stand, the Ideal Father stands. In whatever fashion feels right, share a closing with him: a touch, a hug, a look, a word. As you receive this closing gesture, open your heart and place the Ideal Father into the place in your heart where you will hold him forever. You turn to walk away; let yourself feel whatever comes up. As you move into the distance, you look over your shoulder and see that the Ideal Father is gone from that place. He is now in your heart. You silently move away, returning to this place, to this time in the present, preparing yourself as you have learned to return from this visualization.

Journaling

Take out your journal and write whatever comes up from the imagery, the information you received on life issues, the answers to your questions, the emotions you experienced throughout your contact with the Ideal Father, and where you are at now. Write freely, don't try to be organized or make sense.

Sharing (if done with other men)

We ask men to maintain silence at this point in the process. We would not want you to talk away the gifts you have just received. One exception is when a man has reached a deep level of emotion or he needs support and connection with other men over a specific piece of work. Even in this situation, we will attempt to minimize the number of words and simply bring over a live Ideal Dad image (in the body of another man in the workshop) to listen, make contact with, perhaps hold the man doing the work.

Real Dad

This portion of the process calls for men to represent father images. All other men participating in the process line up with the following instructions. You have just had the opportunity to meet, learn from and bond with the father that you've always wanted. You will now have this image for the rest of your life. Here's the catch: you didn't get to pick your real father. Much of your life has been about facing the father you actually got, measuring up, recovering from, connecting with. You will now be faced with a reality in your life, a mixed blessing—dad will choose you. Before you, stand the Real Fathers. Each of you will be chosen as a son by a man who will use his criteria for selection. You have no input about who chooses you, when you are chosen, or why you are chosen by this man. When he chooses you, you must go with him and do as he says, It is time to look at the father you got. (Men are now selected by the Real Dads, usually volunteer "mentors" who have been through these healing processes themselves. Each mentor uses whatever criteria speaks to him to make his selection and firmly instructs his "sons" to follow him to a private corner of the work space.)

You will be looking at your father's Gold and at his Shadow; the parts of him that were loving gifts to you, the parts that he avoided or denied which he inflicted on you, and how you used his gifts and recycled his pain as your own. Begin by closing your eyes and preparing for imagery as you have learned.

See yourself as you are today, and begin to return to the safe place that you have already created in your imagination, a place that actually exists or a place only in your mind's eye. As you walk back to this place, you see another figure in the distance. As you approach, you realize it is your real father. (Men who never met their bio-dads will have a picture of how they imagined their real father, men with multiple father figures may repeat this exercise on several occasions.) Stop at the distance that feels safe for you and greet him. Listen to his response. You realize that you are in this place to gain focus on what you received from your father, as a child, as an adolescent, as an adult. He sits and you sit across from him. You become aware that he is going to review all that he taught you, in his words, his actions, his inaction, his presence, his absence. What did your Real Dad teach you about:

• *Men*	• *Courage*	• *Honesty*
• *Women*	• *Alcohol and Drugs*	• *Family*
• *Children*	• *Anger*	• *Success*
• *Love*	• *Fear*	• *Money*
• *Work*	• *Sad*	• *Fathering*
• *Play*	• *Shame*	• *Closeness*
• *Sex*	• *Marriage*	• *Belonging*

What did Dad teach you about you? What were his hopes and dreams for his own life, for your life?

It is your time to ask Dad all the questions you have needed to ask. Take as much time as you need. Ask all of your questions. Listen carefully to his answers. Does he answer at all? Are his answers complete; are they what you need, what you hoped to hear?

Finally, it is time for you to leave. Let yourself feel whatever comes up as you prepare to leave your dad. Be aware of what answers and blessings you received. Be aware of the sense of incompletion, the knowledge that Dad doesn't have all of what you need—he never did. As you prepare to leave, give your good-bye in whatever manner feels OK to

you. Can he receive your good-bye? Can you give him what
you most want to give? Turn and begin to walk away, back to
this place and time. As you walk away, you take a final look
over your shoulder and see that Dad is gone. You carry in
*your hands all you learned from him today. These are **your***
***gifts, this is **your** baggage. Continue to return to this time and*
this place, using the skills you have learned. When you are
ready, open your eyes.

Each man now faces his Real Dad figure (the mentor). Speaking from his heart, the Real Dad will give his sons the reality of his limitations in the following way:

> *I cannot be everything you want me to be because. . . .*
> *The limitations of what I can tell you about becoming a*
> *man are. . . .*
> *I cannot carry your baggage, even that created by the ways I*
> *wounded you, because. . . .*

Each man, in turn, now shares with Real Dad his truth about what I call The Waiting, my waiting for Dad to give me the rest of the information about manhood, my waiting to grow up, my waiting for Dad to finish helping me grow up. **Tell Dad what you are waiting for.** Real Dad answers each man from his heart in the following manner:

> *I don't have what you're waiting for because. . . . (Let yourself*
> *feel what comes up as Dad leaves you to wait for what will*
> *never occur; or decides to move on from The Waiting.)*

You are excused by Dad. He has given you everything you will get from him this day. Return to the circle of men (the Dads leave).

Journaling

Write about what you learned from the entire process: waiting to be selected by a Real Dad, how you felt about who selected you, what you learned from the imagery and from your Real Dad figure, with a particular focus in mind. Be aware of the gap between what you wanted from your Ideal Dad and what you perceive you got from your Real Dad. This is your Father Wound, your Father Hunger. Healing the feelings that arise from living in this gap is a powerful part of your journey.

Sharing

After journaling and de-roleing the Real Dad figures, take time to discuss with the circle of men, the role-players, and the facilitators what direction this process gives you in your work, what gifts you received from your Ideal Dad that will strengthen you for the work. Share from the heart. Avoid giving details of the images. Focus on what you learned, what you feel, what you will do with the information. Share how this information will affect your relationships with your own children and the children of other men. Be specific and make a commitment to check-in with the men in group about your success in these matters and the responses of those around you.

Sexuality

I spend a great deal of healing energy in my practice on sexual abuse recovery, sexual addiction, sexual function difficulties, and general sexual confusion. Although this is not a book on human sexuality, many of you will use the processes contained in these chapters to heal your sexual self physically, emotionally, and spiritually. In keeping with this focus, I offer exercises that I have found useful in group.

Blaming the Child

It is common knowledge that most men who are sexually assaulted as children take on the guilt and shame of the perpetrator. One tool I recommend in working through this issue is the worksheet titled "It's Not Your Fault" in my book, *Double Jeopardy* (Islewest Publishing, 1994). This is an exercise written for adolescents but applicable for any man working on this wound. Additionally, men's group can assist in this recovery.

The Real Child

List the qualities of greater power that the perpetrator(s) possessed, including age, size, life and sexual experience, family relationship, intelligence, and trust. Pick a role-player to be the perpetrator. Sit in front of him or her and state: "I blame myself because . . . (finish the sentence)." Then listen to the perpetrator give the list of how he or she was more powerful than you at that point in life: "You couldn't stop me because . . . (give the list)." Repeat this interchange until you begin to get a different sense of the power differential that *was* in place. At the end, look at the perpetrator and state: "This is not (the years of the abuse), this is . . . (the current year), and you will never abuse me again." *If you repeat that statement with power, this may be the entry point to a major piece of healing anger work.*

Ask a man to role-play the perpetrator and have him stand on the carpet. If your fear is strong, position men you trust in front of the perpetrator, giving you the knowledge that symbolically these men that care about you could and would prevent him from hurting you. Be aware that if you feel a strong need for men in safety positions today, there is no way you could have stopped this perpetrator as a child or adolescent. If putting men out as support and safety eases your fear, go to the next stage. Moving onto the carpet go to a place in front of the perpetrator. Put yourself in the body position that indicates the size you were the *first time* the abuse took place (by kneeling down and making other shifts in your body; get yourself as close as possible physically to the size you were at the time of the abuse). Look up to the offender and make contact with the difference in size, age, and other characteristics that you *know* put this person in a position of power over you. Again, if you are ready to do anger work, get the perpetrator down from his or her position of physical superiority with your anger. *You Can Do It!*

Some of you will, even after these processes, struggle with feelings of self-blame:

> *"But I eventually was old enough and big enough to stop him, and still didn't!"*
>
> *"But I was the oldest one in the house and should have been able to protect my brother and sister."*

The next stage is for you. Ask someone to role-play You as you were the first time the abuse occurred. Observe the child you were as he describes why he couldn't stop the perpetrator. Let yourself feel whatever comes up and see how much you still blame this child. If you still feel blame, look at the child and listen as he tells you what it has been like to both be the victim of abuse and blamed for the actions of the perpetrator. Listen as he describes how it feels to have your Adult blame your Child. Take this in and feel it. Now have the child assume the position of his age just after the abuse stopped. It is your time to explain to him why it is not his fault and to begin to forgive him. Own the ways that you have shamed and abused yourself for the actions that another person is truly accountable for. Again, making contact with these insights may take you to your anger. Go To It Now!

In addition to finding your anger in the process, many of you will connect with the sudden grief that often comes from the "Aha" experience of "It really wasn't my fault." This realization can bring to the surface a flood of grief about the shame, the self-blame, and the defensive reactions to those who knew before you did that you were not at fault. Go with the feelings. Collect your support, and fall into the arms of men and women who love you. Be nurtured in your sadness, grief, the lost time and opportunities. And then, put that boy you were in front of you and make amends for blaming and shaming him. Let him know what your commitments are to his safety and growth now that you see his truth.

Note: Forgiving you child may lead you to a deeper understanding of others you have abused. Beware that if you are a survivor and perpetrator, holding the adult accountable will lead to holding your Adult accountable.

What I Didn't Get to Talk About

I discovered an interesting phenomenon among clients that is best described by a statement I have often said in sessions. "It amazes me that many of us learn to talk about sexual trauma with relative ease. Many of us have engaged in lots and lots of sex in lots and lots of ways with lots and lots of people, and what I find most folks have the most difficult time talking about is nonabusive sex or sex in our present-day lives." Getting good sexual information can be extremely risky: for men who operate off any of the following rules:

> *Guys are just supposed to know this stuff.*
> *Sex is dirty and I just shouldn't talk about it.*
> *It's OK to do anything I can get away with as long as I don't talk about it.*
> *Everybody except me probably already knows this stuff.*
> *I can't let anyone know I . . . (struggle with impotence or ejaculatory control, have basic questions, feel I can't satisfy my partner or myself); real men don't have those problems.*
> *Any other rule you operate from that keeps you from sharing who you are and what you struggle with.*

Men often tell me that some of our most useful group sessions are group discussions of the many issues that men avoid. The following simple processes are offered in this light.

Ten Questions

The instructions for this activity are simple: go home this week and write down the ten questions about (sex or any other topic) that you have never gotten answered. Bring them next week and we will discuss them. Upon returning, the group may choose to allow each man to ask one question at a time. We may take pieces of paper and throw the questions in the middle of the room, with each man selecting one at a time to pose to the group, or a man may go through his entire list one question at a time. The questions may be biological (issues of penis size, male and female orgasms), relational (questions not only about the act of being sexual, but about romance, what men and women really want and like), dating, romance, the differences between men and women, safe sex issues, how to put sex back in your life after a period of abstinence (particularly for sexual addicts, abuse survivors, and divorced men), how to deal with sex if married to an abuse survivor, and much more. Any question can be asked. Any man can offer an opinion with regard to an answer.

In this exercise, I am often given the opportunity to offer quality information as a result of my training and years as a therapist (and also find the questions I still seek answers for). This process often brings to light concerns that can be dealt with by referring the man to certain literature on the subject. There is excellent information available not only on the mechanics of sex, but also on healing sexual/erotic dysfunction and on learning to integrate the erotic aspects of sex with intimacy, sensuality, communication, and romance. In addition, these discussions have no absolute answers to many of the questions, and men begin to see that many of these issues are about what is positive, loving, and stimulating for *different* men and *different* partners.

This non-shaming, open discussion emphasizes the importance of non-shaming, open communication with partners and with yourself. There are many benefits to breaking the taboo against open exchange between men on these topics. A little good information can prevent a lot of bad experiences. We often identify and correct bad information that may have been directing a man's sexual behavior for years. Men commit to begin more open communication with their partners and to educate their children. Shame-based information is corrected. Acquiring knowledge about basic tools can immediately improve the quality of sexual relationships. Participants have a greater awareness and non-shaming understanding of the differences and similarities between men and women. Finally, this exercise always reminds me that not all of the healing must be hard-fought, gut-level confrontation of past trauma. Sometimes men simply get a new piece of information and say, "Cool, I can use that right now!"

Ten More Questions

This process is a slightly different version of what you have just read and is directed at going to a level that includes past trauma. Take out your journal and write down the ten destructive pieces of sexual information you received that still affect you. These may include issues of sexual trauma but often will also highlight poor or shaming sexual education from a variety of sources, along with impaired decisions that you may have made based on the information you had. Bring this list to group or to men you trust. The list can be shared using one of the methods offered in the previous process. This exercise provides all of the possibilities described in Ten Questions, with one addition: many of you will find direction in healing sexual trauma from this list. From this work will bloom a focus on the who, what and when of some of your sexual misinformation.

> *Ray knew that he had been molested by his mother. He had confronted and healed this pain in his life, but he still carried a deep shame about being sexual without a clear understanding of the origin. During his journaling on destructive sexual information, he came upon a particular trusted priest, who deeply shamed him about early sexual behavior. Ray felt the loss of trust. He had specifically chosen to disclose to this man because of his trust and admiration, and he carried the belief that God, in the form of this clergyman, had condemned him to a life sentence of sexual shame. In his shame work, Ray confronted the specific messages given to him by the priest, confronted the exaggerated amount of power he still gave one man over his sexuality, and connected with the healing, forgiveness, and permission to be a sexual being that came from his Higher Power.*

Necessary Discussions

The majority of time spent in my groups and workshops is devoted to a man's work on specific contracts with the entire group focused on that man's work. We avoid discussions of life issues that would move us away from the heart and toward detached, intellectual discourse. Many men love to wax philosophical, and as I listen to these men, I often see their eyes glaze over as they sink into the numbness of mental masturbation. However, some of my most meaningful groups have been round-table discussions about issues that strike men deep within their hearts and souls, usually stimulated by one man's fear, shame, anger, or sadness.

> *The group had been exclusively heterosexual for some time When Scott, a gay man, joined the group, Cory was faced with his previously undisclosed past of gay-bashing. As he owned his shame and misdirected rage, he worked on the true source of this pain (his father), and faced Scott's deep rage and grief. Each man, in turn, began to expose his homophobia. We covered such ground as the sexual abuse survivors who had confused child molesters with homosexuals,*

survivors who equated homosexuality with loss of manhood, men who had been raised in, and bought into, the homophobia of their rigid, shaming families, and the wide range of fear-based messages given to children about homosexuality. Each man, including Scott, faced a part of his Shadow, owned it, and gained access to new information about gay and straight people. For Cory and Scott, this work was the beginning of a strong relationship. I cannot truly capture the power of the truth in the room that evening. In my estimation it brought a new dimension into the group that forever changed this circle of men.

Entire evenings have been dedicated to heartfelt discussions of sexuality, religion and spirituality, parenting, addictions, and career choice. These are times not only to share information, but also to disclose strengths and Shadows, Adult beliefs and Child fears. This is not a political forum, but the opportunity to speak from the heart.

Honoring Elders and Mentors

As I have discussed in earlier sections of this text, I live in a youth-oriented culture that casts aside what is old, even people. One outcome of this work in my life is a greater appreciation for what I have in my life at this moment, rather than what I wish I had. I value long-term friends more than ever. I see new friends as opportunities for the long haul. My mind drifts more often to my parents and siblings scattered throughout the country. Even as a man of many words, I find I have no adequate words to describe to DiAnne, Carly, Aimee, and Nathan, how deeply I hold them in my heart. My ability to see the big picture has grown significantly, the importance of each tree, bird, river. I buy fewer things, I use my possessions longer, and I am less emotionally tied to *ownership.* Some of you may have been living all, or part, of this process for many years; but for me, and for many of the men I come in contact with, these changes in values resulted from men's work.

One of the ways in which this part of the journey takes on significant meaning is in the honoring of elders and mentors in your circle of men and in your life. Since our first participation in an Elders' Ceremony, most men's workshop lead by Chris and Jim have included this ritual. Honoring the elders of the community is a natural part of closing each circle.

Elders' Ceremony

I have participated in many variations of elder rituals in recent years. I find that the content is less important than the attitude. This is not the presenting of a gold watch for years of service to a man who is being sent away; this is a process of breathing new life into the wisdom, experience, strength, and Shadow of older men who are continuing to put themselves on the line at men's gatherings. This is not the automatic process of respecting or devaluing men of advanced years; this is the ritual of respecting generations: wise men raise wiser men. One example of this ritual as a closing ceremony for men's retreats is as follows:

> *All men over the age of fifty remain in the meeting room with Jim (who is the Elder Facilitator), and all other men leave the room with me. When we return, we find that the Elders have formed a circle, facing out. The remaining men are asked to form an outer circle, facing in. Jim describes the process something like this. "These are men who bring time, experience and wisdom to this gathering. They have chosen to share some of this wisdom with you. By listening and taking in the words of these Elders, you are acknowledging their position of honor in this circle." One at a time, the Elders stand, and each shares any knowledge he wishes to impart to the younger men, most often insights the Elder feels he needed, but was deprived of in his earlier life. The Elder is free to move about and make contact with the men. After each Elder has finished sharing, the men in the outer circle each have the opportunity to stand and share with one or more Elder, about how he intends to use the wisdom given to him in this ritual. The final stage happens when the men of the outer circle are invited in by the Elders, bringing all of the men together in the center of the room in what has been called a "group hug." Although we close the workshop at this point, it often takes some time for the men to disengage and prepare to go home.*

Days after an Elders' Ceremony I usually receive a host of comments from men about the power of this process. The Elders, particularly those who are new to this ritual, are surprised that younger men are truly interested in what they have to say; this is often not their experience in their families and on the job. Experienced Elders, say they never tire of these rituals. For men like myself, there is often an overwhelming sense of love, respect, and longing as these men take the time to teach us. Many of us have found more loving uncles and grandfathers in this work than ever existed in our families of origin. Many of us have also realized how we have neglected and disrespected the deserving Elders in our families of origin.

Daily Honoring

The honoring rituals I described are powerful moments for many men. They are healing experiences and, like many of the processes I have described, they may lose meaning over time without practice in your daily existence. If you are an Elder, or have made a powerful connection with an Elder, I encourage you to foster eldering relationships in your daily life. For some of us, this has meant a greater commitment to the Elders in our biological families. For others, due to loss or dysfunction, close contact with biological Elders does not fit, and I hope you will find that all of us benefit from the development of elder relationships. I know one man, raised in years of neglect and abuse from his father, who surrounded himself as a young adult with older men, many of them strong and nurturing. I am convinced that without these Elders, this man would not have survived long enough to gain recovery from a devastating addiction, saving his career, his family, his life.

Like all other essential relationships, the kinship of Elders and younger men takes time, effort, and energy. If you are an Elder, keep an eye open for those who need your time and wisdom. If you are a younger man drawn to this work, locate the Elders, spend time with them, listen to their stories (because many of the stories must be passed along to another who will need them). For a moment, perhaps for the rest of your life, these men can lead you forward.

Honoring Mentors

Men and women of all ages have mentored me. Although many of my strongest mentoree relationships have been with Elders, this is not a prerequisite for mentoring as I have come to know it. My first social-work mentor had only a few more years of age and experience but he offered a new therapist a model of this work that was meaningful and *fun*. From this man, I learned to have fun doing what is often painful and painstaking work. If you know you have been mentored, I encourage you to take your journal and write about what you received from each significant mentor: information for the head, work habits, emotional development, spiritual development, skills of the head, heart, and spirit. I encourage you to honor the spirit of these mentors in your work. At several points in this volume, I have given credit to my mentors. I honor their efforts—I honor myself—when I pass along the stories of the good men and women who have tutored me.

If you are a man of some experience in life, in men's work, in your career, I challenge you to find eager men who are available for you to teach. In the twelve-Step programs, the concept of sponsorship is a time-honored tradition that has assisted many in getting and staying sober. A sponsor keeps the best practice of mentorship: A man or woman who has been on a road similar to yours, who has traveled a few more steps, and is willing to support you, teach you, and challenge you. As a mentor myself, I can guarantee you will have the opportunity to be taught as much as you will teach!

Final Notes

This chapter is a testimony to the importance of writing, discussion, and basic information in the healing process. I can recount numerous occasions when, in preparing to leave group, a man will review the many powerful pieces of work and state something like: "But, maybe the most important night in the entire experience was that one thing you said in the group discussion on. . . . That meant as much as all the times I sweated, yelled, and cried on the carpet." In most cases, the man goes on to say he could not have heard this gem of wisdom without doing the other work, but the point is well made. I have often heard men in this work say, "He just needs to get out of his head." I disagree: he needs to establish a connection between his head and his heart and his spirit. Many of us have great heads. We need new information. We need to know how to use our heads in unison with our hearts and spirits.

This chapter is also to prepare you for Moving On. Many of you have been integrating resolution of past trauma with redecisions and new actions. You are discovering that as you heal the past, you focus on it less, accessing new levels of energy and Adult for productivity, giving and getting love, and mission work in your daily life. You are dealing with the questions and challenges that continue to appear with more thoughtful, centered, heartfelt responses. The work on the past may be reduced in intensity just as the passion of your daily life may be intensifying. In the final chapter, I will offer my best thoughts and feelings on this part of your journey. My mission is, "To teach living in the present through healing and honoring the past." You have spent a lifetime doing the healing component. Now it is time to look more deeply at honoring and living the present.

8: Moving On

Moving forward to find a safe
And powerful maleness
You carry the love given
Past and present
You carry the uncertainty
Past, present, and future
You carry
Accountability

Chris Frey
1993

In its inception five years ago, the initial chapter of this book was a few hand-written pages titled, "Movement." Viewing men's work as a call to action, movement, and moving on has remained the cornerstone of my personal and professional life. As you read the final chapter of this guide, I hope you realize each process contained in the previous chapters is about Moving On. Each piece of healing work you have completed has provided you with the opportunity to more fully experience *this moment and the next*. In essence, this chapter is about every step of your journey. The words that follow are simply a reminder to keep using the past to enhance the present and create a vision for the future. As I discuss relationships, spirituality, acceptance and forgiveness, and mission, I hope you will return to your journal, your circle of men, to your family, and evaluate how you are putting the healing of your masculinity into practice in your daily life.

Moving On from Group

If you are in therapy, there is a time to leave. If you are in a men's support group, there may come a time to leave. Should this occur, I find the following two steps to be essential for the transition into the next stage of your voyage.

My Ongoing Self-Care Plan

Each workshop, retreat, course of therapy, and group is a slice of your healing journey, not the journey itself. There was life before the experience, hope for life after. I return to my statement from the early pages of the book. "Therapy is only as good as what you do *between sessions*" becomes, "Therapy is only as good as what you do *with it in the world.*" As you bring closure to any stage of your work, it is imperative to both identify how you will continue to practice the changes you have made, and prepare to meet the new challenges that your Shadow, people, life, God will place in front (or behind) you. Once again, I refer you to *Double Jeopardy* for a detailed format for an Ongoing Self-Care Plan, easily adapted from the original style to your needs. The essence of the exercise is as follows:

> Complete a written review of the changes and growth that have taken place during this phase of your journey. Take time to enjoy the fruits of your labors; take in the hard work and the success.

> Complete two lists, one, an inventory of the issues and relationships you will continue to focus on in your future work and two, ongoing activities to continue in your process of masculine renewal. Be specific. "I will try to stay in touch with some of the guys in group" doesn't count!

> Present your journaling to your circle. Take in the strokes as you review your progress. Take in the feedback, validation, and confrontation as you present your plan for continuing your work. Make your decision on a date to leave the circle only when your plan incorporates the feedback and satisfies your Adult.

Graduation

Each workshop and group must include some form of celebration. In workshops, as we prepare for the Elders' Ceremony, we often create guided imageries that pull together the powerful strands of healing that have taken place through the weekend—we often dance! In group we hold graduations to honor the man—his sweat, his recovery, his future—and to send him back to the world with our love and hope! I have often said, that for many of us, leaving meant sneaking out the back door, hating good-byes, or leaving in anger, "I'll see you at your funeral, maybe, now get out of my life." This graduation is about sharing our joy for work well done, along with openly grieving the loss we will experience by not having this man in our physical presence each week.

The graduation ceremony I began using years ago originated in the *coin passings* I participated in at chemical dependency treatment centers, a ritual in which an individual who had completed the recommended treatment program was given a coin, usually with the Serenity Prayer somewhere on it, as a token of his or her efforts and early recovery. In its early form, my ritual included the opportunity for the man who was leaving to share any final thoughts and feelings with the group as a whole or any other individual, the opportunity for each group member to share his final thoughts and feelings with the graduate, and the passing of a small token (the token has become a magnetic heart) around the group for each man to squeeze in his love and hope. Over time, the ritual I initially designed has evolved into a process that is about each man's unique presence in the group.

I initiated Kerry's graduation as I often did, with a brief description of the importance of celebrating with our words, gifts, joy, and tears the progress and presence of a man ready to leave group. By Kerry's choice, the men in group shared first. As had become the custom among these men, gifts of words, tears, hugs, cards, handmade treasures, music, and food were presented to Kerry. As is usually my custom, I spoke last and described the difference between the man I had met for the first time and the man who sat before me now. As his time to say good-bye came, Kerry asked each man in turn to stand, presenting him with a beautiful stone and his words of gratitude, love and hope for the men he was leaving behind. The tears and laughter flowed, and then . . . we ate!

For me, there are many meaningful aspects to this ritual. I love to hear the men affirm one another. I enjoy the rituals designed by some men that clearly take time, energy and a great deal of caring. I enjoy the affirmation I receive, the recognition within me that I do care how men see my work. And there is always a moment of laughter when I say, "One of the amazing things about seeing, hearing, and tasting all of these gifts is the recognition that planning a celebration is not genetically based—men can pull it off." (The heartiest laughter always comes from the more traditional males who have relied all their lives on Moms and wives to organize and prepare for these moments.) Perhaps most moving, each time it occurs, is the evolution of format that allows the graduate to invite back for the ceremony former group members who were instrumental in his work. I cannot fully describe the feeling in me as I see men who have been gone from the weekly process for one and two years file into the room to affirm the masculine healing in the graduate's life. For many of these men, it is a given that they will appear to celebrate what has become a connection with this circle of men that is now seven years in the making: "Thanks for coming". . . . "No way I would have missed this." Another message that is reinforced through this process is how Eldering and Mentoring takes place in both physical and spiritual form.

> *Vince returned to bring his energy to Jeff's graduation. These men had overlapped in their time in group and had continued a close friendship since Vince's departure. As we settled in for the evening I overheard Ronnie say, "Vince, I feel like you've been here all along. We've all felt the benefit of your love for Jeff." This led to a discussion that we've had on many occasions: that this group has existed in generations, men graduate and men begin. Just as a family gains power in function or dysfunction over the generations, so has the group gained healing power through the changing of the circle. "The strength of this circle is created by all of us here tonight and by all of the men who have come here before you. Their energy is always with us." Each man, in turn, shared a memory of a man no longer in group who had been an integral part of his healing.*

When I doubt the importance and worth of this work, I remember graduation ceremonies.

Putting the Healing to Work

If you have connected with the spirit of this book, you have been putting the healing to work for weeks, perhaps months. This section, then, is my final offering of a few ideas about utilizing what you have learned. Too many books written for emotional and spiritual healing appear to be action guides but in fact contain many chapters of beliefs and philosophy and a brief chapter at the end on how to put the material to work in your life. I have endeavored to walk our journey together in reverse, to focus on healing actions in the bulk of the text and to bring closure with a bit of philosophy and direction.

Parents

Much of this work has been about confronting significant others about the ways they wounded you. This has not been about blame—although within a specific piece of work you may have used words of blame—this is about accountability. If the foundation of your healing is to accept responsibility for your addiction, your abusiveness, your feelings, your Child, then so must you give responsibility to your parents. Many of us early in our work have gotten stuck in magical forgiveness: "The program teaches that I have to let go of my resentments. I know that Mom and Dad had terrible childhoods. They did the best they could. Even though I don't know how and haven't been able to and am still in incredible pain, I'm just going to let go." As we came to understand that intellectual knowledge of our parents' limitations did not always translate into automatic acceptance or forgiveness, the process of accountability and confrontation became possible . . . necessary. Many of us came to see that more important than confronting a person (Mom or Dad), we were confronting the pain.

Having symbolically, and in many cases face-to-face, challenged our parents and our pain, many men have gotten stuck at the other end of the spectrum; they refused what must come next, understanding and accepting the parent as a fallible human being, taking in the good stuff, letting go of the wounds and forming the most Adult, safe relationship possible. I have seen many men stranded at, "I understand now from my Inner Child work that I was a good kid who deserved to be loved and kept safe. I have to heal the shame of the mistakes I have made because of the ways my parents hurt me. They had no right and I will never forgive them." There are certainly parents who continued to be toxic, even dangerous, people, who perhaps merit no forgiveness, only distance. This point of view may leave you stuck at what many traditional parents tend to believe; that men's work and therapy is a process of teaching you to blame, hate, and reject your family. Even these wounds must be laid to rest.

For most of us, our parents were like us, a combination of good intention and narcissism, positive action and hapless inaction, self-care and self-destruction, love and apathy—they were human. At some point, it no longer works to see yourself as the Golden Inner Child who developed into a damaged man accountable for his actions, but to see Mom and Dad as simply bad parents, perhaps bad people. As a loving man once told me, "It's interesting you always wanted your parents to accept you as you are, but you refuse to accept them as they are. Maybe it's time." Consider these possibilities:

Some of you will create a better relationship with your parents. From this work some of you will eventually call your parents, "friend."

Neal had been abused by both of his parents. In the midst of his work, which involved week after week of rage and grief, he learned of his father's illness. In part, his work clearly became driven by his need to resolve his fear and hatred of Dad before his death. He would complete a piece of work and take it to his dad, complete a piece of work and take it to his dad.

There was confrontation, anger, and denial, but Neal kept coming back and back and back. Did Dad change? No. Did Dad change how he related to Neal? Absolutely.

Some of you will enhance, or finish repairing, what has already been a very positive relationship:

Bob said, "I've always loved my dad and knew he loved me. He showed it more than said it by taking care of us, teaching me stuff, spending time with me. He became an even better Dad when he stopped drinking. He wasn't terrible before, he wasn't mean; he just seemed to tune out for periods of time when he was drinking more. I was confused about how much I loved him, how many great things he did for me, and the lingering resentment I had for him. I was ashamed of my anger, but that didn't make it go away. When I finally confronted him, his drinking, in the men's workshop, I understood that there were times when I knew his drinking was more important than us, or me. Having grieved his alcoholism, I was able to go back and talk to him about it. At first, he avoided me, got angry. But, when he realized that I wasn't there to shame him, he listened. He told me things about himself that I never knew: his childhood, his struggles, his effort to be a good dad. Our relationship is even better than before."

Some of you will create tolerance and acceptance of what happened and who your parents both were and are. From this work, some of you will find peace with the limitations of what your parents can be.

"I now realize that my mom had a worse childhood than I had, and she didn't have the opportunities to heal that I have had. That doesn't excuse what she did. I know other women who had the kind of pain she had who didn't molest their sons. I now know it wasn't my fault, and I would never allow her to be alone with my kids. I also know, because I tried over and over to talk to her, that she is never going to admit what she did. I don't need to be scared of or angry at her anymore. She can't hurt me. In her unhealthy way, I know she believes she loves me, and I have had to accept that she is my mom."

Some of you will accept the events of your life, accept who your parents were (and weren't), and accept that they will not be a significant part of your ongoing journey. From this work, some of you will simply move on.

Theo's grief was immense, "I'm beginning to accept that Dad is dead and is not going to come back to help me with Mom. I was so angry at him for so long that I couldn't be sad about losing him. Mom, wellllll, Mom is Mom and she's not going to change. I feel as if I have done what I can: putting up with her, confronting her, organizing interventions, taking her to treatment. Nothing works. She only calls when she's probably so stoned she doesn't remember the next day. She's my Mom in name, but there's not much there."

A few of you will know that acceptance in your relationship with your parents means as much distance as possible. From this work, a few of you will make us your family.

"My dad is dangerous, plain and simple. If I tried to talk to him about any of the memories I have of childhood, he'd try to hurt me all over again—physically, verbally, any way he could. Acceptance for me is to accept that he's crazy and that every time I went back I got abused. He's my father by biology, that's all."

Forgiveness

I have primarily used the term, *acceptance,* up to this point: acceptance of what occurred, who your parents were and are, of who you are, and acceptance and willingness in forging ahead with the relationship with Dad and Mom as it is available to you. Another step in the process is forgiveness. My definition of forgiveness is relieving yourself of the ongoing need or "right" to punish Dad and Mom for what they did and who they are, *not* absolving them of responsibility for their actions, which is in the hands of a Higher Power. This work is not about forgetting the past. It is about letting go of the need to obsess about and use the past for destructive means; it is about truly letting go of resentments. Along that road, I have encouraged you to learn to forgive yourself for real and imagined transgressions. Many of you will choose to give the same gift to your parent. It is about finding the love you have in your heart for these people, not providing or declining clemency for their past; they must make their own peace with the past. There has been great controversy in this work, particularly in sexual abuse treatment, about the necessity of forgiveness in the healing journey, with many therapists falling on the side of forgiveness being an individual choice, not a necessary part of healing. If you use my definition above, this conflict becomes a question of semantics. Despite what Hollywood teaches, *Revenge does not work!* Hanging on to a need to make others pay for the wounds you experienced simply keeps you connected to the past, the rage, the shame, the fear, the grief—Your Pain. You have confronted your pain. Perhaps you have confronted your parent; perhaps you have even been able to deliver some appropriate consequence for their actions (telling other family, warning others who are not safe, removing your children from their toxic presence, removing yourself). Now, let go, turn them over to powers greater than yourself. Even in the case of parents who change, who own their actions, who make amends, your role is to find whatever love you have in your heart and communicate it to the best of your ability.

Parent Sessions

Over the years my concept of parent sessions has evolved. I once saw these meetings as serving one of two primary purposes: for my clients to gather information about their childhood, their family histories, their parents, or for my clients to confront their parents directly about past wounds. In confronting parents, the intention was not to blame but to give the man an opportunity in his Adult to share his perceptions of the issues and to deal productively with whatever the parental response was: denial, minimization, acceptance, accountability, or simply a different set of memories and perceptions. While these sessions were often beneficial, the concept was limiting. As time marches on I have seen the sessions used for a myriad of reasons, such as:

> A series of meetings between the son and parents to slowly process their differences and confront the past traumas.

> Question-and-answer sessions about the parents' childhood, knowledge of extended family members, adult life before the son's presence, early relationship history, sexual history (haven't seen this one very often), dreams and passions, and key periods of the parent's life (the armed service, other marriages, traumatic events). For example, one of my most informative conversations with my father was about his experience closing the family business and going into corporate life. I found that I had made several key assumptions about the effects of this decision on my dad that were completely erroneous. I learned a lot about him that day.

> A one-shot session for the man to speak his truth directly to the parents, without any expectation of any positive feedback or acknowledgment by the parent.

> A session at the end of therapy, after the man has cleared his rage and shame, to enable the man to see that he had grown.

218

A non-confrontational session early in therapy to enable the man and his parents to establish goals to grow together.

Parent-son meetings masked as fishing trips, golf outings, barbecues, and "just dropping by for a cup of coffee." These meetings with healing intent are *not* to be mistaken for the son ambushing his parent with rage and shame, as I have seen when men attempt this process while the wounds are still too deep and fresh.

A session for the man to make amends to his parents, having realized that all wounds were not directed from the parent toward him, but that he, too, struck out in ways that he must be accountable for.

These encounters may take place in a therapist's office, in a kitchen, living room, restaurant, boat, hospital. If this stage in the work is in your future, plan for it. Pick your time and your safe place, if you are able. Of course, if the opportunity presents itself and your heart tells you this is your time to speak your truth, none of the above rules apply—Go For It! And remember, should you choose to speak your truth, prepare for the possibility that your parent will speak his or hers—the road runs both ways. Some of you will never formalize this process with your parents. You will simply begin to engage in a more mature, responsible relationship. Many parents will respond positively, but never ask where the change comes from. (They are afraid you will talk about men's work.) Accept and enjoy!

As goals vary, so do results. I have seen parents and sons arrive separately with suspicion and defensiveness, leaving arm in arm. I have seen sons arrive with hope, remaining after the parents leave to weep at the emptiness. Each session, better than expected, more painful than hoped for, yields its own reward in preparing the son for his next step in healing.

Couples

There are probably more self-help books written on couples' relationships than any other type, probably, because we know the least about the subject.

Many therapists have told me that they find couples' work to be the most challenging of therapies. Many men have told me that the most difficult place to practice the healing work is in relationships with primary partners, wives and lovers. Perhaps I can assist you in applying the regeneration of yourself into the regeneration of your relationship, present or future.

Open your journal and answer the following questions. If you are not currently in a primary relationship, answer based on what you believe today or how you plan to function within your next relationship.

What is your stance on monogamy? If you have been, or are currently, in multiple romantic and sexual relationships, is this in any way inconsistent with the integrity of your masculine healing work?

How do you define commitment in an age-mate sexual relationship? If you have been, or are currently, in multiple sexual relationships, how does the issue of commitment play out in those relationships?

If you are married or in what you define as a committed relationship, how do you finish the sentence, "I will stay in this relationship if. . . "?

Is your partner involved in men's or women's work? If so, how do you feel about his or her process? If not, how do you feel about this?

On a scale of 0-10 (10 being highest), how high would you rank yourself on acceptance of your partner as he or she really is?

Make a list of the five most powerful changes you have made in your life as a result of your healing process. Now, list how you are practicing these changes in your current primary relationship.

There are several common pitfalls that I find among the men who do this work as it pertains to committed partner relationships.

Many of our partners are not involved as intensely in the change process. This may be because they have been focused on their work in the past and have less need at this time. Perhaps this person is already in a healthier space. Often, the partner simply does not value his or her change process in the same way or does not value this type of healing work. Conflict may develop as you attempt to control the other person's change process, as your partner tries to speed you up or slow you down, as one partner solidifies in the stance that the other is the one with the "serious" issues.

Second, even when both of you are intensely involved in this journey, you may be on different paths, at different speeds. You may work on the same issue, but at different points in your struggle. You will often work on what you believe is most important, in spite of the message from your partner that he or she knows a more crucial place you should be putting your energy. Perhaps most often, especially if you are in a relationship where both of you are working through severe early trauma, one or both of you will have periods of time when you act out the pain of your recovery within the relationship, just as you have acted out the pain of your avoidance previously. A home in which both partners are working through their issues can be a fortress of support and validation. It can also, at times, be a temporary natural disaster.

Third, some partners feel threatened by the invasion of support that you may have created through your circle of men. You may be away from home more, going to men's meetings, the content of which your partner has limited detail. New men are calling, coming by, perhaps at odd hours. Your partner may wonder why you no longer try to get most of what you need from him or her. Women may feel as if you have joined some new form of secret men's club, a threat of returning to some patriarchal man-child fraternity of the past. Finally, imagine living with someone, often for a period of years, only to wake up one day and find that within a brief time he has become someone new. He looks familiar and he still has a lot of the same quirks, but in some ways he is dramatically different!

I offer a series of strategies for addressing these issues. As you read these recommendations for the first time, keep your journal next to you and refer to the information you generated on the couple's questions:

Monogamy works in men's work. If you are in what you and the other person believe to be a committed relationship, your integrity, stability, and new identity is at stake if you maintain multiple partners, sexually and emotionally. My definition of an affair in a committed relationship includes going outside of the relationship to establish a secret "he or she doesn't understand me, but you do" bond, even if there is no sex involved. Many years ago, when I was a fledgling social worker, I heard Sam Keen speak on couples' relationships and, if I remember correctly, he proposed that in couple's relationships there are certain levels of certain emotions that can only be shared with one person at a time; you cannot spread this kind of commitment around. That statement had a profound impact on me and has been a foundation for much of what you read in this chapter.

If you are not currently in a committed relationship, you may be saying, "Great, none of this applies to me." Not so, my friend. Become more aware of how multiple, or serial, partners affect your sense of self, the healing work you are involved in, your place in the world of men and women who are affected by your relationship decisions. If you are a sexual addict in

recovery, you have probably already given this issue considerable thought. If you are not, I still recommend you look at how
juggling multiple partners (especially if more than one involves sex) fits into the direction you are moving in your life.
A female friend of mine has often said that she believes many
men learn to practice a new level of honesty and integrity
through recovery, but they exclude sex and business from the
process. Sadly, I often find men of great integrity who put couples' relationships in a separate box and maintain great se-
crecy, manipulation, risk, and deception (of self and others). I
encourage you to put your romantic relationships with women
or men into your healing process, not apart from it.

Get clear on the level of your commitment to your current
partner(s) and their level of commitment to you. Love and
commitment are *not* synonymous for everyone, and loving
someone does not guarantee the amount of effort necessary
to take a relationship through times of significant stress. If
you are married, engaged, cohabitating, in a monogamous
dating relationship, get clear on the conditions of that commitment. What are your bottom-line expectations.

*Frank was married for several years prior to beginning
men's group, and he had struggled with the conflict and distance, often wondering if he made a mistake by marrying. As
he proceeded in his work, Frank became clear that he still
loved his partner and wanted to commit to the marriage on a
deeper level. He was clear that he would not stay in a marriage
in which violence or infidelity was present (a commitment to
his Child that came from his early trauma). He was ready to
pledge his ongoing presence and effort in the relationship. He
would live with the knowledge that he was always going to
come home to this woman and consistently focus himself on
strengthening his part of the marriage.*

Frank closed the exit doors out of the relationship by connecting with a person who did not engage in the behaviors
prevalent in his childhood and by making his decision to
commit apart from his wife, not in response to his wife. In his
situation, his wife brought similar commitment and conditions to the table. He had never envisioned really getting what
he wanted from a marriage before, and never envisioned,
then, having to deliver his part of the commitment for the

long haul. At last conversation, he was less scared, more secure, and still hadn't created the perfect romance.

If you are in a relationship where a significant imbalance in commitment exists, take this issue to your support system, talk with men, talk with men who have positive relationship experience through success and failure. If you have a man or woman who has "waited for you to get well" and you have fed him or her hope or mixed messages, while maintaining other relationships or withholding commitment, what is this about? If you have hung on to someone who has moved on or who is giving mixed messages, what is this about? Becoming a man in most of your dealings, yet leaving your Child in charge of couples relationships, will keep you stuck in dependence, unable to find solid ground to stand on. I need the playfulness of that child to fully engage in parts of my relationship, but having a little boy in a man's body trying to get close and be intimate is not a big turn-on for most partners. If it is . . . Run!

Give your partner (whether you are the man doing this work or the partner reading this book) the room needed to pursue his or her own journey, establishing pace and priorities. One of the greatest gifts you can give someone you love is to support the effort rather than standing as judge, jury, and executioner. Your partner may seek your valuable input regarding the work; this is not permission to become Parent and determine his path. Be cautious of *knowing* better than your partner what his change process should be; look more to your own healing work than to his. If you have an urgent need, such as in the case of a man who is being violent toward himself or others, state this need along with your boundaries: "I cannot control what you work on now; however, I will no longer tolerate your violence, and if you continue, the action I will take is to . . . (leave, have you arrested, ask you to leave)." I am not asking you to be in danger to support your partner's journey. I am recommending you be aware of when you are paying closer attention to his or her work than your own.

Use your support system to ventilate concerns, frustrations, and fears about your partner's work. Staying out of the way of my partner's growth is not easy, and men in my circle often assist me in understanding when to give active support, when to give input, and when to shut up! Many of us are afraid that the process of change will draw us away from our partners when, in fact, our goal was more intimacy and, if you are in this work for awhile, you will meet someone who had exactly that experience. Your support system can help you stay focused on healing your own wounds and on being a more functional person in your relationship, rather than attempting to control your loved one's process. This does not mean passively standing by and watching your spouse or lover grow away from you. It means directing your efforts toward becoming—not creating—a stronger partner. Finally, your circle of support people will assist you in knowing when it does make sense to confront your loved one if you believe that person's actions will hurt him or her or the relationship.

Give your spouse or lover time to adjust to your new support system. Listen to concerns about the time you are away from home and be clear about your goals in being away. This is about positive change, not about running away from home or responsibilities. Don't give in to demands about sharing details that may breach the safety of the circle, but do state clearly the healing—not blaming—intent of the work. Share your changes, in words and in actions. Some of your partners were there for you long before anyone else. Feelings of being replaced may lead to jealousy and competition rather than acceptance and excitement. When possible, give your partner the opportunity to meet the men within your new support system. If you are in therapy, give your spouse or lover an opportunity to meet your therapist, to feel like he or she is *a part of, not apart from* the journey you are on.

Give your companion time to adjust to the changes you make. Some of your work may be so transformative that your partner literally feels as if a new man is living in the relationship. Don't assume that because the change is positive, the other person will immediately be able to adapt to who you've become. Perhaps one of the most difficult adjustments I have seen in long-term relationships is when a man changes in the way the spouse or lover has been pressuring him to change: "I wanted you to quit drinking, but I didn't know you would start wanting all this input into spending the money and taking care of the kids" . . . "Why did you change this when your group suggested it? I've been telling you this for years and you never listened to me" . . . "I didn't realize when you changed one thing it would start changing so many other parts of our relationship" . . . "I always thought you were the only one who needed to change. Now all your work has brought stuff up about me." Be patient. Allow space for mixed feelings and mixed messages. Demonstrate your ability to be committed to your individual journey and to the relationship. One of the great fallacies of this work is that I can either take care of myself or I can take care of you. In fact, I (speaking for myself) must learn how to travel my masculine road as a separate self within the knowledge of my love and commitments to my wife, children, and other loved ones.

Honor your partner's path. As I stated, many spouses and lovers do not choose the type of work I have described within these pages. Many will seek no assistance outside of their immediate circle of family and friends. I have seen many people heal through many methods. Any path that offers all of the answers scares me because all of the healing roads that we are provided have been interpreted to us by other humans, not by omnipotent beings. If the course that you take diverges far from your partner, a separateness that challenges the continuation of the relationship may occur. Take time to look at the effects of your individual travels on the relationship. Look for the common ground. Be open to learning the other's way, perhaps incorporating some of their style, perhaps only understanding it. In the extreme, I have seen relationships dissolve as a result of this work. Sometimes, this was best for both persons, but at times, only benficial for one. More often, when each person's personal path was honored and each person moved on this path within the context of the relationship, I have seen partnerships renewed, strengthened, and secured.

I hope I have provided you with guidelines to blend your work into the primary adult relationship in your life, not a how-to manual for hetero- or homosexual relationships, but a picture of seeing your personal pilgrimage in connection with the journey of your spouse or lover.

What About the Kids?

Much of what I described can be applied to your relationships with your children. Some of you will find that the adaptability, flexibility, and unconditional love of your children create a rapid acceptance of and adjustment to changes that you make. I know when I have completed significant work that creates within me a greater sense of joy, energy, serenity, or passion, Nathan responds almost immediately, and almost always positively. Likewise, when I connect with anger, he responds. At other times, with other children, the response will be more cautious, tentative, perhaps even negative. I find that the older the child (the longer he or she was accustomed to you as you were), the more time necessary to catch up with Dad's changes. Several guidelines for assisting your children are:

> Again, be patient. Remember, the kids are playing catch up. They may or may not have seen the need for the change.

> Take time to discuss your changes with your children, at their levels of understanding: answer questions, give information about how this work will help you be a better father. It is not necessary to give most children graphic details of your trauma. If your kids have specific questions or knowledge about your trauma, addictions, or behaviors, get quality information from your support system about how to discuss these issues adequately, with the child's stage of development in mind. I'll never forget the adolescent who came in and told me, "I thought I was pretty OK and I had pretty good parents until Mom and Dad started telling me all about their therapy and apologizing for everything. If they were that screwed up, maybe I am too." These folks had done some good parenting in spite of their childhood trauma. Their guilt-ridden, poorly-thought-out confessions did nothing to benefit their son. Learn the territory between secrets and boundaries. There's considerable room.

> Be patient with negative reactions to what you see as positive changes. It takes time for some kids to adjust. It is also a reality that what is positive for you may be seen as a negative by others:

> "All of a sudden Dad cares where I'm going, who I'm with, when I'll be home. Where was he when I was little? I don't need him on my back now."

> "He speaks up now. He says no. In a way I like how much tougher he is (laughs); as long as he is tough with someone else."

> "The only thing I think about all this stuff is that my brother will get a decent Dad and it's too late for me—and I'm mad. He wants to talk; it's too late."

> Not every kid will respond quickly in a positive way. Not every kid will respond at all.

Once again, allow your kids the opportunity to connect with your new circle, meet the men, come to a family session. Many of the children of the men in my circle have new elders, and future mentors; many of them simply have new friends. The work grows as we introduce our children into a healing circle of adults early in life.

A Note About Couples and Kids

As you incorporate your work into the family system you live in, as you have read and probably experienced, the reactions are often mixed. For many of you, there will be grief work on arriving "too late" for some relationships to be substantially improved by your growth. A marriage may still end, a child may continue to use drugs, a lover may not trust you, a son may ridicule men's work. Take this work to your circle. Grieve what will not be. Grieve what may yet be, but not within your timeframe. And connect with the stories, yours and other men's, about the relationship that was saved, the child who was assisted in getting sober because Dad was present, the lover who followed you into this work and did his own healing, the son who stood by your side at the last men's weekend you attended.

Spirituality

I hope you have found work of the spirit and soul throughout this book. Yet I find myself starting this final section with a clear sense of inadequacy. I am not a scholar of the spirit, the soul, of religion or God. My inadequacy, however, is tempered by a deep and abiding belief in my presence on this planet, your presence on this planet, and in the sacredness of this healing work, based in nurturing ritual and nourished by powers greater than any individual can muster. Therapy is no longer simply about one person resolving a symptom or concern, no longer about one person getting what he or she wants out of life, no longer simply about the "me" that has become so prevalent culturally and in the therapy subculture. This work, as described throughout, is based in healing myself as a method to bring healing into the lives of family, friends, other humans, and even extraterrestrials, if they ever really show up. Aspects of this work highlight the essentially spiritual nature of men's work that I believe bear mention as guideposts for the continuation of your journey through this life, and whatever comes next:

> Continue your work with a focus toward *wholeness* of self, integrating your intellectual, emotional, physical and spiritual being into one.

Continue your work with a focus toward connectedness with others, integrating your growth with the journeys of family, friends, and future friends.

Integrate healing ritual into your daily life. Many of you will pursue, perhaps more vigorously, organized religion or spiritual directions. Some of you will meditate, pray, journal, create affirmations, participate in sacred ceremony. Give yourself the space to practice a daily process.

Give yourself permission to investigate new spiritual directions and methods. Honor the healing directions of others who chose different paths. In my life, I have been exposed to significant doses of Christianity and Twelve-Step philosophy, with more recent offerings of Native American and mythopoetic perspectives and ritual. I have been taught by men using Jewish, African, and other philosophies. Conversant with none, I have been affected by each. Some of you will pick one direction. I encourage you to find the common ground upon which each stands. One of the great gifts of this work for me is to stand in a room of men from every region of our country (and several other countries): Jewish, Catholic, Protestant, Twelve-Step, Eastern, undecided, secular faiths; White, African-American, Native American, Asian-American, white collar, blue collar, no collar. We need each other—not enough of us know that yet!

Beware of men and women who claim to see all and know **THE** truth. True Kings and Queens give blessing and direction.

Establish a mission statement, a declaration of purpose and action that serves as your working guide for contributing to the greater good. What is your contribution to life beyond taking care of yourself? What are you truly here to accomplish beyond successful completion of your daily routine? How will other people, other creatures, the planet, be impacted by your healing journey? How will you pass on what you have received in this work?

I hope that you have seen every exercise in this book as part of your spiritual journey. I believe any man of any loving faith I am familiar with can use these processes in some form on the healing road. As we meet in our circles, we may then be reminded of all the other circles around us, and around us, and around us, reveling in our differences, joining in our sameness.

Other Books By Islewest

SEE WHAT I'M SAYING: *What Children Tell Us Through Their Art*
  Dr. Myra Levick, Ph.D $15.95
Is your child in good emotional health? Struggling with a problem? Typical for his or her age? Dr. Levick says that the answers to all these questions can be seen in how and what your child draws. A leader in the field of Art Therapy, Levick gives expert help in understanding what children communicate through their drawings, and offers practical tools for assessing a child's intellectual and emotional development.

DOUBLE JEOPARDY: *Treating Juvenile Victims and Perpetrators for the Dual Disorder of Sexual Abuse and Substance Abuse*
  Chris Frey, MSW, LCSW $36.95
Because it has become common for clients in treatment to present both childhood sexual abuse and substance abuse experiences, it is essential that helping professionals be well-versed in the dual disorder as they work to provide comprehensive recovery services. Double Jeopardy is a highly successful dual disorder treatment program that was originally developed for Boys Town of Missouri.

OUR CHILDREN ARE ALCOHOLICS: *Coping with Children Who Have Addictions*
  Sally and David B. $13.95
The authors tell their own personal story of how they found health and serenity in the midst of the chaos caused by the addictions of their four children. They provide hope for parents, along with practical suggestions and successful methods on how to deal with addicted children of any age.

THROUGH THE INNER EYE: *Awakening to the Creative Spirit*
  Jan Groenemann $19.95
Explore the expression of self as you are guided beyond self-imposed boundaries and reach within to your true self. Find more passion, purpose, and productivity in your life as you become free, creative, and whole.

RIGHT SIDE UP! *Reflections for Those Living with Serious Illness*
  Marlene Halpin $10.95
The clarity and warmth of Ms. Halpin's poems and photos portray a sense of peace and well-being. One reflection per page makes this book manageable for those who are unable to focus for prolonged periods of time. A Perfect Gift!

THEY DO REMEMBER: *A Story of Soul Survival*
Sandy Robins $13.95

A story of survival, recovery, and hope for victims of abuse. This poignant autobiography will help abuse victims and survivors realize they do have a choice; they can choose to move from trauma to understanding and healing.

THERE'S A SPOUSE IN THE HOUSE: *Get 'Em Out*
Patricia Schnepf $5.95

Do you have a spouse in the house going through the throes of retirement? Let *There's a Spouse in the House* help you and your spouse make the transition to retirement a creative and adventurous time in your life. This resource will help you make the rest of your life the BEST of your life as you discover a variety of ways to redirect your time, talent, and resources.

THE TOAD WITHIN: *How to Control Eating Choices*
Dr. James Weldon Worth $12.95

Dr. Worth's mythical creation, the Toad, is a metaphor for our appetite when it becomes difficult to control. By envisioning our runaway appetite as a mischievous and persistent Toad, who bullies us with food temptations, we have an adversary that can be visualized, confronted, and captured. Dr. Worth shows us how to engage in imaginary struggles with our Toad and defeat him or her by choosing wisely and courageously. Humorous and Insightful!!!

HUNGER OF THE HEART: *Communion at the Wall*
Larry Powell $19.95

A powerful photo documentation of the healing impact that the Vietnam Veterans Memorial has on those who journey there. Award-winning photojournalist Larry Powell, himself a Vietnam veteran, offers a unique historical record of life at the Wall. His poignant photographs remind us that for thousands of suffering souls, their war is not over. *Hunger of the Heart* brings the healing power of the Wall to all those who are unable to personally visit the memorial.

RESTORING AMERICA'S FUTURE
Gene Gordon $9.95

The author offers fundamental solutions, that have been used successfully by independent businesses, to help our country become once again a financially secure world leader.

To Place a Credit Card Order Call
1-800-557-9867
Mention this ad for Free Shipping

Or send order and payment to: Islewest Publishing, 4242 Chavenelle Road, Dubuque, IA 52002   Fax:319-557-1376

Name _____

Address _____

City _____ State _____ Zip _____

Phone _____

Name of Book _____

Price: $ _____

Quantity _____

Shipping & Handling* $ _____

Sales Tax (IA Residents 6%) _____

Total Enclosed $ _____

Credit Card Information

☐ Visa   ☐ MasterCard

Credit Card # _____

Expiration Date _____

Signature _____

*$3.00 for first book
$.50 for each additional book

Call 1-800-557-9867 Now and Receive Free Shipping

Chris Frey is available for speaking engagements,
workshops, and seminars.

Write to him at
10918 Olive Blvd., St. Louis. MO 63141
or call (314) 997-1403.